Agricultural Urbanism

Handbook for Building Sustainable
Food & Agriculture Systems in 21st Century Cities

Janine de la Salle
& Mark Holland with contributors

Agricultural Urbanism: Handbook for Building Sustainable
Food & Agriculture Systems in 21st Century Cities

Editors and Contributors:
Janine de la Salle
Mark Holland

Contributors
Robert Barrs
Steve Clarke
Patrick Condon
Kelsey Cramer
Don Crockett
Bud Fraser
Joaquin Karakas
Peter Ladner
Kent Mullinix
Edward Porter
Bob Ransford

First published by Green Frigate Books
www.greenfrigatebooks.com

Copyright 2010 © HB Lanarc Consultants Ltd.
www.hblanarc.ca

FIRST EDITION
1. Agriculture. 2. Food Systems. 3. Urbanism. 4. Planning. 5. Design.

Cover illustration: Cory Cleaver, Adrian Irwin
Printed in Winnipeg Manitoba Canada on 100% recycled paper
Distributed by Independent Publishers Group
www.ipgbook.com

ISBN 978-0-9812434-2-9

This book is dedicated to all of the farmers, thinkers, academics, community activists, planning and design professionals, government staff, elected officials, gardeners, chefs, businesses, and individuals who are making daily decisions to support local food and are working together to imagine and create a future where sustainable food and agriculture systems are a vital part of our day-to-day experience.

Agricultural Urbanism will likely become an essential reference for planners, community activists, and others interested in developing vigorous local food and agriculture systems in our communities. This book is much more than a list of methods of growing food in the marginal nooks and crannies of the city, or even a catalogue of needed policies. Instead, it delineates a philosophy and plan for shifting and broadening the focus of urban design such that a sustainable food system can blossom and flourish.

- *Plan Canada Winter 2010*

This book pushes the frontier by showing how steps in the food chain – from food production through food waste disposal – can be enhanced using planning and design principles to create a more sustainable community food system. Ambitious in scope and imaginative in design, it's an important read for communities as they consider the importance of their food systems.

JERRY KAUFMAN
Emeritus Professor
Urban and Regional Planning Department, U. of Wisconsin-Madison
Co-author of the American Planning Association
Community and Regional Food Planning Policy Guide.

Agricultural Urbanism. These are not words that sit comfortably together – at least not until now. Any decent oxymoron makes you think.
Pastoral, productive agricultural landscapes and energetic, dense urban landscapes appear diametrically opposed, until you look behind these images and think about how things could work in detail. The authors of this book help us see that our world could change with agriculture and urbanism working together. This dynamic tension is at play throughout this highly readable, informative and, at times, provocative book.

MOURA QUAYLE
Professor
UBC Sauder School of Business.
Former Dean, UBC Faculty of Land and Food Systems

This book's introduction to 'Agricultural Urbanism' will tackle the one remaining blindness toward urban sustainability - the dramatic impact of food production and delivery. I hope it fosters a renewed interest in personal food production, a localized food economy and a revival of placemaking based upon cuisine.

LARRY BEASLEY, C.M.
Professor
Planning University of British Columbia.
Founding Principal, Beasley and Associates, Planning Inc.

Garlic
Photo: Claire de la Salle

Acknowledgements: Collaboration in Practice

Building sustainable food and agriculture systems requires a new approach that is based on cross-sectoral collaboration and creativity. This book would not have been possible without the strong spirit of collaboration that stimulated the creativity and ideas that help set a trajectory for sustainable food and agriculture systems. Specifically, we would like to thank the following people and organizations for their contribution to the movement and for not only asking the hard questions, but also for dreaming up practical solutions.

We are indebted to many people for their work envisioning 21st century cities and supporting the important discussions about how food and agriculture need to be integrated back into cities in this century, including Larry Beasley C.M. for his championship of food in Southeast False Creek in the early 1990s; the Congress for New Urbanism and the offices of Duany Plater-Zyberk & Company; the City of Vancouver – Mayor Gregor Robertson, Councilors Andrea Reimer and Heather Deal, Director of Planning Brent Toderian and Director of Social Policy Mary Clare Zak, Manager of Engineering Southeast False Creek & Olympic Village Project Office Robin Petri; Metro Vancouver – Johnny Carline CAO, Theresa Duynstee, Policy and Planning, and the staff at Central Area Parks for defending the value of food lands in a growing metropolis; the City of Edmonton – Gary Klassen, General Manager of Planning and Development, Mary Ann McConnell-Boehm, Senior Planner, Planning & Policy Services for pushing forward on some of the most progressive food systems in planning in Canada; the City of Albuquerque – Mayor Martin Chavez and his sustainability staff team of John Soladay, Mary Lou Leonard and John O'Connell who supported the progressive food agenda; the Resort Municipality of Whistler who pursued food in their Olympics concepts; and many others we have worked with who are weaving food into the policies and vision of their towns.

We are very grateful for the support and intellectual commitment and leadership of many institutions, including the Real Estate Foundation of BC – Karin Kirkpatrick, Stephen Mullock, and Tim Pringle; the University of British Columbia group of academics moving the food agenda forward – Art Bomke, Mark Bomford, and the many professors in both the School of Architecture and Landscape Architecture and the School of Community and Regional Planning; Simon Fraser University-Mark Roseland, Herb Barbolet, and Janet Moore; and the Institute for Sustainable Horticulture at Kwantlen University – Deborah Henderson, Kent Mullinix and Arthur Fallick.

We are only one small piece of a much larger and longer drive for sustainable food systems in cities and the early seeds of this movement have been being led for decades by other visionaries in our region including those associated with City Farmer; Farm Folk City Folk; Local Food First; the Vancouver Food Policy Council; Vancouver Farmers Market; and so many others.

We also want to thank leaders in the development community who have embraced the power of food in their projects taking risks to bring it forward in unconventional ways, sharing their vision of sustainable development, first and foremost including Sean Hodgins, his team at the Century Group and the amazing group of people on his Southlands Community Planning Team; Stephen Hynes; and our other courageous clients.

The concepts in this book have emerged from many discussions over many years, and it could not exist without the co-authorship of every one of our contributors. We are very grateful for their generosity in sharing their ideas and precious time to write the chapters of this book to share with the world the threads of their thoughts and many discussions.

We are grateful for the time, patience and insights from Moura Quayle who as a past and current professor and Dean at UBC not only influenced a whole university and many of us on how to see food and cities differently, but also gave generously as an external reviewer for this book.

Few would have access to this book without the effort of Robert France and Rob Abbott as the two men at the helm of Green Frigate Books and their relationship with the great people at the Independent Publishers Group and we are honoured to have their imprint on the book.

We also need to thank Barbara K. Adamski for her patient work with us as our copy editor – all typos and grammatical mistakes in this book are entirely ours, likely from last minute revisions that did not benefit from her exceptional command of the English language.

And finally, we owe a deep debt of gratitude to the partners and staff at HB Lanarc Consultants who covered all the costs for this book out of their own pocket in support of the company's mission to create sustainable cities in the next four decades. No consulting company can easily rationalize such costs and even less so in the darkness of a global recession and it is their personal vision and generosity that has made this possible. Beyond the staff noted as authors of chapters in this book, we need to also thank our design and layout team, Adrian Irwin and Cory Cleaver, for their talent and great work in turning all these ideas and words into a book one might actually want to pick up and read.

Foreword by Michael Ableman

In the mid nineteen-eighties I sought funding to set up an urban agriculture project in the city of Los Angeles. Community gardens had been flourishing in many neighborhoods across North America, but I felt that we needed to create models that demonstrated that unused urban plots could be converted to economic enterprises as well, providing jobs and production quantities of fresh food to communities that were seriously lacking in both. Most of the foundations I spoke with were polite but somewhat confused by my request. After all didn't agriculture take place on farms, and aren't farms far from cities? Urban and agriculture were in most people's minds a contradiction of terms.

At the time I was farming a small piece of land that had become totally surrounded by suburban development. That twelve and a half acres produced close to a hundred fruits and vegetables, fed 500 families, employed 30 people, and generated close to a million dollars in gross income. As an island floating in a sea of suburbia we nourished people as well through annual festivals, workshops, tours, and public meals for young and old.

The majority of those who shopped at our produce stand wore security badges from nearby companies like Ratheon, Applied Magnetics, and Delco, the high tech research companies that designed the so called "smart bombs", and tank turrets and whatever else the US military required to maintain its military power. But while our beets and carrots nourished the engineering minds of US military endeavors, the land around where they were grown was quickly being gobbled up by tract homes and shopping centers, and unintentionally I had become an urban farmer.

We were not alone; our experience was emblematic. Thirty seven acres every hour of prime agricultural land is gobbled up for development in North America, fewer and fewer of us grow the basic nourishment for the rest, and food travels further and further to reach world populations who as of the turn of the millennium are predominantly living in cities. Our industrial attempts to feed growing world populations are failing, resulting in staggering rates of diabetes, obesity, and hunger coupled with equally staggering rates of soil loss, aquifer depletion, and groundwater pollution.

But awareness around food and agricultural issues is increasing; there is an explosion of books, films, lectures, meetings, and conferences all with the spotlight on food. Everyone seems to be talking the talk. But talk is cheap. The gap between those who have access to good food and those who do not has not changed, and the gap between those who have become aware and excited about this movement and those whose hands are actually in the soil doing the work has not changed either. Only one and a half percent of us are actually growing the nourishment for the rest.

In 1989 Cuba faced a food crisis of monumental proportions when they lost access to food and agricultural supplies from the former Soviet Union. The Cubans responded by creating one of the most impressive national models of low input agriculture. But most remarkable was the urban agricultural systems that came out of that time, a system that employed two hundred thousand people and provided close to forty percent of the food that urban residents consumed. The Cubans did not choose to create this world-class model because it was a good idea; they did it because they had to.

We are in the midst of a food crisis as well, but the impacts of our current industrial food system have not become personal enough to force the kinds of structural change that are so desperately needed.

Some of the most exciting work being done to address these issues is happening in our cities amongst those who live on the margins, growing food in the most unexpected places; next to railroad tracks, under power lines, in neighborhoods and backyards and abandoned lots, on rooftops, in and around urban spaces where we typically do not think of the word farm.

Just as in Cuba, necessity drives ingenuity and creativity. When the food system no longer fulfills the needs of the people, whether for economic or distribution reasons or because of concerns for food safety, or simply because people want corn that tastes like corn, or potatoes that are more than just a tasteless medium to convey ketchup and salt to their mouths, they take the responsibility back into their own hands.

Urban residents are developing and implementing creative strategies for producing food closer to where they live, and in the process addressing a multitude of issues; economic, ecologic, social and nutritional.

What began as a handful of individuals responding to a need in their own back yards is now being embraced by planners, architects, developers, and city governments.

For some developers the farm has become the new tennis court or swimming pool, a sexy addition to development plans that might help grease the wheels of the permit process. Mayors and city managers and city councils are jumping in as well, some because it is politically expedient, others because they recognize that the food security of their constituents is fragile at best.

Some are embracing urban food systems for deeper more philosophical reasons, some simply because food grown closer to where it is consumed simply tastes better.

Whatever the reasons what was just a few years ago a radical idea is now becoming part of the public lexicon.

What initiatives are real and based on practical possibility and which ones are fluff? How much do we dare to dream a world where not only does no-one go hungry, but where all of us can share equally in the pleasure of food grown well, food grown by neighbours and friends who are paid a decent wage and whose work is changing our whole idea of what we see in our minds eye when we imagine "city".

This book provides us with strategies and ideas that might help us rethink and redesign our cities to incorporate food and food enterprise. It provides us with a compendium of working models that are happening now, and a range of possibilities that might inspire us for the future. It is written from the unique perspective of those who design and plan the places and the spaces where we live, folks who have recognized the value in melding the range of disciplines that will be required to navigate a future where our cities are not just endless mindless expanses of concrete, steel, and glass, but healthy, happy and nourishing places to live.

Michael Ableman is a farmer, writer, photographer, and founder of the Center for Urban Agriculture and the Centre for Arts, Ecology, and Agriculture at Foxglove Farm where he currently farms. He is the author and photographer of From the Good Earth (Abrams, 1993), On Good Land (Chronicle Books, 1998), and Fields of Plenty (Chronicle Books 2005) and the subject of the award winning PBS film Beyond Organic narrated by Meryl Streep.

www.fieldsofplenty.com
www.foxglovefarmbc.ca

Contents

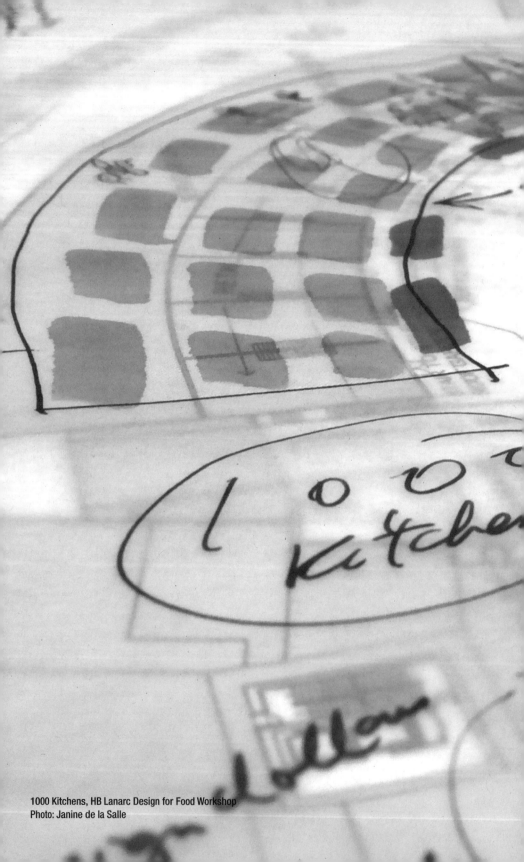

1000 Kitchens, HB Lanarc Design for Food Workshop
Photo: Janine de la Salle

Preface

Agricultural Urbanism (AU) is an emerging planning, policy, and design framework for integrating a wide range of sustainable food and agriculture system elements into a community at a site-, neighbourhood-, or on a city-wide scale. In short, it is a way of building a place around food.

In recent decades, there has been an increase in awareness of sustainable food issues, and much work has been done to promote urban agriculture and farmers' markets. However, little of this work has had a real impact on city planning and design, and where it has, it has focused almost exclusively on community gardens and farmers' markets. AU was created to be a larger, over arching concept and framework to support a much broader and deeper approach to food in a city than gardens and markets, although there is a central place for both in AU. AU looks not only at growing food (urban agriculture, **artisan agriculture**), but also at food processing, packaging, distribution, wholesaling, retailing

(including farmers markets), restaurants, education systems, a local culture of food, and finally, **food security**. It then considers the opportunities for promoting all of these aspects of the food system in all areas of a city.

This book gathers together the goals, principles, strategies, insights and ideas developed by a group of academics, professionals, writers and activists working together on issues of food in cities to lay the foundation for the development of an AU.

It is hoped that this book will start a conversation amongst all those committed to a sustainable and whole systems approach to food and cities. In light of the challenges ahead in the 21st century including climate change and increasing urbanization, we need to work together to restructure, plan, design and govern our cities to achieve the sustainability performance we need and the abundant quality of life that a sustainable urban and regional food system can offer.

Okanagan Farmer with Raspberries
Photo: Claire de la Salle

Part I: Introduction

By Janine de la Salle and Mark Holland

The need for a new approach to food and agriculture is becoming increasingly evident with the failings of the 20th century food and agriculture system. Part 1 provides a synopsis of what agricultural urbanism is, orientation for how to use this book, a vision for what a 21st century food system may look like, and an overview of why a new approach for food and agriculture is needed.

1. Introduction

This book is not intended to be the final word on any topic. Rather, we hope that it will be some of the first words on a very exciting topic, stimulating new thinking, design, and economic development around the movement that we call Agricultural Urbanism.

Agricultural Urbanism (AU) is an emerging approach to community and city building that weaves together the many threads of urban planning and design with the many threads of sustainable food and agriculture systems. AU plans and designs to optimize performance on food and agriculture systems, within a sustainable community perspective, into all aspects of community planning and design. AU is a framework for inviting food and agriculture back into our communities, and back into our lives.

Agricultural Urbanism does not replace any other approach, philosophy or movement. Rather, it adds the strengths of planning and design to the momentum and excitement behind sustainable food and agriculture systems. In the following chapters, planners, designers, government staff and elected officials, educators, students, and non-profit groups will learn core definitions and approaches for AU. The contents of this book are intended to stimulate thinking around how to infuse planning and design practice with a renewed food and agriculture consciousness.

Origins of Agricultural Urbanism

As we crossed into the 21st century, we have collectively become aware that the food system we take for granted has problems — problems so big that we might have to reinvent the food system altogether if we want the world's population to stay fed and healthy for another century. Many authors began to make us aware of the seemingly surreal systems that provide us with what we now call food and the massive petroleum, corn, chemical, and agribusiness network that controlled every aspect of those systems.

In response to this emerging awareness, the alternative food systems movement found new life and moved from the radical fringes into mainstream consciousness. Organic food went from rare and expensive to ubiquitous and price-competitive, and community gardens went from the domain of off-the-grid hippies to that of government policy makers and marketers looking for branding opportunities. Collecting food to give to the poor, once the responsibility of churches and charities, became an initiative supported by city engineering departments as part of a larger strategy to divert the food industry's unused but still-edible products from landfills to food-recovery agencies. The list goes on.

This book attempts to continue this trend of rethinking the 20th century food system, and provides a practical approach to reintegrating all aspects of the food system into our communities.

The AU movement weaves together many threads, with the intent of directly informing urban and regional planning and design.

The intellectual and practical foundation of AU includes individuals and organizations that have worked to address both sustainable food systems and urban planning and development. The growing number of AU proponents pay homage to those who have strived to make both our food systems and our communities more sustainable. AU is a movement that weaves its fabric from their work.

What is exciting about combining the wealth and richness of community planning and design with food and agriculture systems, is that these two streams of knowledge inform each other to the benefit of both.

Through understanding food systems better, we can preserve and enhance the diverse and attractive aspects of the food system and integrate it back into our urban lives.

By threading planning and design in with the cloth of sustainable food and agriculture systems, communities, governments, businesses and organizations are better equipped to build culture around taste and health, develop effective policy, strengthen local economies and generally bring food and agriculture back into our communities.

Table 1.1 Threads of Agricultural Urbanism

URBAN PLANNING AND DESIGN	SUSTAINABLE FOOD AND AGRICULTURE SYSTEMS
■ Agricultural land preservation and farmland security	■ **Urban agriculture**
■ Sustainable communities	■ **Farmers' markets and direct marketing for farmers**
■ **New Urbanism**	■ **Organic agriculture** and **permaculture**
■ Smart growth- and transit-oriented development	■ **SPIN farming**
■ Green and sustainable infrastructure systems (energy, water, liquid waste, solid waste)	■ **Food security, food sovereignty**
■ Sustainable transportation systems	■ **Artisan food** and the **slow food movement**
■ Green buildings	■ **100-mile diet**
■ Community consultation and capacity building	■ Education on all aspects of food
■ Local economic development	■ Farmers' succession planning
■ Many others	■ Co-operative farming approaches
	■ Local food economies
	■ **Community-Supported Agriculture (CSA)**
	■ Wildlife and agriculture integration
	■ Wide range of education on food
	■ Gourmet food and celebrity chefs
	■ Composting
	■ Many others

Past Trends

In the 1980s, several significant positive trends began to emerge that form some core themes of AU: New Urbanism; urban agriculture (and its many facets); gourmet, local, organic food; and others. There were also many well-documented negative trends involved, including urban sprawl, **genetically modified organisms** (GMO) - driven food biochemistry, globalization of food systems through **transnational agribusiness**, and many others. Agricultural Urbanism is at the heart of how we focus planning and design practice on creating towns and cities that are connected to food and agriculture.

Atwater Market, Montréal Quèbec
Photo: Keltie Craig

New Urbanism, based on the leading work of Andreas Duany, Elizabeth Plater-Zyberk, and Peter Calthorpe, among others, began reversing the belief that cities were evil, dirty, crime-ridden places where only those with no other opportunities lived. The movement brought forward a convincing and exciting vision for an urban pattern of development and living that offered a highly desirable quality of life. While some of the results have been overly nostalgic, the New Urbanism movement has been successful in building upon the work of Jane Jacobs, Christopher Alexander, and many others in restructuring how we think about cities, urban planning, and design.

Humans are now officially an urban species, with more of us around the world living in cities than in rural environments. Because of this, cities continue to grow and push into agricultural areas, damaging the environment and compromising the stability and diversity of the urban food supply.

A deep and unspoken assumption that food comes from far away in a processed and pre-packaged form to a store that we drive to, has crept into city planning. With this assumption as the dominant perspective on food, it becomes acceptable to ignore all aspects of the food system in our urban planning and design. However, those who are looking ahead into the 21st century are seeing that this assumption will not hold for the next 100 years and, more importantly, that by locking food out of our cities, we are missing enormous social, cultural, and economic opportunities.

This book plans to stimulate thought and catalyze action around policy development, urban and open space design, community engagement, economic development, and growth management that reintroduce all aspects of our food and agriculture system into urban planning and design in a coordinated, strategic, and visionary way.

Apiary at Brickworks, Toronto Ontario
Photo: Emory Davidge

How to Use This Book

This book is organized under five main themes, each comprising several chapters. Each chapter draws on definitions and concepts from other sections but may also be read as a stand-alone piece. A glossary for key definitions is provided in the last part of the book and key terms are bold/italic.

PART I: INTRODUCTION

Chapter 1 provides the context for AU and gives an overview of the book. Chapter 2 offers a vision for 21st century food systems and provides an end-point for what AU is attempting to help build. Chapter 3 outlines how the planning and urban/open space design professions are waking up to the fact that 20th century food systems are unsustainable and how community planning needs to respond proactively in order to bring food and agriculture back to the urban experience. Chapter 4 is an overview of AU as defined by its goals and principles. Chapter 5 presents the eight dimensions of a food and agriculture system.

These dimensions form the foundation for assessing the best way to integrate food systems into urban planning, including:

- Farming;

- Processing and packaging;

- Distribution, transportation, and storage;

- Retail and wholesale marketing;

- Eating and celebrating food;

- Waste recovery (water, energy, organics);

- Education, training, and skill building around food and agriculture; and

- Integrated infrastructure systems for sustainable food systems.

Chapter 6 summarizes global trends in food and agriculture and what local responses could be.

PART II: AGRICULTURAL URBANISM, CORE CONCEPTS

In Chapters 7 to 14, we explore the landscape of AU and define its core concepts. We then introduce and begin to explore the concept of AU, its origins, the scope of its considerations, and how it weaves together the many other existing movements around food in a way that is useful to city planners and designers.

PART III: PLANNING AND DESIGN FOR AGRICULTURAL URBANISM

This section provides approaches and ideas for integrating food and agriculture into community planning and design. Chapter 15 discusses how infrastructure systems may be planned and designed to increase energy, water, and waste efficiencies in the urban-to-agricultural zones. Chapter 16 examines the matter of Human Scale Agriculture and Chapter 17 looks at open space and urban design for food and takes an illustrative approach to demonstrating how food and agriculture can be integrated into planning and design processes.

Chapter 18 introduces the exciting concept of an agriculture and food hub or precinct, a special area of the city or community that is focused entirely around growing, processing, retailing, educating about, and celebrating food. Chapter 19 takes a close look at how transition areas between different land uses can be designed and programmed to encourage true integration.

PART V: PERSPECTIVES

The combination of the food system and the sustainable community development agenda raises many interesting issues. In this section we explore some of these issues and perspectives. Chapter 20 uses case studies to explore the emerging field of urban agricultural entrepreneurialism. Chapter 21 outlines a draft Agricultural Urbanism Charter that provides a check-list

ACCESSIBLE COMMUNITY GARDENING FOR ALL ABILITIES AND AGES.

Raised beds for seniors
Drawing: Co-Design Group

of requirements for AU projects to meet. Chapter 22 explores how shifting focus away from the battle between urban development and agricultural land to focus on sustainable communities and sustainable food systems offers some unconventional opportunities that can work in some areas to meet the needs of both systems. Chapter 23 focuses on the community engagement prospects around food and explores perspectives and strategies on engaging the community with an agricultural and food-driven project.

PART VI: CONCLUSION

Chapter 24 concludes by looking at the next steps and offers suggestions for a path toward integrating food systems more fully into any city, neighbourhood, or project.

Local Blueberries from Surrey, BC
Photo: Janine de la Salle

Why Launch a New Movement?

The next century will require a new approach to food in North American cities.

The continued growth of cities, combined with the significant need to increase the sustainability of the food systems in cities and their surrounding regions, creates converging forces. These forces collide everywhere, and the food and agriculture system is losing. Because this is not sustainable, we are seeking a way to integrate urban development and the food system in a healthy way.

Sustainable community planning is a high priority now for many cities[1]; however, planning for sustainable food systems is generally not addressed around the planning table. Creating sustainable cities demands an aggressive and integrated approach to merging urbanism and sustainable food systems.

Agricultural Urbanism draws together the philosophies, principles, practices, design ideas, and management strategies from both streams into a coordinated approach to sustainable cities and sustainable food systems.

2. Vision of a 21st Century Food System

Picturing the utopia we seek to build is a necessary exercise for any person working in the field of sustainability. By defining a point on the horizon that we are navigating towards, we may guide our policy, shape our thinking, and change our behaviour toward a more sustainable food and agriculture system. Sustainability is a destination and a journey, a means and an end. But what is the end? The following pages outline the key elements of a 21st century food system that the practice of AU seeks to help build.

There are no good guys or bad guys, just people working together to increase the sum of global happiness. In the 21st century food system, the private,

public, and non-profit sectors engage in meaningful collaboration to address our sustainability challenges. Corporate responsibility is a cornerstone of business plans, and the public sector invests in and regulates research and development of agri-food technologies for the public and environmental good. All players adhere to ethical practices that promote environmental health and social justice through accountability and transparency. New partnerships are formed between public, private, Non-Government Organizations (**NGO**), academic, and community organizations that work together to institute **market transformation** that de-commodifies food while bolstering the agri-food economy with long-term investment in **resilience**.

Soil is rich in nutrients and is a significant resource for carbon capture. Soils that have been degraded due to intensive production methods are reconstituted through land stewardship practices and become the number one resource for absorbing atmospheric carbon on the planet. Soil management practices see the shift away from heavy use of synthetic fertilizers, pesticides, and herbicides. Crop yields increase over time as a direct result of sustainable land-use practices. Intensive production practices shift toward an ecological health model to manage pests and weeds, integrate with wildlife and human habitat, and adapt innovation and technology to support low-till methods, integrated pest management, sustainable harvesting, and soil health.

Land-based aquaculture. Swift Farms, Agassiz, BC
Photo: Janine de la Salle

Meat is a treat. In 21ˢᵗ century food systems, North Americans, Europeans, and others eat less meat, and the meat that is eaten is produced ethically and sustainably through free-range and pasture-fed livestock methods. Livestock farmers are able to fetch a premium for their meats and are able to slaughter and process their meat locally. Cities explore sustainable urban protein options such as *urban aquaculture* and *aquaponics*.

Emergency preparedness & local resilience. Local areas are able to respond to emergency events, including adaptation strategies for climate change and increasing local production, processing, and storage capacity. Families and individuals are primary responders when disaster strikes and community networks ensure that people are taken care of. Government is quick to respond to emergency situations through preventative policies, prepared contingency plans, and supporting research and development of emergency food provisions.

Food comes from near and far. While much of our food supply will be produced locally,

some will also travel from afar via energy-efficient means of transportation (such as light rail or fuel-efficient ships). Value-added local products are sold on a global market for a premium, and farmers manage lucrative operations. Global foods are celebrated and provide a way to learn and appreciate other cultures. Food is farmed in places that make the most sense and what is grown locally is processed and eaten locally, with surplus being traded with other areas for items not grown in the local region.

Food is food and food is medicine. Food is prepared with human and ecological health in mind. It is whole, tasty, and delicious. Harmful additives are banned or at least more clearly labeled on foods to empower consumers. People re-learn how to cook and re-discover the deep satisfaction of feasting together. Food is no longer a commodity, even though food businesses maintain high profit margins. Traditional foods and harvesting practices of First Nation peoples are learned and celebrated, offering unique insight into resource management and the cultural history of being connected to the land, plants, and animals that sustain us.

People have investments and livelihoods in the food system. The 21ˢᵗ century food system provides a wide range of economic opportunities. Niche agriculture operates alongside larger farms that grow staple crops. There are new careers in food and agriculture system planning and design, and a new cohort of farmers is attracted to farming because of the many opportunities it offers. Human labour is used more often on farms to support the ecological health model of agriculture as well as to create jobs. A new generation of urban farmers is born and urban agriculture skill-building programs enable low-income residents to develop marketable skill sets. Economic opportunities in food processing, distribution, and storage is kept local where possible. Education and skill-building in emerging

Michael Pollan picnic at the University of British Columbia 2009
Photo: Janine de la Salle

markets (agricultural technology, local processing, urban agriculture, and artisan agriculture) become part of university, college, and technical institutions' programs.

Everyone can afford good food. The cost of food reflects the real cost of sustainably growing, transporting, distributing, and storing the food. People who are not able to afford good food are supported through other means.

Nikko watering in the community garden downtown Vancouver, BC
Photo: Keltie Craig

Technology supports closed-loop systems, land stewardship, and ecologically-just practices. Technology is developed and used to support healthy food and agriculture systems. No- to low-till machinery is used to build and maintain soil health and *carbon capture* while also enabling the production of large amounts of food. *Biotechnology* is regulated through a democratic process that allows farmers to maintain sovereignty over their seed stock and traditional farming practices and the broader community to choose engineered food products or not. Urban infrastructure systems are *looped*, and there is no such thing as waste. Waste heat and water are recycled for use in urban market gardens or aquaculture operations, and solid organic waste is diverted from the landfill and composted for backyard gardens and urban agriculture operations.

The use of solar and alternative energy is maximized to capture the cleanest, cheapest, and most powerful source of energy on our planet. Harnessing solar and alternative.energy is the main input into the 21st century food system. From *photosynthesis* to *photovoltaics*, food is primarily grown, processed, transported, stored, and sold based on a solar and alternative energy system. National, international, and global infrastructure systems are upgraded to accommodate this new energy source. All countries cooperate in shifting to a solar and alternative energy source.

3. Waking From the Coma:
The End of the 20th Century Food System

It's that time of year again. Hunchbacked figures rummaging in the bushes alongside highways, train tracks, and overgrown city-gardens mark an important annual event. It's blackberry season and everyone is braving the thorny vines to procure the sweet, tangy fruit of the British Columbian (actually Himalayan) blackberry. This yearly happening speaks to the human urge to hunt and gather food from nature, the innate connection between people and their food. While we are no longer hunters and gatherers, these modern-day impulses to eat off the land are based on an innate animal connection to sustenance, or as humans call it, food.

Food shapes our lives, for better or worse. The way we grow, store, and eat our food creates cultural, ecological, and economic patterns that form how we as individuals and societies live and relate. The transformative power of food is absolute. George Orwell comments in <u>The Road to Wigan Pier</u> that "changes of diet are more important than changes of dynasty or even of religion". As Orwell notes, this power can be observed in the evolution of food preservation and in the lowly tin of canned fish that saw a new era of warfare by enabling soldiers to survive far away from any secure food source.[2] Indeed modern civilization is often dated back to the era when humans discovered a static food source, grain, and began to settle in fertile areas where agriculture flourished. However, our connection to food is not a simple sustenance question and, historically, food has shaped our relationships to each other and food has shaped our cities.

In a 20th century North American context, food has formed our lives in new and sometimes invisible ways. This chapter examines what 20th century food systems are and how our lives have been forever transformed by fundamental shifts in what we eat and how we relate to food. This relationship to food on an individual level also determines how we plan and design for food in our cities. Twentieth century food systems have largely stripped the meaning of food from our lives, reduced food to a collection of molecules, and severed the psychological and functional connection to the rural hinterland where most of our food originates. This has caused one of the greatest oversights in city building in human history. As food- architect and author Carolyn Steel notes, "The relationship between food and cities is endlessly complex, but at one level is utterly simple. Without farmers and farming, cities would not exist".[3] Agricultural Urbanism explores how to re-invite food to the 21st century city and ultimately how to re-connect people to food and place.

After an era of human agricultural history focused on the domination of nature, reductionist logic, short-term high yields, and dependence on technological solutions, 20th century food systems are rapidly becoming a relic of the past, and symptoms of an unhealthy food system may no longer be ignored. These symptoms can be quantified and observed by looking at trends over time. For example, the quality of our food has plummeted in the past fifty years, with a sharp decline in the nutritional content of proteins and produce.[4]

Another symptom is the increased risk in food, with livestock pandemics becoming more of a threat and the rapid increase of antibiotics in meat.[5] The incidence of obesity in North America has more than doubled over the past 30 years due to a diet high in fats, sugars, salts, and carbohydrates as well as sedentary lifestyles.[6] Other preventable diseases directly connected to diet and lifestyle include Type 2 diabetes, heart disease, and some cancers. Paradoxically, in a marketplace inundated with low-fat foods, the raging obesity epidemic in North America is costing the health-care system billions of dollars. In Canada alone, the treatment of these diseases is estimated conservatively to be two billion dollars.[7]

Consider also that the lack of stewardship of farm soils also contributes to an unhealthy food system and has been cited as one or several causes of the world food crisis.[8] Land degradation, including soil erosion, salinization, and desertification, has undermined agricultural productivity worldwide.

For most people in North America and Europe, the day-to-day experience with food is of extreme abundance and choice; the answer to what's for dinner? represents infinite possibilities of food combinations regardless of seasonality, locality, or a meaningful understanding of what is in our food or what impacts it may have on our own and the ecosystem's health. In reality, the sense of choice is largely an illusion, with the vast majority of food in the grocery store, including most organic labels, owned by a handful of powerful multinational corporations. While we seem to be overwhelmed with choice and abundance, an exploration of the dark side of our food system reveals quite the opposite.

Food has been relegated to the margins of our lives where the experience of food is reduced to a simple formula: buy food, eat food. Seems simple, except the gatekeepers of the 20th century food system care little for health and people and more about how to sell you more food than you need or could possibly eat.[9] The divorce of food, land, and people has been concurrent with the exclusion of food from city building. From the urban patterns that encourage car-dependence for grocery shopping to the distinct lack of food in how we treat and use public spaces, food has indeed fallen off the table as a fundamental consideration in our policy, planning, and design practices.

The 20th century food system is made possible only through unsustainable means, such as non-renewable resources. This chapter focuses on setting the context for the challenges we face in food and agriculture today by looking at how the 20th century food system has divorced people from a meaningful connection to their food and, by extension, how the beauty and permanence of food has been forgotten in city building practice.

De-evolution of Cities: Rapid Urbanization and the Car

How did we get here? How did a basic need such as tasting and celebrating food become a commodity that is produced and traded with very little consideration to human happiness and ecological health? There was a myriad of causal factors for the disconnection between food and people, but this section will focus on the way cities responded to two main trends that helped to eliminate food from our cityscapes: urbanization and the car.

As cities increasingly became the hub of human activity, more and more people moved (and are moving) to urban centres, leaving behind the family farm.[10] The implications of this shift are that cities are not only growing as a result of population growth but also because of migration from rural areas. The demographic shift from rural to urban has generally left the world with a

The Global Hinterland: Kumquatification of Urban Food

In an era when we need investigative journalists like Michael Pollan to retrace the epic journey our food takes, the modern experience of food is highly dysfunctional, and we all need therapy. Twentieth-century food systems saw a shift away from producing fresh produce and meat relatively close to cities toward centralized processing and distribution facilities in disconnected off-limit areas. While food has always been traded and imported/exported, the advent of scaled-up international trade made it so that cities no longer depended on the surrounding hinterland for their food needs. Instead, they grew to become dependent on the *global hinterland*.

The divorce between urban and rural areas is reflected in the entirety of city building elements, namely the urbanism, architecture, form, and function of the city as a whole. This is readily apparent in transportation networks of pre-auto cities, in which the central nodes were near transportation corridors such as rivers and roads, where food markets flourished as a necessary part of everyday life.

Greenbelt "leapfrog" effect causing suburban development in rual areas. Portland, OR
Photo: Aaron Licker

deficit of rural farmers, which has not been a prevalent issue because large industrial farms have taken the place of the independent family farm. Out of this demographic shift to cities, a new class of farmer has emerged, the urban farmer, specifically in cities that have experienced dire economic conditions and the collapse of sources for agricultural inputs.[11] However, even the best, most innovative practices of urban agriculture fall short of being able to produce enough food for subsistence. We require a more comprehensive approach to sustainable food systems that includes aggressive urban agriculture strategies.

We will not discuss the entire bibliography of the impacts of urbanization and the car. Suffice it to say that cars enabled a new wave of change where urban settlement patterns, which were once closely bound to key transportation nodes, became spread out, undiversified, and most of all, completely dependent on the car. The car not only facilitated new patterns of urban development but also enabled food sources to be centralized in large stores, often only accessible by car. People began to drive long distances to buy their food from grocery stores instead of growing it themselves or trading it with neighbours. In this way, people have become disconnected from their food, where it is grown, and who has grown it.

Large format food retail
Photo: Mark Holland

In the context of the modern-day global hinterland, the average person living in a developed country may procure an infinite combination of a vast range of foodstuffs from the grocery store. From coffee to kumquats, our food travels more than we could ever hope (or choose) to. The persistent availability of tomatoes that bounce instead of squish engenders an illusion of abundance that conceals gross inequity in the way food is controlled and regulated globally. While food is truly abundant and the planet has never produced as much food as it does now,[12] new systems are needed to ensure the democratization of foods around the world.

The **food miles** metric is imperfect: it only measures **greenhouse gas (GHG) emissions**, one of many dimensions of sustainable food and agriculture that must be considered. A simple food-miles and associated GHG emissions analysis does not consider the embodied energy of foods and can provide misleading results. For example, research shows that what we eat has far greater impact on GHG emissions than how far the food travelled and that eating less meat cuts emissions more than reducing food miles does.[13]

Take the BC hothouse tomato: the natural gas energy required to produce vine-ripened tomatoes in February (in an albeit mild Canadian winter) may take more energy per tomato than a field grown tomato in Mexico, even after accounting for travel. So, which is the better tomato? It depends on what you see as the most important factor. Taste? GHG emissions? Local economic development? Or, perhaps questioning if we should be eating tomatoes in February at all.

Food has become part of the global hinterland in that it is grown, processed, transported, sold and eaten through a complex global system. While not a new phenomenon or necessarily an unsustainable system, the global food system must refocus on using less energy and re-building diverse scales of agri-food infrastructure.

Post-Apocalypse: Carbon Counseling for 20th Century Food and Agriculture Systems

One way of characterizing food system changes from pre- to post-20th century food systems is to look at the embodied energy of food. Energy input into growing or otherwise obtaining food has shifted from human-animal-solar inputs to largely fossil fuel-based input. In terms of how food shapes our lives, 20th century food and agriculture is highly mechanized and takes less human energy, and as a result, only a relative few people work to grow the foods we eat. In this way, food has shaped our lives by its absence, and we fill the void it left with other activities, such as shopping. This shift to a fossil fuel-based food system has increased the amount of embodied energy that is in our food. The energy it takes to produce, process, distribute, store, and sell food is now far greater than ever before. Consider that out of the total ten units of energy needed to produce a given unit of food, we get one unit of energy out of the food. This means that nine units of energy are being used to grow, transport, store, and prepare food. Nearly a quarter of all trips in the city (most of which are done via motor vehicle) are associated with purchasing and consuming food.[14] Emissions have also increased by 21 percent in Canada's agricultural sector between 1990 and 2006, which represents 9 percent of the country's overall increase in GHGs over the same period.[15] Many farmers and advocates are now looking toward organic agriculture, which involves using energy from the sun as the primary source of energy for growing food.

From an energy conservation standpoint, this appears to be a gross inefficiency. With the advent of a fossil fuel-based agri-food system, industrial agriculture has become an energy hog. Inputs used to produce food at the industrial standard scale require new and more inputs as well as global distribution and marketing chains. In this way, 20th century food systems have witnessed a dramatic increase in the energy that goes into food, despite the fact that we are still drawing the same amount of energy out of it (human digestive systems are finite and don't increase simply because of the excessive amount of food available to the average person in North America or Europe).

From the petroleum needed to produce nitrogen fertilizers and packaging for food, to the gas in the car for going to the grocery store, the main ingredient in dinner is oil. Given the trends of rapidly increasing oil prices, this extravagant use of an exhaustible resource creates a significant vulnerability in our food system. What happens to our food supply when the oil is gone (or when food becomes really expensive)? One could speculate on these future scenarios, but underlying all of them is the need for a more energy-efficient food and agriculture system.

Related to the shift to fossil fuel-based food, the culture around what we eat has also changed. While meat used to be a luxury, it has become a regular three-times-a-day indulgence, signifying over a tripling of meat consumption over the past one hundred years.[16] Newly developed or developing countries such as India and China, who historically tended to have more plant-, fish-, and legume-based diets, are now eating more and more animal protein.

The **foodprint** of producing this amount of meat, not only poses significant land, energy, and GHG-emission concerns, but also ethical ones (the horrors of factory meat farming will not be retold here). Consider that the average foodprint, the amount of land it takes to grow food for one person per year, for a meat-based diet takes approximately almost five times more land than does a vegetarian diet, 2.11 and 0.44 acres (0.85 and 0.10 ha), respectively.[17]

Our Relationship to Food: Fear and Loathing in the Grocery Store

We have become slightly terrified of our food — and for good reason. Over the past five to ten years there has been an alarming number of food contamination incidents in produce and meat products. The impact of these outbreaks is exacerbated by the central organization of processing and distribution. Consider this: all the spinach grown in California gets shipped to one facility for washing, packaging, and distribution. If one farm sends leaves laced with harmful bacteria, and this spinach is then washed with the other spinach, all of a sudden the problem becomes a continent-wide health threat with significantly more people being affected. Such incidents of lethal and toxic foods have betrayed people's trust in the food they buy and have ultimately created a culture of fear around food.

The mad cow and avian flu pandemics have threatened entire industries, caused much suffering in animal stocks, and, perhaps most importantly, compromised the health of people to the point of sickness and even death. Without analyzing the underlying causes of these pandemics, it is hard to say if the industrial food system is behind the mad cow and avian flu outbreaks (although feeding ground-up animal parts to herbivores is repulsive and wrong). However, it is safe to say that these threats to the food system have driven another wedge between people and their food.

Another way that we have been alienated from our food is that we no longer know what it contains. Ingredient lists of food made in labs instead of kitchens do not tell us what exactly is in the food and how it affects our health. Also, in North America, food labels need not disclose genetically modified ingredients, so not only do we not know what

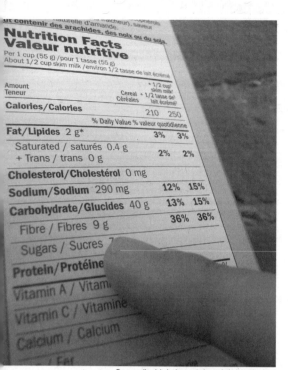

Nutrition Facts
Valeur nutritive
Per 1 cup (55 g) / pour 1 tasse (55 g)
About 1/2 cup skim milk / environ 1/2 tasse de lait écrémé

	+ 1/2 cup skim milk Cereal + 1/2 tasse de Céréales lait écrémé
Amount Teneur	
Calories/Calories	210 250
	% Daily Value % valeur quotidienne
Fat/Lipides 2 g*	3% 3%
Saturated / saturés 0.4 g + Trans / trans 0 g	2% 2%
Cholesterol/Cholestérol 0 mg	
Sodium/Sodium 290 mg	12% 15%
Carbohydrate/Glucides 40 g	13% 15%
Fibre / Fibres 9 g	36% 36%
Sugars / Sucres 7	
Protein/Protéine	
Vitamin A / Vitam.	
Vitamin C / Vitamine	
Calcium / Calcium	
Fat	

Even reading labels does not always help to understand what is in the food we are buying and eating.
Photo: Janine de la Salle

we are eating when it is listed, but we are not even given the choice of whether or not to feed ourselves GMO products. But the food must be safe, right? We hope so, but increasing bacterial outbreaks, pandemics, alien ingredients, and untraceable commodity chains are making it more and more difficult for shoppers to unquestioningly trust food on the shelves at the grocery store.

It is becoming more common for people to not even know the right questions to ask around food. Increasingly, and not very surprisingly, researchers are finding that children do not know where their food comes from.[18] Well, that is not totally accurate: they know that it comes from the grocery store. What does it mean when generations of young people grow up not knowing that eggs come from chickens not rabbits, that carrots grow in the ground, not on trees, and that meat is a dead animal that somebody

had to kill? Many people in the global north have switched from being eaters to being consumers and do not have the ability to assess what foods are good for them. Food and food-like substances are no longer an essential source of health, pleasure, and community. They are merely a well-marketed collection of molecules that have no meaningful relationship to land or people: farmers are now producers, people are now consumers, and food is now a commodity.

The decrease in social capital around food (for example, agricultural land stewardship and knowledge of how to grow, process, and celebrate real foods) has put us in a temporary comatose state that we are just waking from. For example, we are now realizing in Canada the average farmer is approximately sixty years old, and many young people do not carry on the family-farm torch that has been passed on through several generations. This predicament, if unaddressed, will see a complete disintegration of Canadian agriculture as we know it (or knew it) within the next fifteen years.

The sterilization of our food, under the auspices of health and safety, have altered our expectations of what good food looks like. We never see imperfect vegetables such as "girl" or "boy" carrots in the grocery store or farmers' market, because we consumers have been conditioned to accept only perfectly shaped and coloured produce. Our dislike of unusual-looking foods has led to unnecessary waste from the farm to the dinner table.

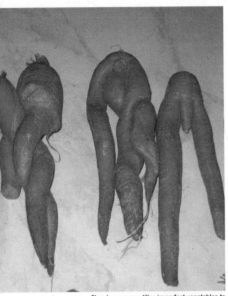

Gleaning groups utilize imperfect vegetables to make dried soup mixes for people in need.
Photo: Harvey de la Salle

Implications on City Building

The emergence of the global hinterland that characterizes 20th century food systems has unmistakably transformed the form and function of cities. The disconnection from food that we experience on an individual level is also felt by professionals in the practice of city building. The following section outlines at a high level how the disconnection from food has shaped our 20th century cities in terms of land use, transportation, growth management, buildings, open-space design, and local economy.

Food processing and storage facilities, such as slaughterhouses, canneries, and warehouse, have been moved from the city core out to industrial zones or even to other countries. Because food processing and storage have migrated from the **public realm**, there is no longer policy or development guidelines for how these facilities can be part of the urban fabric.

The traditional marketplace and small shops have faded away, replaced by large-scale grocery stores. Where we procure food has moved from open-air markets that characterize some of the most interesting and vibrant parts of a city to large, sterile megastores, where shelves are lined with rows and rows of over-packaged foods that arrived in the country shortly before being put out for sale to the consumer.

The agri-food industry simply is not very good with people, hence the alienating landscape of the modern grocery store. (Critique from a design perspective may point out that these megastores are detrimental to sustainable communities as they are not connected, do not create a sense of place, are not designed with people in mind, and only have a single purpose).

The refocusing of transportation networks on cars and shopping malls has made it all too necessary to drive virtually everywhere. Pre-automotive cities had road networks that radiated out from a high-activity area. This area focused on the buying, selling, and trading of goods — food being an important one. As noted in <u>Hungry City</u> by Caroline Steel roads in old cities were named for what was on them. The names of roads near and in the historic food-market area of London are an example of this.

Transportation networks no longer connect to where the food distribution centres are because these areas often receive goods by truck for wholesale distribution to those who serve the large grocery-store chains.

Building form and character no longer reflect food and agriculture uses because buildings no longer have a connection to either. The majority of buildings that do have a food and agriculture function, such as your not-so-local supermarket, do not have the appearance or function of anything other than a warehouse. From space on a rooftop or balcony to grow herbs to communal areas with shared kitchens and eating facilities, residential buildings are only now starting to consider food at the planning and design phase .

Accommodating growth of cities through low-density development on farmland sadly continues to be the industry standard in many regions. Even though development in growing areas is inevitable, creative new ways must be explored to ensure the preservation of agricultural land as well as the increased density in cities to ensure complete communities.

Open-space design has also forgotten food and, until the recent advent of the urban agriculture movement, the public realm has largely comprised inedible plants, vacant soccer fields, and volcanic rock. The public realm in a city presents a key opportunity for integrating food back into cities.

The great local economic development opportunity around locally farmed and processed foods has only begun to be realized. In 2008 alone, the direct impact of farmers' markets on the Canadian economy was 3.09 billion dollars.[19] However, to fully capture the value of the local economy around food and agriculture, we need to establish systems for sustainable-food processing, distribution, celebration, education, and waste.

Summary

It's a great time of year when the humble blackberry picker emerges from the prickly understory clutching yogurt containers that spill over with the dark purple fruit. For a short time, the urban gatherer is able to experience the rare joy of finding, harvesting, and above all, tasting fruit that goes directly from plant to eater.

The generalized lack of such intimate food experiences and a connection to food in life and city building has made it clear that we need to start doing things differently and more sustainably. There is great hope and possibility for reconnecting to the true abundance of food in the global hinterland, and a clear first step is to integrate food and agriculture back into how we plan and design communities. Through planning, policy, and design strategies, AU considers how to re-invite food back into the city and re-forge the connections to the rural hinterland. While the practice of AU is still in its infancy, there is much to glean from how we are currently addressing food and agriculture system sustainability in terms of what is working, and what is not.

At Fairmont, chefs grow herbs on the rooftop garden and use them in the hotel kitchen, Vancouver BC.
Photo: Janine de la Salle

4. Agricultural Urbanism in a Nutshell

What is Agricultural Urbanism?

Agricultural Urbanism (AU) is a planning, policy, and design framework for developing a wide range of sustainable food and agriculture system elements into multiple community scales. AU refocuses economic development, community identity, and urban planning and design on all aspects of food and agriculture systems.

AU focuses on integrating the widest possible range of food system elements into a community in a manner appropriate to that community. From field to fork, the entire food and agriculture system is the unit of analysis for AU, which establishes a rich and comprehensive "food program" in planning and design process.

The challenge we as a group of planners, designers, academics, activists, and policy analysts began to note over the past few years was that the planning and design of cities and regions greatly impacted the success or failure of a region's food systems and vice versa. However, there was no organized philosophy, approach, or movement to lead the way on how best to address sustainable food systems in urban and regional planning despite significant and complimentary parallels between AU and other movements seeking to create more sustainable communities such as

Figure 4.1: Bringing food & agriculture back into the city
Source: HB Lanarc

New Urbanism, the local food and agriculture movement, among many others. While much effort was being focused on urban agriculture and farmers' markets, the rest of the urban and regional food system was all too often missed. And thus AU was born.

Why Agricultural Urbanism?

As discussed in this book and in books by other authors,[20] the current model of the global industrial food system has offered some benefits but is generally considered unsustainable. In considering an alternative or more sustainable model, it is important to note that the global industrial market and regulatory systems are structured to perpetuate the current unsustainable system.

Simply put, unsustainable food systems are a serious government and market failure. We recognize that the approaches to agriculture and food systems explored in this section are at times fully viable in current economic realities and at other times face significant challenges. Because cities change slowly, we must begin consciously planning for a sustainable urban and regional food system to prepare cities and regions to pro-actively respond to change and opportunity.

Ten Principles of Agricultural Urbanism

In order to define the goals of AU and meet them in any particular the project, the following principles can be used to inform any issue, decision, or action. An AU approach to any project or plan needs to:

- **Take an integrated, food-and-agriculture-system perspective**. Promote the greatest range of food-system elements possible in every community planning and design process or project, including production, processing, distribution, retailing, education, celebration, infrastructure, food security, and others.

- **Create a rich experience of food and agriculture**. Use *placemaking* design strategies to make food visible and enhance the experiences that involve growing, harvesting, tasting, selling, buying, learning about, cooking, and sharing food.

- **Build the food and agriculture economy**. Plan into any project or neighbourhood the widest range of food-system elements possible to increase the economic activity and profile of the food system.

- **Increase access to food**. Plan and design to make food available to everyone in every neighbourhood by providing access to growing space, food stores, restaurants, and other outlets.

- **Educate about food**. Embed formal and informal education opportunities around food and agriculture into the plans, designs, and programs for every neighbourhood to provide the opportunity for rich engagement with all aspects of the food system in daily life.

- **Manage to support sustainable food systems**. Integrate sustainable food-system goals and considerations into government policy, programs, and institutional mandates as well as into all development plans. This includes integrating key food-system stakeholders into all decision-making processes.

- **Provide food and habitat for other species**. Integrate urban habitat considerations into the food and agriculture agenda for both rural and urban spaces wherever possible, recognizing that birds and others are not always a good mix with crops or other food activities.

- **Organize for food.** Forge and maintain partnerships and organizations to take responsibility for managing successful urban food systems, policies, programs, and physical spaces because food often falls between the cracks of typical governance and jurisdictional platforms.

- **Construct sustainable infrastructure for food and agriculture.** Consider the needs of urban food systems and the many opportunities they offer to community infrastructure systems. Address energy, water, wastewater, and solid-waste management.

- **Bring food and agriculture into the full suite of climate change solutions.** Develop a deeper understanding of how food and agriculture can contribute to climate mitigation and adaptation strategies.

University of British Columbia Farm Charrette, 2008.
Photo: Janine de la Salle

Agricultural Urbanism Strategies

The cornerstone of implementing AU is to integrate the systems and opportunities of food systems into urban planning and design to create an urban environment that activates and enhances all aspects of a sustainable food system through the integration — not separation of — people, their living environments, and food.

AU IS ABOUT PROVIDING OPPORTUNITIES TO:

- Grow food.
- Experience food.
- Support local processing and distribution systems for food.
- Plan in a wide array of wholesale, retail, and restaurant or food-service opportunities and experiences.
- Embed a rich tapestry of formal and informal learning opportunities around food.
- Create a culture of celebrating food and those who make it.
- Ensure that everyone in the community is fed.
- Reduce food and agriculture waste.

The implementation of the principles of AU into a wide range of city planning and design opportunities raises many opportunities. A summary of some covered in the book are included below.

FOOD PRODUCTION STRATEGIES:

- **Preserve parcels of agricultural land.** Preserve viable agricultural land wherever possible through appropriate land use decisions and by spreading density around the neighbourhood.

- **Create community gardens and productive landscapes.** Plan community gardens and appropriate supporting infrastructure into all urban areas, especially multifamily areas, and pursue ways to use productive plants in the landscape. Include more commercial food production facilities, such as greenhouses.

- **Integrate the widest possible range of food-related land uses**. Plan for a wide range of land uses related to food to accompany any agricultural areas, including processing, retail, restaurants, educational institutions, and festivals or events. This approach will increase the local food economy and support entrepreneurial farmers and the business case for farms. The essence of this approach is described as artisan agriculture.

- **Production for charity**. Develop systems that utilize unused land and glean from waste food streams to support local food banks and soup kitchens in their work to ensure that no one in the community goes hungry.

FOOD PROCESSING STRATEGIES:

- **Production diversity in land use and design**. Consider and integrate into the planning and design of the community a wide range of food-processing opportunities, including supplying large and small industrial spaces for a variety of companies.

- **Building upon existing food leaders**. Consider existing food production industries connected to the site, neighbourhood, or region as a starting point around which to build a land-use or tenant cluster. This can create an "identity" for the area.

- **Tenant casting**. Cast local smaller-scale regional food producers into a role of participating in a specific food precinct or development whose location and facilities or identity might benefit them.

- **Transparency or "back of house is front of house."** The concept in development of hiding any messy activities is traditional, but in a sterilized urban world, those activities often are the most interesting aspects to observe. Make these messy, authentic activities as visible as possible. Design production facilities to show as much of the production process as you can, through windows, displays, and other means. The informal education value of this approach can be significant.

- **Including retail in the production facility**. Wherever possible, include some form of producer-direct retail in a production facility to more directly integrate the producer and consumer.

- **Solid waste management opportunities**. Consider company and land-use synergies related to the management of packaging, including the re-use of packaging, composting of biodegradable packaging, and others. In addition, stacks of various types of agricultural and food containers can offer an interesting and authentic character to an area.

- **Water, wastewater, and energy infrastructure**. Promote the development of innovative infrastructure systems to supply the significant amounts of water a food system needs to treat its wastewater for re-use, and to both supply energy and harvest waste energy where possible.

- **Transportation needs**. In urban areas focusing on food, consider the many different logistic needs that may apply, including design for larger trucks, farm equipment if the site is adjacent working farm areas, and parking for retail visitors.

FOOD SALES STRATEGIES:

- **Support small- to medium-scale wholesalers**. Small- to medium-scale food wholesalers are the key link between regional and local producers and retailers or restaurants. Because of this, warehousing and other supporting land uses and facilities are needed wherever possible. These spaces can often fit into other land-use areas so long as the impact of the trucking associated with moving products in and out is dealt with appropriately.

- **Cluster wholesale and retail outlets**. Large wholesale-style retailers, such as Costco, can serve as an important anchor in a retail cluster around which many specialty food suppliers can gather to benefit from customer traffic. Integrating small or occasional retail outlets into wholesale outlets can increase the profitability of the wholesaler and offer a different food experience to customers.

- **Avoid food deserts**. Plan food retail outlets into every area to avoid *food deserts* that have no food retail outlets and force people to travel long distances to access food.

- **Integrate supermarkets into the urban fabric**. The typical supermarket business model includes a large, boxy building surrounded by parking lots. Alternatives exist in many areas, however, to integrate supermarkets into the urban fabric and make them more pedestrian friendly and a part of the city.

- **Support farmers' markets**. Ensure that every community has a central plaza, street, or open space to support a farmers' market. Include outlets for power and water, and access to public washrooms.

- **Don't be too tidy**. The visibility of activity involved in the shipping and making of food adds a strong sense of authenticity as well as educates customers. Let some of this "messiness" shine through.

- **Food banks**. Secure sufficient infrastructure and land to provide food banks in the community to support access to food for those who cannot afford to buy.

RESTAURANT AND FOOD SERVICE STRATEGIES:

- **Many extroverted restaurants**. Restaurants are a central part of an urban lifestyle, and a diverse community can support and benefit from many restaurant options. Wherever possible, ensure that restaurants have a visible patio to further increase the profile of food in the local culture.

- **Connect restaurants and caterers to their suppliers**. Support the opportunity for restaurants to be located close to their supply chain, such as having a brew pub or a waterfront fish and chip stand close to a commercial fishing dock. In addition, direct links and relationships between restaurateurs and agricultural producers increase the local food economy and the local food culture. Institutions can establish procurement policies to purchase as much local produce and food as possible and can build relationships through these agreements over time.

- **Restaurant waste management**. Develop environmentally friendly ways of managing the significant waste streams from restaurants, including composting, conversion of waste fryer oil to biodiesel, and others.

- **Create celebrity chefs**. Work to enhance the profile of local chefs in both the media and the community to support their economic success and celebrate their skills and creativity in general.

FOOD EDUCATION STRATEGIES:

- **Diverse education opportunities**. Develop a strategy to offer the widest possible range of food-related education in the community, including formal and informal training in growing and cooking food, general food knowledge, and business opportunities in the food industry.

- **Profile of food and agriculture**. Plan and design communities to make visible as much of the food system as possible to support curiosity and informal learning on all aspects of the food system in the community.

- **Youth education**. Support youth who are interested and motivated to start-up farm operations. Encourage educational institutions to develop flexible programs that facilitate a hands-on learning experience.

FOOD CELEBRATION STRATEGIES:

- **Visibility of food in the public realm**. Design the public realm to have all aspects of the food system visible, including growing, processing, packaging, transporting, selling, making, eating, and learning about food. Making the food system visible includes programming food into plazas, parks, and streets; ensuring buildings have windows to make internal food operations visible from the street; and more.

- **Food events throughout the year**. Support the greatest range of food events possible throughout the year in the community. Celebrating the food aspects of each season. Design spaces for large festivals. The list of food events in towns and cities in North America is enormous, and events cover all seasons and nearly every imaginable type of food or drink.

Therefore, each community can have at least one good food festival based on some aspect of the food system or some agricultural or food product in which the community excels.

- **Home and garden design**. Ensure that all homes have great kitchens and access to gardening space nearby to support the celebration of food in each home.

A vibrant food system is one of the most important elements of a great quality of life in any community and needs to be strategically planned and designed into the community. Great urban food systems do not happen by accident. AU offers a coherent approach that enables planners and designers to support the development of sustainable urban and regional food systems.

5. Unit of Analysis: The Food and Agriculture System

While most people think only of the eating and possibly the farming aspects of a food system, a number of elements that make up a sustainable food system should be integrated into planning strategies. Indeed, a food system is the cycle of farming, processing, transporting, distributing, celebrating, and recovering food waste in the context of larger natural, social, political, and economic driving forces. Specifically, a food system includes:

1. **Farming & Management** — the growing and raising of food, including rural and urban agriculture.

Figure 5.1: Elements of a Food and Agriculture System
Source: HB Lanarc

2. **Processing** — the process of altering raw foodstuffs to create a different, more refined product. Examples include preserving, cooking or baking, preparation, meat processing, grain milling, and other value-adding operations.

3. **Transportation & Storage** — the distribution and storage of both raw and processed food products.

4. **Selling & Buying** — the retailing, wholesaling, and purchasing of food products. This takes place from the farmgate, to grocery stores, to farmers' markets, to restaurants.

5. **Eating & Celebration** — the act of consumption and enjoyment of food. This can include food-related events, and eating in both the public and private realms.

6. **Waste Recovery** — the diversion, management, and utilization of organic waste (for example, as an energy source or as fertilizer using recycled nutrients).

A sustainable food system is built on principles that further the ecological, social, and economic values of a community and region. A sustainable food and agriculture system is:

- Secure and therefore reliable and resilient to change, and accessible to all members of society.

- Energy, water, and waste efficient.

- An economic generator for farmers, whole communities, and regions.

- Environmentally beneficial or benign.

- Balanced in food imports and local capacities.

- Climate adaptive, with agricultural practices and crop choices being regionally appropriate.

- Highly productive in urban and rural areas.

- Supported by multiple scales of food processing, storage, distribution, and retail facilities.

- Celebrated through community events, markets, restaurants, and more.

- Biodiverse in agro-ecosystems as well as in crop selection.

- Educational to create awareness of food and agricultural issues.

- Ethical, ensuring quality of life for livestock and providing a fair wage to producers and processors both locally and abroad.

All sectors including, public, private, non-profit, and academic will need to collaborate in building sustainable food and agriculture systems. These systems are complex and constantly changing, which is a key barrier to action. Government policy has one of the most central roles in creating and supporting sustainable food and agriculture systems. While food and agriculture policy at the federal and provincial/state levels is an essential part of a path forward, AU focuses-in on the city scale to proactively address the challenges and opportunities for food and agriculture.

6. Macro Trends, Local Reponses: Food and Agriculture System Planning at the Local Level

The topic of food and agriculture is unfamiliar territory for many local governments. Planners and decision-makers have traditionally focused on more familiar concerns, such as roads and infrastructure, water and waste, and managing land and development. However, the pressing concerns of sustainability are encouraging municipal governments to think more creatively about how they can address issues of community resilience and livability, and food and agriculture consistently showing up and providing some of the most interesting opportunities.

The various stages of food production, processing, distribution, and consumption are related to many issues that municipalities are grappling with. For example, the food system impacts and is impacted by land use, urban design, transportation, economic development, waste management, cost of living, and health. Moreover, municipal governments across the continent are beginning to recognize the enormous opportunity provided by a more thoughtful consideration of food and its relationship to local community development. Sustainable food and agriculture system planning and design is an opportunity to increase the sustainability and quality-of-life of their communities, and it can be a critical lever for achieving other planning goals and strategies. Cities across the country and around the world are recognizing, creating, and capitalizing on the benefits of sustainable food systems as they are now understood to be an integral part of the planning practice.

Trends and Impacts on Local Sustainability

The world is rapidly changing and so is our food system; implications for cities has never been more significant. Local governments are increasingly on the front lines of sustainability and are key players in building sustainable food and agriculture systems. The following section outlines key trends and local responses. Figure 6.1 depicts action areas for food and agriculture system across from urban to rural areas.

ENERGY SECURITY

Our food system is almost completely dependent upon fossil fuels. Production, transportation, packaging, processing, refrigeration, preparation, and other food-system components — excluding household cooking — require ten units of energy for every unit of energy produced in the form of food. In short, food systems in North America consume ten times more energy than they produce, and depend on existing, relatively inexpensive, readily available fossil fuel. Award-winning novelist, historian, and essayist Ronald Wright sums it up as follows:

> We tend to think of the looming energy crisis in terms of cars, factories, heating, and air conditioning, but the first thing to keep in mind is that fossil fuels are feeding us.... how many are aware that we have literally been eating oil and gas for more than a hundred years?[21]

Action Areas for Food: Urban to Wild

WILD	RURAL	SUB URBAN	URBAN
• Resource Managment	• Wildlife Integration	• Urban Containment	• Urban Agriculture
• Sustainable Harvests	• Agricultural Area Plans	• Perl-urban agriculture	• City Food Plans
• Traditional Food Culture	• Processing Infrastructure	• Retro-fitting suburbia	• Food Precincts
	• Farmer Housing		• Celebration
			• Waste recovery

Figure 6.1: Action Areas for Food Urban to Wild.
Source: HB Lanarc

Local governments and communities are beginning to examine the opportunities for becoming more self-reliant when it comes to energy. Areas where local governments and communities can begin to address the energy challenge include:

- Encouraging the production of local foods to reduce transportation-related energy use.

- Building/retrofitting for energy-efficient infrastructure, such as using waste heat recovery for agricultural production (for example, to heat greenhouses).

- Increasing access to food markets for residents and purchasers, and decreasing trips generated from food procurement.

- Exploration of alternative energy sources, such as solar, wind, and geothermal.

- Re-introducing local food and agricultural infrastructure, such as processing facilities, in order to create more resilience in the supply and demand system for food and agricultural goods.

GREENHOUSE GAS EMISSIONS

A by-product of the energy-intensive food system is the substantial amount of greenhouse gases (GHGs) that are released into the atmosphere. A main source of GHG emissions in the food and agriculture system is the transportation and storage of goods. Nearly one-quarter of trips in the city (most of which are done via vehicle) are associated with purchasing and consuming food.[22] Many farmers and advocates are now

Family Gardening in the Strathcona Community Garden, Vancouver BC.
Photo: Milisa Gardy, Honey Bee Photography.

looking toward organic agriculture, which involves using energy from the sun (rather than high-input conventional agriculture that depends on natural gas and petroleum-based fertilizers and pesticides) as the primary source of energy for growing food.

Local governments and communities can begin to address the climate change challenge as it relates to food and agriculture by:

- Allocating and protecting land for urban and peri-urban agriculture and related activities.

- Encouraging the growth of medium- to small-scale food outlets in order to make pedestrian and transit access to food sources a more convenient option.

- Supporting initiatives that aim to increase awareness and market access for local foods.

- Promoting and encouraging the transformation of agriculture to an industry that uses clean energy.

GROWING CITIES AND TOWNS

Accommodating population growth sustainably (that is, without increasing ecological impacts) is probably one of the greatest challenges for local governments and communities. Protecting agricultural land as populations rise requires urban growth to be well-managed and focused on existing built areas.

Approaches to managing growth and protecting agricultural land at a local level include:

- Creating urban containment boundaries to limit the expansion of urban area onto undeveloped lands.

- Defining areas where infill and intensification are possible and desirable, and encouraging new growth in these existing areas.

- Protecting agricultural land specifically for agriculture through local zoning regulations. (Ideally, this would be supported by provincial legislation similar to **British Columbia's Agricultural Land Reserve**.)

- Building higher density, sustainable communities that are transit-oriented, mixed-use, walkable, and livable.

- Integrating urban residential and farm uses at the urban-rural interface.

LOCAL ECONOMY

Local food and agriculture can be powerful economic drivers whose true potential has not yet been fully realized. The majority of the agricultural products that are grown in North America are exported for processing in distant (including foreign) markets. Because of this, most of the potential value of major crops is lost to an export-based agricultural economy that has less to do with local people and the bioregion, and more to do with single bottom-line economics. Processing, selling, and celebrating food locally can create a powerful economic multiplier effect for the local economy. Furthermore, in recent decades, it has become increasingly difficult for farmers to maintain their livelihoods on the prairies, and the average age of farmers increases every year. The absence of a vertically integrated local economy that specifically addresses agribusiness represents a future risk to sustainability and economic competitiveness.

Strategies for economic development and bolstering the local agri-food system will grow from the establishment of a planning system that places value on agricultural land and promotes vertically integrated agribusiness. This will help to ensure that towns and cities will grow to be resilient in the event that global socio-economic or environmental conditions disrupt the globalized food markets.

This approach at the local level may include:

- Creation of an economic development strategy focused on agriculture and food.[23]

- Scaling up local food infrastructure, such as value-added processing and distribution centres.

- Supporting initiatives that are focused on increasing market access for local foods, such as chef-to-farmer networking events.

- Increasing new farmers' access to farmland.

INDIVIDUAL AND COMMUNITY HEALTH

Many people in North America and globally do not have access to healthy food choices, which has resulted in a dramatic increase in obesity and diabetes rates in both adults and children. Other population health issues associated with a lack of healthy food choices are certain types of cancer, cardiovascular disease, and type-two diabetes, which is now prevalent in children. These illnesses are very costly for health-care systems: In Canada, the treatment of diet-related illnesses is estimated at over one billion dollars in direct costs and over three billion dollars in indirect costs.[24] Often, foods high in saturated fats, salts, and carbohydrates are more easily available and less expensive than nutritious foods. The effects on urban sustainability include reduced quality of life and a growing number of unhealthy and under- or over-nourished residents.

As with all of the trends documented here, health is a multi-jurisdictional issue. While health largely falls under the purview of the federal and provincial governments, local governments and communities are also able to contribute to food security through:

- Creating urban forms that promote health, such as walkable communities.

- Increasing access to local food markets by allowing a range of market types in a range of land uses.

- Supporting community gardens, demonstration gardens, and other forms of urban agriculture as key recreational, therapeutic, and community-building activities.

COST OF FOOD

Relatively speaking, North America has largely been shielded from the 2008 world food crisis that saw a dramatic increase in the cost of basic food staples in most countries. However, the protection from this type of price increase is temporary, and Canadians should be considering how to mitigate these price shocks through diversification of agricultural goods and greater self-sufficiency. Also, food in Canada is comparatively cheap, in part because not all the costs of production, transportation etc. are included in the prices consumers pay at the till. For example, there are environmental, health, and other externalities associated with feedlot beef, including methane emissions and concentrated waste streams. Conversely, the pricing of fresh, high-quality local foods better reflect their real costs, including paying farmers a fair price for their labour and stewardship of their land. While the market transformation toward normalizing more sustainable food that is priced to cover the true costs of the product will be gradual, social justice and access to healthy food must be considered and planned for.

Some ways to address the increased cost of food while ensuring access to a healthy diet for all people include:

- Exploring food subsidy programs for low-income individuals and families.

- Examining areas in the local food system where increased energy efficiency could result in market efficiencies and lower costs for consumers without adverse effects on the integrity of the food system or return on investments for farmers.

- Facilitating and encouraging urban agriculture so that people are able to grow a significant amount of their own food. This may involve but is not limited to retrofitting industrial buildings to support rooftop farm operations, enterprise around urban aquaculture, market gardens, or greenhouses.

ECOSYSTEM HEALTH

Agriculture can be an important element of ecosystem health (for example, crops are food for migratory birds; old field habitats are hunting grounds for predatory birds; hedgerows are songbird habitat; and riverbank areas are home to fish and amphibians, soil microbes, voles, and more).

Local governments and communities can support sustainable agriculture by:

- Allocating land for small plot intensive (SPIN) farms within town boundaries

- Setting guidelines for human- and ecosystem-friendly agriculture that would occur on land within town boundaries (examples include a ban on chemical pesticides, fertilizers, and herbicides and the limiting of odours and dust generated from farm activities)

Summary & Opportunity

Food-system planning is quickly becoming mainstream. While all city departments are increasingly collaborating to achieve sustainability goals, food and agriculture systems are often led by planning departments. Good land-use planning is the primary ingredient to any sustainability initiative at the local level. The growing attention to food in planning has been recently discussed in the journals of both the Canadian Institute of Planners and the American Planning Association. Similarly, a study of planners' perspectives on their role in the food system revealed an understanding that it is critically important to planning sustainable cities.[25] Responses included:

> "Food . . . is a public good that transcends the market."

> "We're realizing more the need for holistic planning to go beyond the built environment; social issues like food are related to the built environment."

> "[food] is a critical part of neighbourhood revitalization."

> "We need to get more involved in nutrition issues — it's important for healthy residents in healthy cities."

> "We need to recognize food as an important aspect of our local economy."

> "Better access of low-income, inner-city residents to less expensive, quality grocery stores needs to be achieved."

Local government can capitalize on efficiencies made possible by an integrated planning approach, which brings together different systems (for example, infrastructure, energy, and buildings) that perform different but synergistic functions to meet common sustainability goals. Understanding relationships between different systems' elements is a first step.

Table 6.1 on the following pages outlines a menu of food and agriculture sustainability strategies from the local government perspective. Through creating a matrix of food-system elements and key performance areas of local government, we are able to show how food and agriculture are local government opportunities. Note that use of the term "planning" here refers to the coordination of all municipal departments in achieving common sustainability goals. The matrix reveals how a food and agriculture system can be strategically integrated into other planning efforts to deliver on a community's sustainability objectives.

Lunching in the Railway Community Garden, Vancouver BC.
Photo: Janine de la Salle

Table 6.1 The Food System: Opportunities for Integrating Food and Agriculture into Sustainable Community Planning

| Agriculture & Food System Elements | Key Performance Areas of Local Government | | | |
	LAND USE & GROWTH MANAGEMENT	TRANSPORTATION	URBAN DESIGN	ENERGY & INFRASTRUCTURE
PRODUCTION	Contain urban growth and protect agricultural land Permit community gardens as a use in all land-use designations	Provide end-of-trip cyclist facilities (secure, weather-protected bike storage) near community gardens	Enhance the public and private realms through food amenities, including community and private gardens, edible landscaping, green roofs, etc.	Use production space to manage stormwater Use waste heat from infrastructure (e.g., sewer lines) and other as an energy source for greenhouses
PROCESSING	Permit context-appropriate scales of food processing as a use in all land-use designations	Provide end-of-trip cyclist facilities (secure, weather-protected bike storage) for processing facilities Ensure good transit access to processors	Provide community-scale processing options (e.g., bread ovens, fruit presses) as amenities in private and public developments	Use waste heat as an input into processing activity, and/or as an output for other processing or industrial uses
TRANSPORT	Cluster various food-related uses (e.g., processing, retail, etc.) to reduce transportation pressures for goods movement and to increase walkability	Ensure that transportation master plans include a food transport component	Design for convenient yet pedestrian-friendly food drop-off/loading areas at the rear of buildings containing food retailers and restaurants	Promote biodiesel or other alternative energy-powered vehicles (including people-powered) for the local transport of foods.
STORAGE	Permit food storage in all land-use designations as part of food-secure/resilient neighbourhoods	Create multi-functional underground parking areas for cool storage (e.g., root cellars, beer cellars, etc.)	Include food-storage components in site and neighbourhood design (e.g., root cellars, beer cellars, etc.)	Use renewable and/or waste energy to cool large food-storage areas

Key Performance Areas of Local Government

BUILDINGS & HOUSING	PARKS & OPEN SPACE	WASTE MANAGEMENT	SOCIAL/ECONOMIC DEVELOPMENT	
Insulate buildings and provide urban habitat through the use of green roofs and vertical landscaping	Integrate edible landscaping and permit gardening as a use and recreational opportunity in parks and public open spaces Ensure required gardening infrastructure, including water hook-up and secure sheds	Provide composting space in gardening areas to help divert waste from the landfill	Use all food-system elements in social programming (e.g., skill development and education) and as part of a larger economic branding/ marketing strategy (e.g., food precincts and related destinations)	
Design community centres to accommodate community kitchens for processing activity (canning, preserving, etc.)	Provide community-scale processing options (e.g., bread ovens, fruit presses) in parks and public open spaces, where appropriate	Support food-processing waste-diversion programs to reduce organic waste		
Provide food drop-off and distribution areas in multifamily and possibly other buildings (e.g., community-supported agriculture drop-off points)	Provide end-of-trip facilities (secure, weather-protected bike storage) near gardens in parks Ensure good transit service to garden areas	Support waste-collection efforts that also rescue quality organic waste from retailers and restaurants (i.e., unused, nearly expired food) for emergency organizations		
Provide food-storage areas in units and buildings (e.g., pantries)	Consider integrating community root cellars into parks and other public spaces	Co-locate or incorporate waste-diversion facilities/ areas near or in food-storage areas		

Table 6.1 The Food System: Opportunities for Integrating Food and Agriculture into Sustainable Community Planning

Agriculture & Food System Elements	Key Performance Areas of Local Government			
	LAND USE & GROWTH MANAGEMENT	TRANSPORTATION	URBAN DESIGN	ENERGY & INFRASTRUCTURE
RETAIL, WHOLESALE & MARKETING	Support food retailers as important in complete, mixed-use neighbourhoods	Provide end-of-trip cyclist facilities (secure, weather-protected bike storage) in food retail areas Ensure good transit access to food retailers	Ensure food retail outlets are designed to a scale and character appropriate for walkable, vibrant neighbourhoods	Use renewable or waste heat from infrastructure as an energy source for retailers/ wholesalers
EATING & CELEBRATION	Support restaurants and other eating venues as important in complete, mixed-use neighbourhoods	Provide end-of-trip cyclist facilities (secure, weather-protected bike storage) at eating establishments/ venues Ensure good transit access to eating establishments/ venues	Encourage sidewalk cafés and other opportunities for food celebration in the public and private realms through pedestrian-oriented design guidelines	Use renewable or waste heat from infrastructure as an energy source for eating establishments
NUTRIENT RECYCLING & WASTE MANAGEMENT	Support composting as an important activity in all land-use designations	Utilize biodiesel and/or waste oil as a transportation fuel (e.g., green fleet)	Design composting facilities into the public realm (e.g. appropriate receptacles) to divert organic waste from the landfill	Use waste oil (e.g., vegetable oil) in a digester for power generation

Key Performance Areas of Local Government

BUILDINGS & HOUSING	PARKS & OPEN SPACE	WASTE MANAGEMENT	SOCIAL/ECONOMIC DEVELOPMENT	
Incorporate food retailers (e.g., grocery stores) into residential developments as part of complete, mixed-use neighbourhoods	Co-locate food retailers and parks to support complete, vibrant communities	Support food-retailer waste-diversion programs to reduce organic waste		
Ensure community centres are designed to accommodate community kitchens for processing (canning, preserving, etc.)	Design and integrate celebration opportunities (e.g., picnic tables for food fairs, community dinners, etc.) into parks and other public open spaces	Support restaurant waste-diversion programs to reduce organic waste		
Ensure all multifamily and other buildings in which food is consumed include organic-waste separation stations and/or storage	Use composted organic waste as a fertilizer in parks and other public areas	Use biodiesel and/ or waste oil as part of garbage pick-up.		

Bees on the "Queen Excluder", Cambridge,
Photo: Emory Davidge

Part II: Agricultural Urbanism – Core Elements

By Mark Holland and Janine de la Salle

Agricultural Urbanism brings many elements and ideas together across a wide spectrum of disciplines. Part II details the landscape of sustainable food and agriculture systems. This discussion is organized into the food and agriculture system elements that form the framework for AU.

7. Agricultural Production

The first dimension of Agricultural Urbanism is the cornerstone issue of farming, or agricultural production. All food starts with some form of agriculture and, therefore, the pursuit of sustainable, high-intensity agriculture is paramount. Some of the key elements of agricultural production to address when planning an urban or regional food system are land, farmers, agricultural practices and business models, equipment, and land-use controls. This chapter provides a special focus section on urban agriculture types and requirements.

Land

The first and most obvious element of agricultural production is land. There are three areas of consideration regarding land: The preservation of farm land, the size of land parcels and land tenure options.

AGRICULTURAL LAND PRESERVATION

High-quality agricultural land needs to be preserved wherever possible in order to retain the important soil capital that underpins any sustainable regional food system. Agricultural land is protected in some jurisdictions by various land conservation systems and in other jurisdictions, there is little to stop development from encroaching on farmland. Low-quality farmland has a variety of agricultural uses in more rural areas, but not in urban and urban-edge environments, where the highest priority for preservation should be high-quality arable land. As discussed in a later section, where development and increased land value have

impeded a farm's ability to legitimately function, we may need to consider a strategic approach that allows some development, in order to return the largest possible amount of land back to agriculture. This approach would involve appropriate ownership, subsidies, and institutional management systems.

Tractor on a Rutland Farm, BC
Photo: Claire de la Salle

PARCEL SIZE

The issue of parcel size is becoming critical in supporting the full diversity of agricultural production desired in a region. Large parcels, while more expensive to a farmer, can support a wide range of agricultural production, but often specialize in a small number of products. In and around urban areas, parcels are almost always smaller, requiring strategic education in unique and creative business models for high-value, small-scale agriculture in order to make these smaller parcels work financially.

TENURE

Purchasing land can be financially challenging for a new farmer. Traditionally in Canada, farms were often passed down through the family or, in cases of colonization, land was given free by the Crown, the executive government in Commonwealth Countries. Because of this many farmers in past centuries did not have to start their farm with a significant outlay of capital to simply acquire land on which to farm. Today, access to farmland for farming is much more difficult as it is largely held by private land owners who largely determine the degree to which farming happens on the land. Where ownership resides with those who decide not to farm or to try to convert the land to another use, agricultural capacity can be lost. A sustainable food and agriculture system will offer farmers a range of tenure opportunities to support entry-level and experienced farmers, as well as large and small farms.[26] In addition, the role of agricultural or land trusts to hold farmland in perpetuity for the express purpose of farming is likely to be needed to ensure that key parcels of land in highly contested areas remain for agriculture uses.

Livestock hauler, Abbotford BC
Photo: Claire de la Salle

Farmers

The focus of pro-agriculture efforts has largely been on the preservation of farmland, which while important as discussed above, is now being eclipsed by the challenges of finding farmers to farm food in our North American economy. There are a number of considerations in this regard, including: Demographics, the perceived attractiveness of farming as a career, knowledge of advanced farming techniques and securing farm workers.

DEMOGRAPHICS

The average age of farmers in North America is rapidly increasing. Currently in British Columbia, the average age is approximately fifty-seven years. The United States Department of Agriculture (USDA) reports that the proportion of farmers over fifty-five rose from an appropriate 37 percent in 1954 to 61 percent by 1997, and has continued to rise. Concurrently, the proportion of farmers under thirty-five declined from 15 percent in 1954 to 8 percent in 1997.[27] While the short-term impact of this aging trend has been somewhat offset by mechanization and **agribusiness human resources models**, the future of sustainable regional food systems depends on making farming a much more attractive and competitive career for youth.

Interestingly, a counter-trend is appearing in the more progressive areas of agriculture. In 2008, the Organic Valley cooperative of over 1300 farms in the US and Canada reported a much lower average age, with over 35 percent of farmers under forty. The average age of Organic Valley farmers in 2008 was forty-nine, with 14 percent under thirty, 20 percent under forty, and 39 percent under fifty years of age.[28]

ATTRACTIVENESS OF FARMING

A sustainable regional food system will have a full range of farmers at different stages of life. A key element in keeping a robust and diverse group of farmers in our regions is making farming a desirable career for today's youth. In the face of significantly greater financial rewards, certainty, and societal respect associated with any number of other careers, it takes a seriously committed young person to choose farming over other options. Some regions in North America are focusing on attracting immigrant farmers more than trying to draw their current youth into farming. This is one approach, but it misses the point that farming is not a competitive career choice for many local families. In order to attract younger farmers, a region will have to celebrate farmers, turn them into minor celebrities, and work to ensure farming has a low barrier to entry and an income level competitive with that of many other career choices.

KNOWLEDGE OF ADVANCED FARMING METHODS AND INNOVATIVE BUSINESS MODELS

Knowledge of advanced, high-productivity, and high-value approaches to agriculture, in addition to organic farming techniques, becomes critically important to a sustainable regional food system. Currently, most instruction in agricultural schools focuses on large-scale agribusiness and not on the alternative approaches such as high-intensity, high-value, organic farming techniques and business models that AU requires.

FARM WORKERS

Farms require affordable labour, and supplying these farm workers and meeting their family-housing and other needs can be formidable for a farmer, especially a new farmer. A range of initiatives is required to address the labour requirements of a sustainable regional food system, and these will require many stakeholders to address the varied issues in a coordinated manner. For instance, in some areas, the housing required for farm labourers is not permitted by local agricultural zoning. Also, with the advent of Canadian federal policies designed to attract immigrant farm labourers, ethical considerations on the health, safety, and treatment of these farm workers is increasingly coming under scrutiny by advocacy groups and others.

Agricultural Practices and Business Model

The next set of issues and challenges in the production dimension of AU includes the agricultural practices and business model that underpins production.

AGROECOLOGY

Essentially, any discussion of AU needs to start with the principles of agroecology.[29] This may or may not include the official certifications of organic as these designations can be diluted in their institutionalized and bureaucratic realities. However, the principles of safe, organic agriculture are a near requirement for any serious food production that occurs in and around villages and cities. Agroecological principles are also a foundation of a sustainable food system and as such,

Loading the truck at Foxglove Farms Saltspring Island BC.
Photo: Janine de la Salle

Much has been said about sustainable approaches to agricultural production, starting with the organic movement that gained momentum in the 1970s in North America and has since gone mainstream, with General Mills and others being major producers of organic produce. Formal guidelines for organic production were established in the USA in the 1990s following a hotly debated process. We leave the debate between large and small organic production and all its associated discussions on embodied energy, emissions, economics, and the culture of food to others. For the purpose of this book, we make the observation that AU is predisposed to small or human scales of agricultural production due to its inherent focus on the local, urban, and regional scales of settlement and economy. AU is predicated on integrating food production and cities and, therefore, the agricultural practices must be as safe and benign as possible and even offer the "delight" that McDonough and Braungart refer to above, to allow them to integrate, with the best possible outcomes, into an urban or village environment.

should be promoted everywhere. Currently, the dominant model of the interface between city and agricultural areas is one of **"buffers"** — a focus on putting distance between them.

The reason is obvious enough. If agricultural practices include liberally spraying poisons and fertilizers, and using tillage methods that cause significant clouds of dust and particulate, machinery that causes excessive noise, and manure-management systems that inundate large areas with noxious odours, then few of us would want our children to sleep or live in that environment. As McDonough and Braungart note in their book, Cradle to Cradle: "Rather than being an aesthetic and cultural delight, modern agriculture becomes a terror and a fright to local residents who want to live and raise families in a healthy setting."[30]

MARKET ORIENTATION

An AU approach to the market includes a primary orientation to local food markets in the business model for farms. Conventional agriculture has largely focused on export markets and the industrial, regulatory, and educational models have evolved to support this approach. By no means is export-oriented agriculture wrong or unnecessary. Indeed, there are many significant benefits to it, and the essential truth of economies of scale will always remain. It is likely that, in the future, export-driven agriculture will be essential in a sustainable development scenario, with sustainable energy, water, and transportation systems in place. However, the land use, market orientation and culture of food that forms the foundation of AU are a locally-focused milieux. The focus of

Okanagan Vineyard.
Photo: Claire de la Salle

FARMING EQUIPMENT

The requirements for equipment on the modern farm can be formidable. The scope of equipment required to run a contemporary industrial farm matches or exceeds the requirements for any other major industrial corporation.[31] Alternatively, in smaller-scale agricultural models, equipment may be replaced by sound management practices and human labour.

> ### FARM EQUIPMENT/ MANAGEMENT PRACTICE REQUIREMENTS:
>
> - Soil cultivation and preparation.
> - Planting.
> - Fertilizing & Pest Control.
> - Irrigation.
> - Harvesting/post-harvest.
> - Hay making and mowing.
> - Loading.
> - Many others focused on specialty crops.

the business model for farming in an AU paradigm is on high-intensity, high-value, organic (safe), and value-added food businesses. Agricultural production is seen as the first step in a vertically integrated approach to food production. In short, AU focuses more on food and farming than on simple agricultural products.

Equipment

The next element in agricultural and food production is the issue of the equipment required to manage a modern farm. There are a few issues of specific importance here including: Farm equipment, management systems and, equipment ownership.

When a farm includes a major livestock operation, such as beef, hog, or chicken farming, the scope of barns and equipment becomes infinitely more formidable, complex, and expensive.

MANAGEMENT SYSTEMS

In addition to the physical equipment required, computer, software, and support systems are also required to achieve optimum performance and provide data for management decisions in farming operations.

EQUIPMENT OWNERSHIP OPTIONS

A significant amount of equipment is needed for many farm operations, large or small, export or locally focused. This investment can be prohibitive to a new or small farmer, and alternative ownership or financial models may be required for a sustainable regional food system to ensure the diversity of farmers and the robustness of the region's food supply. Based on one study from the University of Saskatchewan on Québec-based farm equipment cooperatives, the cost of having access to a full range of modern equipment and technology could be lowered by over 30 percent by using a cooperative equipment ownership model.[32]

Land Use Controls

The final dimension of production to consider involves the critical issue of land-use controls as exercised by any number of local, regional, or senior governments and other related agencies. Two issues in particular are worth addressing, agricultural land conversion and zoning.

AGRICULTURAL LAND CONVERSION

In areas where there are no controls on agricultural land, development tends to sprawl rapidly outward onto large and inexpensive parcels of land on the edge of a city. This is visible across North America, and has many well-documented negative implications. In some regions, states, or provinces, there are more stringent controls on agricultural land, such as British Columbia's Agricultural Land Reserve. These controls typically establish a commission to oversee any application to change from agricultural use to another. They can be very effective at preserving farmland but may not be agile enough to respond to the unique requirements of a successful regional food system because they focus solely on land, and there is not enough for a sustainable regional food system.

As a general rule, development must respect agricultural land-use restrictions. However, in some cases, the particular nature of the land controls may hinder a strong local food agenda that could respond to unique locations adjacent existing urban areas, many of which are permanently compromised in their value to conventional industrial agricultural business models. In these cases, there exist significant opportunities that maintain or increase average agricultural productivity. Further, special development cases may bring many other sustainable community benefits through development to offer strategic subsidies, unique design approaches, institutional endowments, land trusts, and more.

ZONING

Most local governments have zoning for agricultural land areas, and these zones establish what uses and activities are allowed on the land. Zoning is entirely within the jurisdiction of a local government and can be changed by local politicians. This can be positive if a creative and progressive approach, such as a strong AU agenda, is proposed because zoning can be amended to accommodate the rich array of uses and

Okanagan Farm Worker.
Photo: Claire de la Salle

Beans growing at the Stop, Toronto ON
Photo: Janine de la Salle

Focus on Urban Agriculture

The practice of growing food in cities is a cornerstone of Agricultural Urbansim. Urban agriculture is experiencing a renaissance in North America, where community, government, learning institutions, and developers are increasingly collaborating in creating food-growing spaces in urban areas. This section examines the many expressions of Urban Agriculture in North America and how to design for food growing in cities. (Please see Appendix B for a case study on Southeast False Creek that was awarded the top LEED rating for neighbourhood design that included urban agriculture features)

EXPRESSIONS OF URBAN AGRICULTURE

Urban agriculture is a highly adaptable and functional characteristic of towns and cities and is rapidly becoming a central element of livable and complete communities across North America. Borrowing from the success of urban agriculture systems in countries such as Cuba and Zimbabwe, a wide range of urban agriculture types have begun to emerge as an important and permanent characteristic of communities.

In planning and design for food and agriculture in cities, it is important to understand the characteristics of urban agriculture in order to develop a program that fits with needs and resources in the community. This overview describes the range of urban agriculture types, programs and functions, and management structures (Please see Appendix A for more detail on design opportunities for urban agriculture).

The following urban agriculture types occur in the public and private realm. Urban agriculture types are differentiated by their unique characteristics and considerations of various types of growing spaces. Often an urban agriculture site will contain a combination of several types such as: Container gardening (raised beds, vertical growing, pots), in-ground planting, rooftop gardens, backyard gardens and planters and edible landscapes.

value-added food industries and activities associated with the project.

On the other hand, if no sustainable food agenda is present and development is considered, the agricultural productivity of the land can be lost forever to a less progressive approach to development.

This section has focused on providing an overview of some of the key considerations related to land and agricultural production that need to be addressed for sustainable urban and regional food systems, and on providing some observations from an AU point of view. The next chapter picks up from where the production of raw agricultural products leaves off and moves into the world of food processing, packaging, and distribution.

Clearly, the emergence of urban agriculture in North American cities cannot be considered solely from a food-needs subsistence basis. Interestingly, however, urban agriculture has been integrated into the political agenda more comprehensively than in the Global South.[33] In Europe and North America, where people are comparatively well-fed, urban agriculture has been linked to a vibrant spectrum of ecological, social, and economic benefits in addition to those of food security.

Potting Shed
Drawing: Kelly Domoni

URBAN AGRICULTURE TYPES:

- Teaching and learning gardens and farms.
- Significant food production.
- Education on growing, preserving, and preparing foods.
- Agri- and aquacultural enterprise.
- Recreation and therapy.
- Community development and capacity building.
- Crime reduction.
- Addiction rehabilitation.
- Open-space management.
- Storm water management.
- Urban greening and biodiversity.
- Waste diversion and composting.

Each unique type, program, and function of urban agriculture is further differentiated by the management structure of the growing space. Management structures for urban agriculture can take many forms, including: Community/resident volunteer management of a garden, garden or farm managed by the farmer, organizational management of a garden (for example, non-profit society, restaurant, school, and/or partnerships between local government, community, and private developers. Expressions of urban agriculture are highly diverse and adaptable to virtually any space, function, and management structure.

URBAN AGRICULTURE REQUIREMENTS

Urban agriculture is commonly understood to encompass a wide range of agricultural activities within the boundaries of semi-urban and urban areas. This section focuses on: Integrating food-producing plants into the planning and design of the landscape; creating new opportunities for urban agriculture through building and landscape design and zeroing in on the supporting elements of urban agriculture that help to make it a viable design and planning option. Appendix A offers design ideas and considerations for urban agriculture.

When incorporating AU into the public or private realm, there are many requirements to ensure long-term feasibility to consider. The following paragraphs outline the core urban agriculture requirements.

Soil type and depth. Soil type and depth will vary widely based on type of garden bed, microclimate conditions, and plant types. It is essential to match the soil to with these conditions (e.g. intensive rooftops may require special light weight soil, or really wet areas need well-drained soil).

Drainage. Adequate drainage for plants growing in containers or beds on non-permeable surfaces is essential to the long-term viability of urban agriculture. Good drainage requires appropriate soil types, as well as drainage trays or other methods to trap and evaporate excess moisture.

Wind exposure. Given that many urban agriculture opportunities occur on balconies, patios, and rooftops, wind exposure needs to be considered. Sensitive plants require a screen against high winds, and enhanced irrigation needs to be considered because wind speeds up the evaporation of moisture in soil.

Access. The transportation of both people and garden materials to and from public and semi-public spaces is another consideration. In a multi-storey building, elevator access from the parking area to the rooftop is critical. AU areas should also be universally accessible. For instance, elevator access to rooftop garden areas from the lower parkade is essential both for people with disabilities and for those transporting garden supplies such as soil, plants, equipment, and non-compostable waste. Urban agriculture spaces such as courtyards, rooftops, and private patios, should be accessible by necessary garden equipment such as wheelbarrows. For at-grade garden space, access by vehicle to drop off materials and supplies should be considered.

Water sources and uses. Irrigation of urban agriculture areas will likely require a potable water source that can be distributed through hose bibs and/or automated irrigation systems. Rainwater collection for irrigation of urban agriculture spaces, while water-efficient, requires monitoring to ensure health and safety standards. Both automated and hand-watering irrigation should be thought of, as hand watering is an enriching aspect of growing plants. It's important to have an adequate number of hose bibs for personal garden plots and large patio areas. Micro irrigation and drip irrigation (which can be set with timers to irrigate at the most efficient times and at the roots of plants) can reduce potable-water use.

Size and dimension of beds. The size and dimension of urban agriculture beds will vary widely, depending on design concepts, available space, and solar exposure. In terms of accessing beds for maintenance, a 0.6 meter, 2-foot, reach is a general guide. If a bed has access from only one side, it can be 0.6 meter, 2 feet wide,; if it is accessible from both sides it can be 1.2 meters, 4 feet wide.

Orientation/exposure. Areas that contain urban agriculture plantings should be oriented for maximum solar exposure and minimum wind exposure. Rooftop gardens may experience high winds. Choose plants that are tolerant of wind and put up living screens (trellises with vines) to shelter people and plants. If practical, place screens on the north side of plants. For container plantings in high-wind areas, be sure to have adequate soil depth and non-porous containers because moisture will quickly evaporate. Consider wind-block walls as part of building design.

Materials. Construction materials for garden beds, planters, and/or containers should use non-toxic materials.

Supporting structures. Structures such as tool sheds, potting stations, root sheds, compost facilities, processing facilities, and irrigation systems are essential components of a urban agriculture program. These structures should keep rain and moisture out, be large enough to accommodate gardener needs, and be secure when located in public areas.

Processing and/or distribution facilities are essential to capacity-building for the community that is stewarding the urban agriculture spaces. Education on topics such as saving seeds, storing roots, and preserving food is a central component of successful urban agriculture. Some small-scale processing and distribution facilities opportunities include:

- Community kitchens. Located in a public building, a community kitchen should be equipped with cold, freezer, and dry storage as well as industrial-standard cooking and cleaning equipment. A community kitchen facility is a great asset to a community and hands-on training workshops on food preparation and/or preservation and other food events can be held on-site.

- Other processing facilities are needed to support processing (such as seed saving, or meal preparation). Similar to the community kitchen model, this facility would provide a locus for education around urban agriculture systems that would contribute to the overall capacity of the urban agriculture program.

- Distribution nodes. Given that gardens often produce more food than needed, neighbourhood distribution nodes should be established so that people can bring their surplus foods for sale, trade, or donation to a worthy charity. Another approach would be to have produce stands set up as a mini-markets where people can pay by donation for produce, a system that would need to be established by the community. These produce stands could be strategically located outside the community demonstration garden or at a school, plaza, or community centre.

Compost provides a way to closing the nutrient loop in gardening and a place to put garden waste. It is also a source of high-quality soil that can be added to gardens to increase soil quality and stimulate plant growth. There are several factors to consider when planning a compost facility.

- Amount of compost. For bigger areas, such as a rooftop or community demonstration garden, a large three-stage composter is important. For smaller areas, such as a private patio, a freestanding bin is sufficient.

- Type of composting systems. There are two main forms of composting. The first is layering green (lawn cuttings) and brown (fallen leaves) organic waste. The second is vermiculture, in which worms accelerate the decomposition process by breaking down garden and kitchen waste. Vermiculture is especially useful for composts that need to be small but productive.

- Aeration. All compost needs to be aerated to let oxygen into the decomposing matter. This can be done through a combination of holes in the lid and sides of the composter or manually with a special tool or pitchfork.

- Drainage. If the compost is exposed to rain, there needs to be somewhere for the excess moisture to run off, evaporate, or be absorbed. Too much moisture hinders the breaking down of garden waste and promotes rot.

Compost Bucket at the Stop, Toronto ON.
Photo: Janine de la Salle

Summary

Twentieth-century town planning has turned its back on the vital element of food in our lives. It has eliminated agriculture in cities, paved over the agricultural land around cities, and centralized the distribution of all food supply in a few supermarket locations that stock foods that are produced on far-away industrial farms and transported long distances by land, air, and water. This pattern is at odds with both the previous several thousand years of settlement as well as with the needs of a sustainable city. Agribusiness-based production, storage, manufacture, packaging, and transportation of food in the city is a significant contributor to energy consumption, greenhouse gas emissions, and the degradation of arable land. Developing local food production opportunities in both urban and rural areas supports sustainability goals and has many other positive economic, ecological, and social benefits.

8. Artisan Agriculture

Agricultural Urbanism focuses on making food and agriculture a central part of planning, designing, and living in cities. The soft-focus images that come to mind when we think of this goal are romantically attractive. However, a closer look at the predominant forms of agriculture in North America today reveals some significant challenges to this idea.

Conventional agriculture today does not integrate easily into the urban fabric because it requires large areas of farmland, significant industrial-scale barns and machinery, and heavy spraying of fertilizers, pesticides, and in some cases, manure. The risk of dust or chemicals drifting into nearby residential areas is always a concern, and the scale of machinery makes it immediately evident that these uses are incompatible.

One response to this dilemma is to create significant buffers between agriculture and human settlement, essentially further separating our cities and the production of the food that sustains them. These buffers are appropriate in many cases and are also being promoted as a partial solution to the ongoing trade-offs between agriculture and habitat. However, as noted elsewhere, conventional buffers tend to sever the physical and psychological connections between people and agriculture.

When we begin to pursue the closer integration of farming and cities, we need to envision or articulate an alternative model of farming that will not only survive being in close proximity to homes, but will also actually benefit from that adjacency.

What is Artisan Agriculture?

The term "artisan agriculture" is offered here to describe the type of agriculture that is compatible in and around cities. The word "artisan" is included because it is already associated with the food movement in a manner appropriate to this discussion, and it infers paying close attention to every detail and using advanced skills. In simple terms, the concept of artisan agriculture includes:

- **Low-toxicity farming practices.** Agroecological farming practices with a minimum of toxic pesticides and fertilizers and other sprays are essential for any farming operation adjacent or integrated into neighbourhood areas. This type of farming reduces risk and the need for buffers.

- **High-value products.** The industrial model of agriculture tends to focus on raw foodstuff as a commodity, with a business model made viable through massive-scale production. The smaller land parcels adjacent a community require a high-value and/or value-added product focus and the adjacency of an urban market makes this focus feasible.

- **Vertically integrated.** The focus of artisan agriculture is on finished food products. Many of the value-added steps to transform the raw foodstuff into the final food product occurs on the farm, allowing the farmer to harvest as much of the profit from each step of the food supply chain.

Artisan Cheese, Farm House Cheddar. Agassiz, BC
Photo: Janine de la Salle

■ **Land and asset collaboratives.** It is common practice for farmers across North America to share ownership of a piece of equipment that they each need but only use once or twice a year. A cluster of urban-edge small, artisan farms can follow this same practice, particularly since the range of equipment and facilities they need for all the steps to create food from agricultural products is quite diverse, and will reduce individual costs and increase financial success.

■ **Integrated infrastructure.** The water, wastewater, energy, and solid-waste management systems of an urban-edge farming operation offer many opportunities to both integrate with urban infrastructure and turn waste into shared resources. Some examples are composting urban food waste for soil amendments, treating urban runoff in ponds and using it for irrigation, and using waste urban heat for greenhouses or buildings.

■ **Positive community interaction and recreation.** Artisan agriculture has a strong business case for connecting urban populations with the sources of their food. In conventional agriculture, there is risk associated with having community members in and around the farm. Artisan agriculture looks to integrate the community into as much of the farm as possible, because it is through these interactions that the community builds relationships with the farmer. Through these experiences, community members can more readily become the artisan farmer's loyal customers, even though similar food products may be available for less in the supermarket. Farms on the edge of an urban area are part of the visual and experiential open space that is needed to offset the intensity and lack of natural areas that characterize a city. Integrating walking trails and other recreational amenities into urban-edge farms is another way to better connect a community to a farmer. Issues of activity conflicts and legal exposure need to be considered and resolved in some of these situations.

■ **Farm ecosystem integration.** The detailed attention to the design of the multi-faceted artisan farm reflects the conscious integration of habitat into the farm structure, supporting habitat corridors where possible and paying attention to the needs of birds throughout the year. Not all wildlife is appropriate in a farm, however, and some can cause significant damage. Where possible, wildlife should be integrated carefully.

■ **A diverse education.** The education of a conventional farmer is a hybrid of practices over generations or that of a college or university focused on industrial farming techniques. The education for artisan agriculture covers agroecological farming practices and a range of small-business management strategies to support the vertically integrated business opportunities required to succeed. Artisan agricultural approaches may not fit the personality of those farmers who prefer to focus on farming rather than on dealing with the public and on being entrepreneurial with the many spin-offs from their farm.

- **Economic diversity.** Artisan agriculture mixes agriculture with processing (manufacturing), retail, restaurants, hospitality, agro-tourism, and education. Because of this, artisan agriculture offers significantly greater economic diversity to a community than does conventional agriculture. While in any individual case, the scale of any given element of these various sectors may be small, with a critical mass of artisan farms, the positive impact on the community could be considerable.

Table 8.1 - Artisan Agriculture Characteristics

Agriculture component	Artisan agriculture characteristics
FARMING PRACTICES	Low toxicity, low impact (minimal buffers required)
FARM PRODUCTS	High-value products for urban markets
FARM ECONOMIC VIABILITY	Small scale, high value, premium
FOOD PRODUCTION SUPPLY CHAIN	Vertically integrated, maximizing benefits to producer
INFRASTRUCTURE	Integrated for efficient use of urban water, energy, and waste by-products
ASSETS, EQUIPMENT, AND LAND	Collaborative investment and management
FARMERS' EDUCATION	Innovative and cross-disciplinary
COMMUNITY INTERFACE	Celebrating, recreating, teaching, learning
HABITAT	Farming and habitat consciously choreographed together
RECREATION	Farming and recreation integrated where possible
ECONOMIC DIVERSITY	Diverse across supply-chain sectors, with increased *local multiplier effect.*

Artisan agriculture may not be the choice of many farmers. However, it is a blueprint to better connect urban-edge farming and food production to a city. Some of the characteristics of artisan agriculture are noted in table 8.1. Additional benefits include a reduction in urban exposure to conventional agricultural problems, such as spraying, noise, dust, odours, lighting, and more. A reconnection of the community to its food sources is likely to occur, particularly where a series of annual events are structured into the farm business model and site design so directly. Farmers' profiles in the community will rise over time, possibly leading to minor "celebrity status" for some. We have celebrity chefs — why not celebrity farmers? The diversity of the economic

business model through vertical integration increases the resilience and probability that urban-edge farms can survive. Finally, it is probable that a slight premium can be charged for agriculture and food products raised with an artisan approach, thereby providing some education on the real costs of producing food.

Today, there are many examples of artisan agriculture around communities in North America, and the number is growing steadily. One interesting example is Little Qualicum Cheeseworks outside of the small city of Parksville on Vancouver Island. Cheeseworks is a family-owned dairy farm that abuts residential subdivisions and shopping centres. Its owners have turned their entire operation into an experience that includes the following:

- **An open farm.** The entire central farm area is open for customers to walk around, and includes a walking trail that reaches out through the fields where the dairy cows spend their days. Customers can walk through certain areas of the barns where calves are raised, manure is mucked, machinery is worked on, and hay is stored. In addition to the animals used in farm operation, others are kept to add to the experience for children. On a typical summer day you'll find families gathered around pens laughing at the animals' antics, with parents doing their best to answer the steady stream of children's questions about the animals.

- **Educational signage.** The publicly accessible areas of the farm are filled with humorous and informative signage. It can take the better part of an hour to walk around and read about the many aspects of the operation, from the dairy operation to the cheese-making process. Respect for the complexity and difficulty of farming grows during this self-guided tour.

University of British Columbia Farm
Photo: Janine de la Salle

- **A diverse economic model with a food focus.** The farm's business model does not focus on the mass production and sale of milk, but rather on the sale of nearly a dozen types of cheese made on the farm. The packaging room is directly behind the cashier in the farm's shop, so on any given day customers can watch the cheese be readied for purchase. The farm recently expanded into growing berries, and opened the Mooberry Winery. The farm shop now includes a fruit wine-tasting bar near the cheese coolers. In addition, a booming trade is done all summer through an ice-cream stand next to the chicken barn. Cheeseworks sells many products both wholesale and retail. The business model includes agricultural commodities, wholesale products, retail of many related things (cheese, local meats, wine, and various food- and farm-related goods), and agro-tourism experiences.

Core Concepts

Underpinning the concept of artisan agriculture are many themes and threads of study on food and agriculture in communities. A few of these are discussed in more detail below.

BORROWING FROM PERMACULTURE

Sustainable agriculture and/or agroecology is defined as a mode of farming that attempts to provide long-term sustained yields through the use of ecologically sound management technologies.[34] Fundamentally artisan agriculture is based on ecosystem design. This is the practice of mimicking ecosystem functions in an agricultural context. For example, establishing grassland set-asides and hedgerows for inviting beneficial insects, birds, small mammals, and amphibians into a productive agriculture area is a key strategy. A more active example is using a portable chicken coop that is

moved over grazing areas to ensure a diet rich in grasses and grubs for the birds as well as to fertilize the land before the coop is moved. These practices have evolved into a philosophy and principles. When we apply the principles and practices of sustainable agriculture from the Permaculture school, we can more clearly see artisan agriculture take shape.

Continuum of Farm Practices

Conventional industrial agriculture typically includes larger land areas, high degrees of mechanization, significant chemical and fuel inputs per kilo of product produced, limited access of the farmer to the value-added steps in the food industry after agricultural production, limited connection of the farmer to the consumer, little interaction between the farm and the community, and highly capital-intensive equipment and infrastructure systems. This model of agriculture has revolutionized farming in the past fifty years, with many benefits. In areas where agriculture interacts with North America's growing cities, agriculture continues to lose ground, and in some areas — such as British Columbia's Lower Mainland — the stresses between keeping farmland undeveloped and the pressures of a relentlessly growing population and economy are becoming significant.

Author and farmer, Elliott Coleman, offers the answer to the question, "how much land does it take to feed one person for one year?" From a management perspective, there is a person-to-land ratio guideline to ensure a high-quality diversified cropping system. According to Coleman, this ratio is 2.5 acres to one person, which is enough land to provide a year's worth of vegetables for one hundred people.[37] Of course, this assumes a high degree of skill on the part of the farmer. From this perspective, smaller-scale, specialty operations are better able to supply the ever-increasing market demand for fresh, local foods on the basis of pursuing farming as a viable livelihood choice.

Artisan agriculture has the potential to be a vital part of urban and surrounding areas. It offers benefits to farmers, farmland, local economies, communities, and ecosystems. Here are some of the advantages of artisan agriculture:

- **Low start-up costs.** Capital investment for commercial artisan-scale farm operations is significantly smaller than for large-scale operations. For a smaller operation, it is estimated that the capital investment in equipment, irrigation, and greenhouses for a 5-acre farm is approximately $20–25,000.[38]

- **Increased land access for new farmers.** There are increasing options for new farmers to access smaller parcels of land through tenure agreements, where farmers pay an annual fee for use of the land. In or near urban areas, where land values are often high and out of reach for most people interested in starting-up a farm, this is an important advantage.[39]

- **Farmland protection for farming.** By activating farming on farmland, more agricultural areas will be protected though legal mechanisms such as

In contrast to a large-scale industrial model, which fits poorly on the edge of a dense urban area, artisan agriculture operations are generally medium to small in scale. While we envision artisan agriculture surrounding and penetrating urbanized areas, in practice these farms operate on small parcels of land. This is partly due to a general lack of large tracks of unfragmented farmland close to cities and towns as well as the fundamental nature of artisan agriculture as a high-value, small-footprint practice.

land trusts or covenants. In particular, protected land around a city may experience less speculation by suburban-oriented developers.

■ **Community interface with agriculture.** With urban and peri-urban farms located in residential and mixed-use areas, direct-purchasing opportunities dramatically increase from the current status of weekly seasonal farmers' markets and some large chain and restaurant procurement. Connecting artisanal products with hungry urban eaters results in a whole new culture and ethos of food. Many farmers are setting up their farm businesses as *community-supported agriculture* (CSA), where people buy shares in that year's crop. This practice has moved from the original fresh box of fruit and veggies, to grain and meat CSA. Other community-agriculture interaction points may be through recreation corridors that use setbacks on farmland for trails, celebrations, education, and skill-building opportunities.

Implementation Strategies

Artisan agriculture may not appropriate for every farmer, crop, or production. However, is does provide a compelling version of what urban-friendly agriculture might look like. Developing this model of agriculture requires a range of innovation, including:

■ Increasing local food-processing, storage, distribution, and marketing capacity.

■ Using restrictive and affirmative covenants/easements on the land to protect the land for farming in perpetuity and to ensure appropriate farm practices.

■ Developing land-tenure and cooperative ownership agreements so that multiple farmers may operate on a single parcel of land.

■ Establishing farm equipment sharing systems to decrease capital investment in farm start-up.

■ Integrating artisan agriculture into regional economic development strategies and agricultural plans.

■ Re-establishing small-business loan mechanisms within financial institutions.

■ Creating incentives, such as ecological goods and services taxes, where the farmer is compensated for protecting and enhancing on-farm habitat.

The essence of AU is the integration of the entire food system into cities in a visible and viable manner. Because the dominant model of agriculture in North America at this time uses practices that are incompatible with urban areas, a new model of an urban-edge farm is required. Artisan agriculture is a concept that can offer an alternative to the industrial model of agriculture and can work in many locations to claim the new opportunities that exist around sustainable, urban-edge farming.

Washing eggs at the De Milne Farm. Salmon Arm, BC.
Photo: Mark Holland

9. Food Processing, Packaging, and Distribution

The food and beverage processing industry is the industry that takes raw foodstuffs and makes them into the food and drink that we buy from a store or restaurant and consume. This part of the food system is significant in size, impact, and importance — socially, economically and environmentally.

The processing and distribution of food and beverages is a critical, but relatively invisible, part of the food system to those not in the food industry. In the past, increased attention has been paid to agricultural production techniques as well as to the health of food products. Recently the profile of food processing and distribution issues have increased since abattoirs and other food processing facilities have been centralized, food contamination or additive problems have emerged, and phenomena such as the 100-Mile Diet have driven home awareness of from how far away much of our food comes.

Field edge processing at Foxglove Farms. Saltspring Island BC.
Photo: Janine de la Salle

The Processing Industry

Processing industries are typically organized by the types of products they process. Other countries organize their industries in similar ways, with some subsectors in these categories gaining higher profile where those industries are of significant size.

ORGANIZATION OF CANADIAN PROCESSING INDUSTRIES:

- Animal food manufacturing.
- Grain and oilseed milling.
- Sugar and confectionary products.
- Fruit, vegetable, and specialty-food processing.
- Dairy processing.
- Meat product manufacturing.
- Seafood processing.
- Bakeries and tortilla manufacturing.
- Other food manufacturing.

Each industry sector has its own rich and complex economic and physical realities. Some tend to have more domestic markets, but most are modeled on production for an international market. Advanced equipment, training, and research have bearing on every aspect of each sector, responding to the need to continuously increase the efficiency of processing in the face of very small profit margins.

Land-Use Perspectives on Food Processing

From a conventional, city-planning point of view, most food and beverage processing and distribution is merely an industrial land use, taking the form of a faceless industrial building in an industrial park, surrounded by trucks bringing in raw ingredients, followed by trucks of various sizes leaving the industrial park and heading into loading docks across the city to deliver their goods. The city has zoning regulations determining where such activities can take place, particularly those that may have a negative impact on neighbouring areas, such as abattoirs. In the minds of most city planning departments, the entire food processing system is like any other industrial industry and is not considered a desirable element or opportunity for most neighbourhoods.

From an AU perspective, food and beverage processing and distribution is of critical importance because it accounts for a significant amount of the economic value in the food system (value-added processing, investment, and jobs). It sets the stage for the local or international focus of the food industry in a region and is a significant opportunity to make the production of food from raw agricultural ingredients a visible part of urban life. At this point, AU begins to distinguish itself from "urban agriculture" and many other more sustainable food movements that have, in the past, focused primarily on agricultural production.

Packaging

The packaging of foodstuffs frequently occurs at the point of manufacture or at a packaging plant for many different types of food. Again, from an urban point of view, these are faceless industrial sites, internally focused, surrounded by trucks with interaction with the community kept to a minimum.

Packaging is necessary to organize food products into sizes that can be shipped and displayed easily and that customers want. Packaging is also a critical part of preserving food. Packaging extends food's shelf life for transportation or storage in our cupboards and is the way we "brand" a food product so it can effectively compete in the no-holds-barred battle for our attention and purchasing choices on a supermarket shelf.

A significant percentage of the municipal waste stream comes from food and beverage packaging. We have successfully installed recycling systems for most beverage packaging across North America; however, recycling food-related packaging poses significant health risks and because of this, the majority of food packaging waste goes straight to the landfill.

While the amount and types of packaging are really the choices of the food company, a more locally oriented food industry can get away with less packaging because of its immediacy — the short time between the production of the food and its consumption. Cookies from the local bakery do not need to be shrink-wrapped in an inert gas to last the thirty minutes between when they come out of the oven and when a hungry office worker consumes them during the morning coffee break. On the other hand, those cookies do need to be preserved if they are to be shipped across the continent and expected to last six months in their package and emerge almost as fresh as the day they were made. Not all local producers of foodstuffs can reduce packaging, because their products have to compete for attention on a grocery store shelf. But it is far more difficult for large-scale food production and distribution systems to effectively reduce packaging.

An AU approach to the packaging dimension of the food system promotes localness and sustainability, including reducing packaging where possible, ensuring that packaging is made of non-toxic, biodegradable material, and working to support systems of packaging take-back for re-use or reprocessing.

Distribution

A main component of any industrial system, including the food system, is the distribution infrastructure (logistics) of moving raw materials to processing locations and subsequently moving processed goods to the market. At previous points in history, the costs of transportation were considered a fundamental element of economic theory and production. The 20th century advent of cheap and massive transportation systems relegated transportation to a relatively minor consideration in a business model, triggering a rapid move to massive and global economies of scale for food production and distribution.

However, the 21st century challenges, such as climate emissions, *peak oil*, and costs of maintaining and replacing highway infrastructure, have returned logistics and transportation to their former level of importance in industry, including the food sector. Concurrently, the cultural momentum created by the "100-Mile Diet" phenomenon and similar discussions has significantly raised the profile of food miles (the distance food travels from its origin to your table), and "local" has now replaced "exotic" as a desirable trait for food products in many areas.

Agricultural Urbanism, as a locally focused movement, is structured less around getting food products out to a dispersed market and more around bringing people (customers, residents, restaurateurs, others) as close as possible to the food's origin. While AU addresses larger-scale movement of food and agricultural goods, it is more interested in a vertically integrated, locally oriented distribution system. Distribution systems in AU are more about creating local food-identity destinations that invite customers to connect as directly as possible with the farmer and other food producers.

On a national or even continental scale, alternate distribution for food is a future opportunity for increasing energy efficiency of food travel. For example, a North America-wide light-rail network that connects regions from north to south and east to west would greatly improve food-distrbution efficiency.

Semi-truck unloading foods for wholesale distribution. Vancouver, BC
Photo: Janine de la Salle

10. Food Sales: Food Wholesale and Retail

One of the most important points of engagement that we have with food is in its purchase. All food we haven't grown ourselves is acquired through a retail or trade process. The retail sector has emphasized in the past few decades the importance of the "shopping experience" and nowhere can it be as rich an experience as in the shopping for food. Images of markets around the world are etched in our memories, from experience or from media images, connecting deeply to the urge for abundance in our lives.

While the modern food supermarket or big box store has moved a long way from the markets of history, the urge to have a great food shopping experience remains strong. In considering how to increase the diversity of food retail and wholesale opportunities, the food sales dimension of a city can be seen as a continuum that ranges from wholesale to consumer direct purchasing.

CONTINUUM OF FOOD PROCUREMENT:

- Wholesale.
- Wholesale-oriented retail.
- Large-scale retail.
- Medium-scale retail.
- Small-scale retail.
- Restaurants and food services.
- Institutions.
- Producer-direct retail (formal and informal) — farmgate, farmers' markets, private garden stands, and more.

Wholesale

Because there are often many steps in the food production process between the field and a local grocery store or restaurant, a range of wholesale companies that connect producers, packagers, and retailers will exist in any region. From an urban planning point of view, these will take any number of forms, but because they are primarily focused on business-to-business sales, they will most often physically be housed in a large warehouse in an industrial area with extensive logistics facilities. In some cases, these warehouses will also have processing or packaging facilities included in them.

Much has been written on the challenges of the sustainability and health of the food supply related to the large-scale production, wholesaling, and retailing of food. The concerns of many researchers focus on the fact that when a very large food retailer or food-service company (that is, institutional) procures sufficient supplies of various foodstuffs to meet their large-scale market needs, they expect to receive reliable provisions and a high degree of consistency in the food. These demands tend to result in brokers bypassing smaller producers. This system then tends to favour industrial-scale farming, centralized processing facilities, significant logistics systems, and an approach to food packaging and processing that keeps food safe to eat for much longer than is natural because of the miles it must travel to reach our neighbourhoods.

From an AU perspective, all sizes of food-wholesaling need to be protected and enhanced wherever possible to maintain regional distribution networks, jobs, companies, and investment, as well as to connect this element of the food system more directly to the urban fabric and experience. The future of industrial lands in increasingly dense cities will likely, over time, require the mixing of industrial uses such as warehousing and wholesaling with other uses. As long as noise, smell, and trucking access are addressed, many other uses can fit around a food wholesale building.

While respecting the critical need to have efficient truck access to and from wholesalers' buildings, wherever possible, these facilities should be pulled into the city fabric with retail, educational, or other uses associated with them, to increase the profile and awareness of the wholesale food system — especially where processing is concerned. In addition, large-scale refrigeration, washing, packaging, or other systems required in many wholesale locations can offer streams of material, energy, and water that can be used by nearby businesses if planned in advance (eco-industrial networks).

Wholesale-Oriented Retail

This type of retail is most typified by stores such as Costco, or other big box, wholesale-style retailers. The rise of this type of retail has been significant in the past few decades and, given its ability to provide food at a significantly reduced price, it is likely here to stay.

From an urban planning and design perspective, these stores generally have a poor sense of place, do not fit in well with the urban fabric, and offer a sterilized shopping experience. However, because they offer pre-packaged inexpensive food, they typically become a core provider of a certain range of foodstuffs for the North American family. While changes in the 20th century economy, culture, and energy flows may affect this form of food retail, it is likely

here to stay for our lifetime and needs to be proactively addressed in the planning of food systems and cities.

Each of these companies has a highly refined model for their outlets that is replicated in nearly all locations. The formula for these regional food retailers tends to be a concrete, walled building with a very large floor area, surrounded by even larger parking lots. One side of the building is devoted to loading bays for delivery trucks. These stores tend to be located in areas that are central to the largest population possible and have easy highway access since nearly all customers drive.

On rare occasions, these larger box retailers will integrate themselves into high-density locations when the demand is high enough to motivate these companies to implement an urban form. For instance, Costco recently installed a full-size store beneath four residential towers (each higher than twenty storeys) in the city of Vancouver, BC. However, the customer catchment in downtown Vancouver is enormous, with several hundred thousand potential customers within a radius of less than eight miles. This type of store occurs only in progressive, high-density urban locations. They normally locate where the regional retail catchment has sufficient population to meet their development formula.

The need to provide large amounts of parking for these outlets in structured or underground forms requires significant demand to rationalize the ten- to twenty-fold increase in cost for each parking space (for example, $3,000 per surface stall to $25,000 to $50,000 per underground/structured parking stall).

LARGE- AND MEDIUM-SCALE FOOD RETAIL

Large- to medium-scale food retail (approximately 3000 to 9000 square metres or 30,000 to 100,000 square feet), such as Safeway, Save-On-Foods, Whole Foods, Choices, and IGA, typically follows a similar format to the wholesale-style outlets: inexpensive buildings, large areas for parking and loading, and a location with central and easy access to a large retail catchment area. These stores are typically chain stores with purchasing policies and practices similar to those of any large-scale corporation.

Decisions on where to locate supermarkets are made in a central corporate location (head office), are based on a highly refined development formula, and depend on many economic factors for location and timing of development. In denser, competitive markets, this can mean the presence of many stores in an area. Conversely, in some cases, cities can experience what is called "food deserts" (fig 10.1) — large areas where no supermarkets are located.

Because food is such an essential part of life, the absence of any significant supermarkets in urban areas can trigger extensive transportation needs and associated challenges. As such, ensuring that sufficient reasonable-sized food outlets are located throughout all areas of a city becomes a planning issue.

AU seeks to encourage the integration of as much locally produced food into the stock as possible, and ensure that the design of the store fits into a neighbourhood so as to make it more walkable, livable, and sustainable. In addition, wherever possible, it is important to build these stores on main transit lines to ensure that those of all ages, abilities, and incomes can access food without a car.

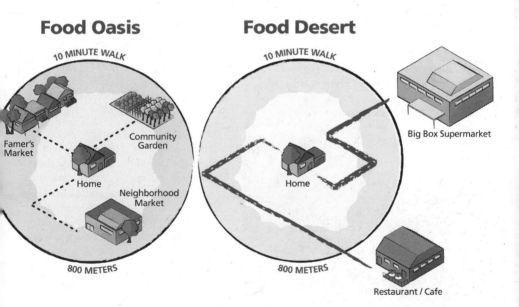

Food Oasis

10 MINUTE WALK

Famer's Market

Community Garden

Home

Neighborhood Market

800 METERS

Food Desert

10 MINUTE WALK

Big Box Supermarket

Home

800 METERS

Restaurant / Cafe

Figure10.1: Walkability is central to access to healthy food source such as small scale food retail
Source: HB Lanarc

SMALLER AND
BOUTIQUE-SCALE FOOD RETAIL

Smaller and boutique-scale food retail (under 3000 square metres or 30,000 square feet), such as corner stores and green grocers) are one of the most challenging but also most lively aspects of food retail. These outlets are typically either neighbourhood-oriented food markets or specialty food outlets. In many cases, specialty stores can be only a few thousand square feet or less in size.

The location of a neighbourhood food store needs to be central to an area having a reasonable multifamily population. The conventional single-family density of around five units/acre, two units/hectare, does not create a sufficient population to support much more than a very small convenience store (about the size of a 7-Eleven or a gas station), which will typically focus on fast or junk food. Multifamily neighbourhoods of fifteen to over one hundred units/acre , fourty units/hectare, can begin to provide sufficient density to support profitable neighbourhood grocery stores.

Vancouver, BC, offers some excellent examples of how neighbourhood grocery stores have moved into the new multifamily neighbourhoods in the downtown core

and along major transit lines with surprising frequency – a new food store every several blocks, in some instances. In this case, the stores are not only smaller scale, but are largely focused on organic produce.

The neighbourhood grocery store of this smaller scale is only offered by certain food retail chains. Many chains prefer a unified large-scale format. The neighbourhood food store can face many challenges given the very small profit margins on food sales and the increasingly high rents in more urbanized areas for retail stores of 1000 to 3000 square metres, 10,000 to 30,000 square feet.

The retail experience of food at this scale is critical. The draw of a mega-grocery store is a guarantee of significant choice and relatively low prices. The smaller store cannot offer the same choice, and often struggles with providing the lowest prices overall, given its reduced level of sales. In response, the smaller retail outlet must be both very targeted in its niche audience and products and, in many cases, spend more time on the food retail experience. Also, smaller-scale food retail may be located in areas otherwise unserviced by grocery stores, thereby increasing pedestrian access to food sources and eliminating food-access challenges associated with food deserts.

The experience of big box food retail is almost identical across North America — enormous, very-inexpensive buildings with a high level of fluorescent lighting. They contain long aisles, a huge selection, a visual barrage of intense primary colours, an expansive presence of the main food brands at eye level in every row, and many checkout stands moving people as fast as possible. It is, all in all, a very clinical experience.

The smaller retail experience is frequently quite the opposite: intimate buildings, narrower aisles, fewer main brands, more ethnic foods visible in the primary food areas, and a more personable interaction with clerks who get to know their customers over many years of working, living, and shopping in the neighbourhood.

Neighbourhood scale food retail. Wilder Snail, Vancouver BC
Photo: Boyd Thompson, Proprietor

The culture of food is different in each city, town, or neighbourhood. This culture will, in some part, determine the presence and character of the smaller food retail outlets. Larger chain stores have aggressive strategies to move into any market they believe is large enough to meet their retail formula, and because of this, they will be found in any town large enough to support them. Smaller retailers respond to the local culture more directly, based on its ethnicity, the culture of walking or driving, the social habits surrounding food that are commonly practised in the community, weather, and many other factors.

For instance, many immigrants from Vietnam, China, and the Indian subcontinent settled in Vancouver, BC, during various immigration cycles in the past fifty years. Many of these new Canadians have established vegetable markets throughout every neighbourhood in the city, consistent with the shopping habits of their home countries. These markets offer the best choice, quality, and price for vegetables — and are a mainstay of Vancouverites' shopping patterns. However, the cities within fifty miles of Vancouver have few such vegetable markets — to the point where Nanaimo, a city of nearly 100,000 people on nearby Vancouver Island, has not a single fruit and vegetable market.

The experience of purchasing food from a smaller, neighbourhood-scale food retailer is a deep and archetypal experience for us all. AU focuses on providing the greatest possible opportunity for smaller, locally owned, general or niche food stores to establish in each neighbourhood to maximize the local trade in food as well as the presence of food on the street and in the community members' lives.

EXPORT-DRIVEN FOOD CULTURES

Food wholesale and retail industries typically comprise several large-scale companies that hold the majority of the market share,

along with a minor percentage of small- and medium-sized producers of niche products. Because of this, the activities and facilities in these sectors are generally centrally planned and managed, with input from many places in the world and products internationally distributed. While this approach brings efficiencies that can keep the cost of food low, it also tends to yield an indifference to the culture and profile of food within the region. A food-manufacturing facility is more likely to be psychologically and economically connected to its parent company's supply chain and sales networks than it is to the city in which it is located and in which its workers live. This corporate predisposition furthers the separation of the food processing industry and its activities from the awareness, culture, and life of our neighbourhoods, cities, and regions. Exceptions to this rule are rare and largely driven by the personalities and leadership of local managers.

A city or region can have a competitive advantage in one aspect of the food processing industry, based on what can be produced in that area or region, for example, grain on the prairies and seafood on the coast. As such, it is entirely appropriate that some processing sectors dominate others in a region, and are focused largely on export. However, what can be lost when a purely export-driven processing paradigm emerges is the connection of that industry with the visible and experiential culture of a city.

Take Vancouver as an example. Although it is a major hub of seafood processing, there is no strong fish market presence aside from the tucked-away fisherman's wharf experience. The seafood processing plants are located in largely inaccessible areas and hide all their operations, and most Vancouverites have little idea of where seafood is processed. There are seafood stores throughout the city, but the culture of the seafood industry is primarily one of export at the expense of a local physical and experiential identity. The only presence of a "fresh seafood culture" is in a few recognized restaurants and in two or three outlets at the Granville Island Market.

Agricultural Urbanism strongly supports the prosperity of the food sectors that have significant export potential, but it also works to foreground the presence of that sector or industry in the local culture and urban form, to celebrate its contributions to the local culture and identity of the city, and to offer additional economic spin-off potential.

Agricultural Urbanism also works, through planning and design, to support the greatest level of local processing possible and to keep jobs and investment in the food industry within the local economy.

The Principle of Transparency

One of the key tenants of AU is transparency and engagement with all aspects of the food system. AU projects strive to make manufacturing processes in the creation of food visible, offer a greater sense of authenticity in the experience of the food, celebrate the local food-production players, and increase general awareness among consumers of where their food comes from and who was involved in making it.

In the past, when our lives were more connected to rural and agricultural environments, the food-production process was highly visible. Around our homes and villages, we could see and smell the cows, chickens, pigs, and gardens where food was grown. We could watch the slaughter or harvest, because these processes were done on people's own homesteads or by smaller village-oriented food producers. Freshness was a prerequisite in the absence of preservatives and industrial refrigeration systems. However, today's world is quite different for most North Americans. Because we have become an urbanized population,

we now hide most of these food production processes and become disconnected from the awareness of where our food comes from and how it is created. As we begin to reinvent our cities over the 21st century to become more sustainable and livable, we have greater opportunity and need to make our food system more visible.

The Irony of Urban Sterilization

The level of sterilization of the urban experience in most modern cities is remarkable and has resulted in the emergence of an urban culture of boredom, distraction, ignorance, and artifice with respect to food. The term "authenticity" has become so overused in the real-estate industry that few self-respecting industry professionals ever utter the word anymore — and yet we all acknowledge it to be one of the most powerful and attractive forces in community development.

The foundation of authenticity in a place is when its form and activity are largely unselfconscious in that the characteristics of the place and the activities that occur there are driven primarily by a purely functional reason – it is not trying to present itself as something that it is not or "spinning" its identity.

Humans have many impulses that drive their work to shape cities to deliver the experiences they desire. For much of the past, the realities of our world were very messy and dirty, and we created the concept of modern, clean, technologically advanced cities. A mental review of any "desirable" futuristic image of cities you have seen will highlight this urge in humanity to create highly ordered, clean living environments. Most urban utopian drawings of futuristic cities do not prominently feature piles of steaming manure, muddy tractor ruts, and chicken slaughtering equipment. They almost never show people eating. And yet, when we look back on our lives and our memories, it is the squishing up of a muddy track in our rubber boots, the smelling the wet earth and grass, and the experience of pulling a carrot out of the ground or eating a messy handful of food at a sidewalk café that burns itself into our memory far more than a walk through an empty, clean, modernist plaza somewhere in a perfect cluster of modernist buildings.

An unintended consequence of our drive to the pristine in city design, where it has been achieved, is a strange creeping level of boredom, numbness, and pathology of disconnectedness. A great quality of life for us as humans, one that triggers a wide array of meaningful feelings and experiences, necessitates direct engagement with what is messy and real in life — including how our food is created.

Interestingly, in the face of the movement to the pristine, we see a reaction to our sterilized North American urban reality. The industry of agri-tourism, where we go to other places and pay large amounts of money to return to the visible, messy, and authentic process of growing, harvesting, and making our own food is blossoming. We now flock to farmers' markets in part because the produce is fresher, but also because we feel a deep, archetypal connection to truth in engaging with the messiness, incompleteness, and the "un-spun" quality of farmers and their dusty pick-up trucks. Within a farmers' market, the producer with piles of amazing-looking produce piled on whatever they brought it in is strangely more attractive than the nearby stall where everything may be perfectly clean, bundled, and in pretty baskets surrounded by custom-made, farmers' market displays — looking a bit too self-conscious and contrived.

Agricultural Urbanism promotes transparency and foregrounding of the food production system in communities. The design and location of processing, wholesale, distribution, and retail facilities in visible and central locations not only increases our awareness of its presence but also contributes to a powerful sense of authenticity and place, increasing the scope of experiences urbanites have and more deeply connects them to the region where they live. Conceptually, and in some cases in reality, AU believes in glass walls that make visible the creation of our food. Agricultural Urbanism promotes the de-sterilization of the experience of food and, by doing so, helps create places that are complex, real, and memorable.

A fine-grained network of places where an individual, family, procurement officer, or chef may purchase a wide variety of foods is a key dimension of Agricultural Urbanism. This section defines opportunities in the restaurant and food-service sector.

Canada Lamb Roast, Karakas Residence Vancouver BC
Photo: Janine de la Salle

11. Food Sales: Restaurants and Food Services

Restaurants and Food Services

The restaurant and food-service elements of a city or town are significant in scope, complexity, and most important, potential. Restaurants and cafés are the cornerstones of great villages and cities and are indicative of their overall quality of life. Restaurants and cafés are where a significant amount of the economics and culture of food unfold and are experienced. In their kitchens, raw agricultural commodities are transformed into art forms and experiences that create memories that last a lifetime. The act of making food, whether by a chef in a restaurant kitchen or by a sidewalk food vendor preparing something fresh in front of you, connects us all to the archetypal experience of sustenance and abundance.

Morning Coffee in France.
Photo: Janine de la Salle

From an urban planning and design point of view, the following are important considerations for promoting sustainable food in restaurants and food services:

MANY CHOICES ARE NEEDED

Restaurants and cafés are a central part of the lives of most in any town or city. We eat out in a wide variety of places (from cheap, fast food to slow, expensive food) on any given day: the morning coffee and muffin (even from a gas station convenience store), the working lunch, the afternoon latte, the drinks and appetizers after work, dinner at a restaurant, and an evening out with friends. The number of times we eat out goes up significantly as our income rises.[40]

Eating out is a staple of our modern, urban existence, and we will often drive as far as necessary to get to a restaurant we want to have breakfast, lunch or dinner at. Of interest is how selective we will be regarding where we eat. Particularly in the United States, it is not uncommon for people to drive for forty-five minutes or more to get to a restaurant of choice. The development company, Intrawest, tells an interesting story about the traffic jams that used to exist every evening at a site they developed in the southern United States. People drove nearly an hour to go out to eat, and did the same in reverse when they all came home at night. Intrawest put in several good restaurants at the resort, and now the traffic jams are reversed, with people now driving to the resort to come to its restaurants and leaving the resort to go home after dinner.

Because our tastes and incomes vary so much, any neighbourhood or development needs to provide the greatest possible range of restaurant and café opportunities that the market can bear. Restaurants, cafés, and pubs offer employment and tax income to a local community, and form the heart of the evening of many towns. They are a location of energy, activity, and laughter and are the key animator of many sidewalks and plazas.

SIZE

Most eating establishments do not require large areas. In fact, some of the most interesting "hole in the wall" eating places can be less than a few hundred square feet. A large restaurant is less than 930 square meters, 10,000 square feet. Each restaurant concept requires a different configuration of space and location. Where a restaurant can be cast as a tenant early on in a development project, the urban design can be structured to best ensure its success. Given the diversity of eating needs, the widest possible diversity of restaurant spaces is needed in any neighbourhood or project.

LOCATIONS AND TRANSPORTATION

Each restaurant concept will have a different customer catchment strategy, which will affect transportation. Chain restaurants, which tend to focus on larger catchments, often have an automobile focus and require extensive parking facilities. This is particularly true of fast food and family restaurants. Restaurants in more urban settings or those that cater to a local audience, especially "lunch crowds," often require less parking and develop strong and loyal personal bonds with their customer base.

ASSOCIATED USES — COLLAPSING THE SUPPLY CHAIN DISTANCE

Typically restaurants or cafés are stand-alone businesses. However, when a more comprehensive approach is taken to the food system, the restaurant is seen as a point along a significant supply chain. The more that the supply chain can be brought closer

to a restaurant and made more visible, the more authentic and unique the food experience can be. For instance, the rooftop gardens associated with some high-end hotel restaurants (such as the Fairmont Hotels in Vancouver and Toronto) have become legendary. Purchasing fish and chips from a shop on the waterfront where fishing boats tie up offers a greater sense of connection to the source of food. Bistros associated with wineries in farmland also shorten the supply-chain distances and connect customers more deeply to their food.

One of the more interesting expressions of a short supply chain in a food establishment is a brewpub. Most brewpubs display their brewing facilities through glass-walled rooms to add to the special ambience of the restaurant. Watching the brewmaster load and check the kettles and tanks, stepping among large sacks of barley and malt in his rubber boots while the glass room steams up, adds a satisfying dimension to enjoying a handcrafted ale.

An AU approach to restaurants will explore and pursue any opportunity available to get the creation and supply of food as close as possible to the eating establishment and to increase the visibility of the food's creation.

THE PRODUCER RELATIONSHIP

Many restaurants and food-service companies purchase their supplies from wholesalers or brokers. On occasion, however, a direct relationship can be created between a restaurant and a farmer or other food supplier. In some cases, the restaurateur will simply purchase directly from the supplier and in other cases, they will work with the supplier around specific products they would like.

The artisan food movement has greatly increased the number of direct links between restaurants and farms, sausage makers, bread makers, wineries, breweries, and many other industries. However, taking the time to search out suppliers or customers who want to build a special relationship can be challenging for a busy chef, farmer, or artisan food maker.

In some cases, special relationships can be profiled as an important part of the restaurant experience and brand. While hundreds or thousands of examples of these special relationships exist in any state or province in North America, two are notable in British Columbia.

"Locals," a restaurant in the small city of Courtenay on Vancouver Island, has created special supplier relationships with local farmers and food producers for most of its main ingredients. The chef has had professional photos taken of the farmers, their families, their farms, and their produce and has filled the café with these pictures. There is little art on the walls, just the smiling faces of the farmers and great pictures of their produce. Eating a plate of exceptionally fresh food and looking up at the wall to see the very same carrots and pea-shoots that are on your plate next to the people who grew them is a rare experience.

THE DELIVERY EXPERIENCE

As discussed in other parts of this book, the misplaced interest in sterilizing our city spaces has resulted in boredom and missed opportunities for vitality and authenticity. One of the interesting parts of this is the "delivery experience" at a restaurant. A modern, conventional restaurant ensures that deliveries are made at the back so as

BISHOP'S, THE PINNACLE OF GOOD EATING
MARK HOLLAND

Hazelmere Farm, that provides local restaurant Bishop's with fresh local ingredients, is located on the rich nearby farmland of the Lower Mainland. Many food authors have explored this relationship over the years and all who have eaten at Bishop's know its unique food is available not only because of the world-class chefs in the kitchen but also because of the fine ingredients that go into the cuisine.

Bishop's is a fine-dining restaurant with white tablecloths great art on the walls and the best service of any restaurant I have ever dined in. I remember one time when my wife and I were eating at Bishop's and Mr. Bishop himself emerged from the kitchen with a pumpkin in his hand walked across the room and gave it to a woman who was having a meal with her family. It was not customary in our experience to have produce given out in a higher-end restaurant so we inquired. Mr. Bishop came over to our table and told us the story: it was a "sugar pumpkin" that was not available in Western Canada so he had arranged for Hazelmere Farm to grow these pumpkins for him. The women who dined regularly at Bishop's was so enthusiastic about the day's pumpkin soup that he found an extra pumpkin in the back and gave it to her to take home. While this story is not a usual occurrence, the experience we all had in the restaurant that evening was unique, memorable and reconnected us deeply with the people, raw ingredients, and artistry required to make great food – from the farmer to the chef to us.

not to disturb customers. This is appropriate for many restaurants; however, it can be a missed opportunity for many others. It is always an interesting punctuation to an eating experience in an urban bistro when the delivery person navigates the front door and the tables with a dolly loaded with boxes of fresh produce.

Visibility of the food-supply chain results in us looking down at our plate of food and being more connected to the original foodstuffs and farmers that made it possible, and thereby makes us more aware — for a moment — of the chef who transformed that box of potatoes into food on our plate.

THE PEOPLE

The people behind the food are a key part of an authentic restaurant experience. The presence of Mr. Bishop on the floor of his restaurant in the story above is a simple example of the power of having a chef, owner, or key member of the team present as part of the dining experience. Overhearing a good sommelier explain aspects of a wine list to a nearby table offers moments of thought and interest to any meal.

The presence of kitchen staff is another key part of the restaurant experience, whether that involves seeing them unload produce, prepare food, or hang out in the back for a smoke. Watching the brewmaster emerge from the steaming brewing room and walk through the pub in his wet rubber boots adds an air of mystery as we wonder what he must know to be able to create the seasonal beer we're enjoying. As diners, we often see a juxtaposition between the often-rough appearance of a line cook covered in tattoos and the refined food she may have just prepared. Food is powerful in its ability to break down social boundaries and make us experience for a moment our connection with each other.

FOOD BANKS AND FOOD PROVIDERS

Recognizing that many people do not have the disposable income to eat out, or to even purchase healthy foods, food banks and other food providers are vitally important to many people's food security. From soup kitchens to health clinics, these services provide reliable healthy food for low-income citizens, and must be managed and funded as part of all community-planning exercises.

WASTE STREAMS

Restaurants produce a significant amount of organic waste that can be turned into a resource. These waste streams can be composted in most cases, and in others, can be turned into biofuels or other useful resources. While turning a waste into a resource is the goal of sustainable-materials management, waste food has a serious economic and environmental impact on most communities.

The Environmental Protection Agency (EPA) notes that almost half of the food in the USA — approximately 100 billion pounds , 45 billion kilos, of food (at a rate of 3,000

Sorting Area, Vancouver Food Bank
Photo: Janine de la Salle

pounds, 1364 kilos, per second) — goes to waste. This accounts for nearly $100 billion overall, and about $30–40 billion in lost revenues from restaurants and convenience stores alone. This massive amount of waste results in about 12 percent of the average municipal waste stream being food related.[41]

This waste stream is not only an economic loss, but it also has significant environmental impact. Twelve percent of the municipal waste stream is a significant amount in costs, fuel, and emissions for hauling garbage. Because food waste is technically an "organic" waste, when deposited into a municipal landfill, it will decompose *anaerobically* and release a significant amount of methane, a greenhouse gas that is twenty times worse than carbon dioxide.

To illustrate the tremendous opportunity in urban organic-waste diversion, the Vancouver-based pilot project, IC3 Community Composting, measured the total GHG emission reduction associated with a relatively small volume of organic composting. From 2003 to 2005, the Strathcona Community Garden and Environmental Youth Alliance worked on a community composting initiative to illustrate the link between throwing out organic waste and the impact it has on climate change.[42] In a partnership with the Quest Outreach Society, a food redistribution charity, bi-weekly deliveries of 2 to 4 metric tonnes, 2.2 to 4.4 short tons, of food waste were brought to the Strathcona Community Garden composting facility, where part-time staff maintained the compost in a system of twelve wood/wire mesh bins. The two-year project had the following results:

- 250 metric tonnes, 276 short tons, of food waste diverted from the landfill creates 280 tonnes, 309 short tons, of GHG equivalents plus all emissions associated with its delivery.

- Produced 50 metric tonnes, 55 short tons, of compost for the Strathcona Community Garden.

- 54 volunteers contributed a total of 1841 hours towards the project.

An AU neighbourhood will directly address the food waste stream and try to divert as much good food destined for the waste bin either to those who need food (see the section on food security) or to a composting site that can create soil amendments or fuel.

THE CELEBRITY CHEF OPPORTUNITY

We have seen celebrity chefs in the past twenty years, such as Julia Child and Wolfgang Puck, rise to the status of rock stars and witness a steady stream of new and younger faces. In Britain, we have seen the likes of Jamie Oliver and Gordon Ramsay become front-page celebrities with multiple TV shows, restaurants, and books. The proliferation of food shows on TV through specialty channels, particularly The Food Network in North America, has raised the level of awareness and enthusiasm for cooking to a new high. Humans love celebrities, and there is significant value in tapping the celebrity machine to promote sustainable food systems in communities.

In a neighbourhood or development project, the easiest way to harness the celebrity-chef factor is to partner with a high-profile chef for a restaurant, café, food store, or food-education institution in some way. They can also be involved in promoting events or festivals.

Restaurants and food services bring food into our lives daily in one of the most direct ways. An AU neighbourhood or development will work to provide a diversity of restaurants as well as a close and visible connection between the supply of raw foodstuffs and the processes and people that turn them into food for our enjoyment.

2. Broad-Based Education on Food and Agriculture

In the British Broadcasting Corporation's (BBC) miniseries Jamie's School Dinners, Chef Jamie Oliver tackles the unhealthy eating habits of British children. Viewers will remember the scene in which Jamie asks a classroom full of children to identify the names of various vegetables. The startling fact, as the scene proceeds and he holds up various vegetables, is how few the children recognize. The scene then cuts to a similar situation in Italy, where even early grade-school children could name 100 percent of the vegetables he shows them, including some we as TV viewers had difficulty recognizing.

These scenes highlight the fact that knowledge of food does not come naturally in today's society. The industrialization of the food system has separated consumers from knowledge of and engagement with most of the sources of the food we eat. This issue is compounded when we consider the loss of knowledge of healthy, organic farming and cooking. In pre-industrial ages, up to 90 percent of people were **agrarian**, with intimate knowledge of all aspects of agriculture, **animal husbandry**, and cooking — knowledge passed down through the generations. In post-industrial times, a modern, fast-paced urban or suburban life almost completely separates us from our sources of food and makes knowledge of food something we must consciously pursue.

While many will cite concerns about the industrialized food system — frequently with good reason — focusing on those problems is not the purpose of AU or a strategic approach to sustainable food

Education on growing food at the Stop in Toronto, ON.
Photo: Janine de la Salle

systems. Pandora's box was opened a long time ago on the connection between industry and food, and it will not be closed. In this context, education on all things food becomes the key opportunity to evolve a sustainable food system. Education on food can be organized loosely into several areas:

- Knowledge of sustainable food and agriculture issues, trends, and policy

- Knowledge of growing, preparing and preserving foods

- Knowledge of sustainable farming

- Knowledge of how to plan and design for sustainable food and agriculture systems

This book focuses on urbanism as a concept and opportunity for food, and explores education on sustainable food systems and opportunities for urban planning, design, and living.

Education Opportunities Everywhere

A general knowledge of food is important to build a community and a culture that values food, celebrates food, encourages careers in food, and generally leads to a healthier population. An approach to raising the knowledge level on food can be organized into what knowledge areas are important to address and the venues we can use to encourage learning.

The areas of knowledge in food that are important for a sustainable community include general information about healthy and sustainable food choices; the diversity of foods available, including local and foreign or ethnic foods; how to make healthy food choices; and others.

In a community, there are a number of ways to deploy this information: through schools (different types), events, visibility of food information or learning opportunities in the public landscapes, and more.

An AU-based approach to food education works to ensure that community planning and design support formal and informal education opportunities around food, as well as promote formal food-related education venues and programs.

For those wishing to pursue a career or learn professional skills in the food or beverage industry, the presence of agricultural and culinary schools is important. Zoning needs to ensure that these are supported wherever appropriate. For those interested in learning more about food as a personal interest, the physical venue becomes less important because classes or tours can be organized in many venues. However, a food-oriented facility with infrastructure and community presence will raise the overall profile of food and become a centre of food activity and education. Food hubs or precincts discussed later in this book explore this idea in more detail. These facilities can include a culinary school or a more community-based facility such as a community or cooperative industrial kitchen facility, or any number of other functions.

Knowledge of food should be incorporated into the curriculum and the school experience for all levels of schooling, particularly in the K–12 years. At one level, this is merely a curriculum strategy to ensure that all school children progress through the stages of knowledge and basic skills in food, gardening, and cooking. On the other hand, it also asks that schoolyards (and possibly greenhouses) include a food production and education program to give children and youth a deeper experience of watching food grow, managing soils, watering plants, weeding, and harvesting.

The need to supply growing spaces in a neighbourhood through community gardens will be discussed in following sections. In short, in any multifamily residential area, most home owners have limited access to sufficient sunny land in which grow food. The educational experience of growing food in a community garden is as important (or possibly more important) than producing significant amounts of produce. Walking through a large community garden is an education in how or how not to grow various things. Having a garden plot that is struggling within sight of someone else's that is thriving is a significant invitation to strike up a conversation and learn.

The Southeast False Creek garden in downtown Vancouver was established as a demonstration how-to garden in a high-density environment where most residents have access only to a balcony or rooftop garden plot. Gardening requires education at the best of times, and in a difficult and space-constrained environment of a high density neighbourhood, many will be watching to see how the educational dimension of this garden evolves.

As noted regularly in this book, one of the most important aspects of integrating food into a community is making as many of its steps in creation as visible as possible. One of the great opportunities in urban design to raise the knowledge level of food informally throughout the community is to make the production and processing of food associated with any store or restaurant visible to patrons and, wherever possible, the passersby. For a child, watching a butcher at work through a store window is an education on where the meat on their plate came from. The urban restaurant chain, Café Crêpe, has the chef making crêpes in the front window, fully visible from the street. The window is designed to open so lunch can be purchased from the sidewalk, and you can watch it being made. This visibility of the cooking process brings a strong presence of food into daily urban life.

Likewise, for every child who sees it, a public pressing of apples in a park or plaza will permanently connect the apple juice at the breakfast table to the glorious mess that

is involved in making apple juice. Watching a fruit bag of apple pulp break its seams and explode apple pulp across the ground through the slats of the apple press is an experience not soon forgotten. Neither is the taste of unpasteurized apple juice coming straight out of the press. Children will immediately and intuitively understand the reality of creating food when they compare that experience and taste to those of the generic, clear bottled apple juice they get from a store.

Notwithstanding the romantic picture outlined above, the very same plaza where the apple pressing occurs likely has a soft-drink vending machine somewhere. Many North American schools are now working hard to ban junk food from their cafeterias because of their influence on children's food choices. An AU neighbourhood will try to lower the profile of unhealthy food, junk food, fast food, and vending machines selling junk food. Because these legitimate businesses are promoted by sophisticated corporate interests, and there is a strong demand for their products, they likely cannot be eliminated. Moreover, an honest appraisal will result in most of us admitting to eating junk food and fast food periodically and rather enjoying much of it. However, a neighbourhood or community that is committed to promoting healthy and local food will work to balance the highly visible presence of these sources of food with healthy and local options.

Overall, the increase in both visibility and educational opportunities around sustainable food systems and their many facets will strengthen the culture of healthy and conscious approaches to food, resulting in citizens making many choices over time to evolve their community's food system.

Agassiz Slow Food Cycle 2009
Photo: Janine de la Salle

Education in Cooking

Culinary institutes exist in most cities as independent schools or as part of a community college. The study of cooking is typically seen as a vocational trade, even though the level of skill and knowledge for an advanced chef would easily be equal to that required by many professions. In the same way that cooking has been a hidden vocation for a long time, so has the presence of cooking education. One exception is the cafeteria or restaurant typically associated with a community college, where culinary students do the cooking, baking, and serving in some cases.

An AU approach to this aspect of education in food would be to first ensure that zoning and possibly incentives exist for a culinary

school, perhaps going as far (in a master-planned community) as actively casting a cooking school as a tenant in the community and searching one out and attracting it with incentives. The second most important effort to make is to ensure that the cooking school and its students are centrally visible in the community. A group of culinary students in their whites, hanging around outside a cooking school, provides a unique energy and reminds everyone of the work and skill that goes into even the most basic restaurant meal.

Community colleges and schools around North America run a busy trade in evening and weekend courses for those wanting to learn more about food. In addition, the proliferation of wine and food organizations also has resulted in many new educational opportunities for interested citizens. The agro-tourism industry has created additional holiday-oriented experiential and educational opportunities in many regions. The Slow Food movement offers a Master of Food program comprising nearly a dozen and a half courses on all aspects of food, wine, and taste.

Planning an AU neighbourhood cannot necessarily trigger groups and organizations to develop and provide educational opportunities, but it should ensure that there are sufficient facilities to support a wide range of food education and agro-tourism events as they arise.

Education in the Food and Agriculture Sector

Beyond education in cooking, there are many other roles, education streams, and careers in the food industry. Many are based on formal education, including any number of academic degrees in agriculture or nutrition, or on-the-job training as an apprentice tradesperson, such as a butcher or meat cutter. The integration of sustainable food systems issues into any food training curriculum is critical to the future of the food system. From a community-planning point of view, the main issue, as noted earlier, is provision of sufficient facilities and spaces to support these programs.

A critical additional consideration is the linkage of open space to the educational institutions, particularly farmland adjacent to a community. Many of the educational dimensions of food connect directly to agricultural production, whether it be a college for agriculture or animal husbandry, or taking culinary training and needing to know the basics of growing vegetables, fruit, or herbs. In many cases, the cost of land and facilities can be prohibitive for one school to handle; however, a partnership between schools or with a developer or a land trust can provide land, facilities, and educational opportunities to the community.

Education in Sustainable Farming

Those who track the rising food issues in North America continually return to the observation that farmland is important but it is no longer the juggernaut of the food system. Activating farming on farmland is. One of the most critical issues going forward is the supply of farmers who are willing to tackle the challenging economic realities of farming as a career. There are a growing number of examples and stories of the next wave of bright agricultural and food entrepreneurs; however, their number is relatively small compared to the scale of the challenge. Beyond that issue, there is also the evolution of farming practices in the face of increasing centralization, industrialization, and **chemicalization** of the food system. Re-energizing organic and sustainable agricultural education is critical to establishing a sustainable food system.

The art of whole-system agroecological farming is complex and interconnected, and includes crop choices, animals, intensive soil management, crop rotations, mixed planting combinations, integrated pest management approaches, and many other aspects. Learning these requires hands-on experience, so having farmland adjacent to urban areas is beneficial.

In addition to land, facilities and teachers are required to bring food education options into the market place, assistance for students themselves is another key issue. Tuition, jobs, and housing are the basics of surviving as a student in any area, including farming communities. Some educational farms such as Intervale and Fairview Gardens have found unique ways of mixing education with enterprise. Where this combination is viable, addressing the requirements for feasibility is an important part of the planning process in a community. Beyond being able to support the needs of farming students and the overall food system, the presence of apprentice farmers in a community, with their dusty clothing and lunch boxes, creates a memory of how we are fed.

Partnerships created in a community or through a development process are central to developing visible and viable training of farmers. Taking an AU approach to a community can set the stage for this better than other types of development, but significant investment will be required by many over the long run to build this capacity in communities.

Education is central to the success of any AU strategy or project, and this involves addressing, in the planning and design process, many aspects of the education process, including land, facilities, students' needs, financial viability of an educational institution, and a general foregrounding of the food system in all ways to provide informal learning opportunities and to celebrate all students of food.

LEADERSHIP IN EDUCATION: DELTA EARTHWISE SOCIETY

A CASE STUDY FROM PATRICIA FLEMING

One of the most pressing issues facing agricultural sustainability and the development of regional food systems is the need to attract, train, and excite youth about growing food. The disengagement of people from food is systemic. It starts at an early age and is handed down from parent to child. How can we inspire future urban farmers if no one understands how food grows or how it gets to the table?

Organizations that so far have driven the movement and engaged people can be effective allies in moving forward the vision of AU. When projects are successful it's often due to the community-level support for the ideas that are top-of-mind for citizens.

Earthwise Society in Delta, BC, is an example of a grassroots community-based organization providing the kind of community engagement that is necessary for the acceptance and actualization of planning initiatives around AU. On a 1.21 hectare, 3-acre site in Tsawwassen, Earthwise has developed an ecological demonstration garden and organic farm that encourages public interaction and awareness in contrast to the current model of urban-edge agriculture that excludes people and contributes to their alienation from the food systems.

Earthwise has developed a new model for urban-edge farms, one designed to educate the consumer, to invite exploration and discovery, and to provide fresh, local food for as much of the year as possible. Earthwise also addresses the issue of disengagement by providing education programs that connect children with growing food, from the preschool years through high school. Students visit the Earthwise farm to learn about seeds, soils, ecosystems, and food.

The Sustainable Resources 12 (agriculture) program provides hands on learning opportunities to high-school youth at the Earthwise Farm. By making these connections, the society seeks to address issues of farming succession by exciting young people about the possibilities of careers in agriculture.

Planners and municipalities can leverage their programs by identifying partners in the community who already have an audience and who possess the expertise and credibility to provide meaningful public engagement. Public apathy and disengagement from government processes, whether manifested through low voter turnout or lack of participation in planning processes, speaks to public skepticism of government-run programs, public input processes for planning decisions, and restrictive legislation. Effective involvement of community-group partnerships with governments and planners can play a key role in driving and supporting grassroots change necessary to effect meaningful progress toward goals of AU.

3. The Celebration of Food and Agriculture

The celebration of food is a cornerstone of Agricultural Urbanism and, more importantly, of any great community anywhere, for it makes visible the values and opportunities of food systems in sustainable communities. The celebration of food begins with making the people and the food system elements highly visible through a program of food-related events throughout a year.

Visibility of Food

The importance of making all aspects of the food system as visible as possible in a community is one of the core principles of AU and is referred to often throughout this book. Not all steps in the creation of food are easily palatable, however, as some involve the slaughtering of animals, oily machinery, manure, mud, organic waste, and many other aspects that are quite messy. However, the experience of food is only complete when we have a greater awareness and connection to all the steps in the food system that gives us sustenance. While there is clearly immense value in promoting the truly celebratory aspects of food, there is a deeper spiritual connection in the awareness of the honest and messy exchange of life celebrating food.

In order to celebrate the entire food system in a community, the full range of steps in food production need to be visible. The AU principle of "back of house is front of house," where the many steps in receiving goods, preparing raw agricultural products into food, and storing the many supplies (crates, traps, racks, equipment, and more) related to these steps in full view is a key

aspect of design in an AU community. The transparency of being able to look into a food establishment and see the work being done by cooks and other staff enhances awareness and implicit gratefulness and celebration of the investment of creativity and energy into the food we eat.

Okanagan Cow
Photo: Claire de la Salle

Celebrating the Seasons

In every month of a year, different aspects of food come to dominance. In most cases, these are based on harvest times. In others, they are based on annual holidays and customs or on the maturing of certain products, such as a fall or spring wine release. Because of the global food supply system, inexpensive transportation, and open international trade agreements, we have become less aware of the seasons of the food supply because we can get almost anything any time of the year at the supermarket. The signs along our community's roads advertising fresh fruit or vegetables that are now in season and for sale at some farm or roadside market are often the most visible reminders we see of the food seasons today.

It is important to plan events throughout the year in a community to explicitly celebrate moments in the agricultural year and remind us of what is fresh and local. Some of the most visible and fun annual moments to celebrate are the Christmas and New Year seasons, recognizing that many cultures have these or similar celebrations at different times of the year. At the famous Christmas markets in Germany, downtown streets and plazas are filled with small kiosks that sell all types of winter foods and mulled wine. A walk along the long, car-free shopping street in Munich during the Christmas season is magical. As the snow falls, thousands, surrounded by Christmas lights, gather to eat baked goods and drink mulled wine among the centuries-old architecture.

The celebrations of the Lunar New Year (Chinese New Year to many) are also known and celebrated around the world with many special types of food. Thanksgiving in North America is a significant food-oriented event, with a particular focus on turkey and ham dinners. The Japanese cherry blossom festival (Hanami) includes extensive consumption of dumplings (dango). Oktoberfest in western and European countries is a time to celebrate beer, sausage, and pretzels. February's Valentine's Day triggers a mass consumption of chocolate, as does Easter in North America. Passover as well comes with special food. And the list goes on. These events use food to mark a season more than they do the harvest cycle, but they strongly connect us to food, time, and each other within the physical spaces of our cities and towns. Communities that celebrate food need to embrace the annual cycle of cultural events and increase the profile of their food elements where possible.

The Public Realm

Beyond making all aspects of the food system and seasons visible, the celebration of the simple act of eating and drinking in the public realm is important. There was a time when many North American cities prohibited café tables on sidewalks. Fortunately, however, most cities now encourage eating in plazas and along sidewalks during certain hours.

Great food cities often have a large area in the downtown full of street food kiosks. Sometimes they are permanent, as in Portland, or temporary and associated with "market days" as in many cities. The English Garden in Munich is world famous for the amazing experience it offers of fresh beer and pretzels in the middle of a large urban park and sitting on benches on the grass under large trees, surrounded by both friends and strangers in conversation.

The spilling out of food stores onto the sidewalk is a key element in animating a city. Possibly nowhere is this more visible than in Chinatowns across North America, which offer the unique experience of an uninterrupted display of many unfamiliar ingredients from the back of the store right out onto the sidewalk. For farmers' markets, it is common for communities to close entire streets or parking areas and devote them to food for the day.

Integrating the food agenda into public art is a key opportunity to support various annual food and seasonal events, but the presence of food-related public art throughout the year keeps these events in the memory of all who live in the community. The integration of a permanent apple press or an oversized feast table into the public realm keeps the presence and memory of a food year fresh, and declares publicly the importance of food in the community. Many older rural communities incorporate old farm machinery into public art installations in their village city centres. In any **agricultural urbanist** neighbourhood, food-system elements need to be incorporated into the public art agenda to further raise the profile and support the program of a sustainable food agenda.

Additional ideas and approaches to celebrating food in the public realm are addressed in the section of this book that focuses on urban design for food.

Home Design

The rise in the importance of food in the middle and upper middle classes is possibly most visible in the growth in popularity of the "trophy kitchen." From the 1940s to the 1970s, the kitchen in the average North American home was designed as a small and separate room. Since the 1980s, we have seen the rise of large, custom-designed, high-tech kitchens. Today, restaurant-grade kitchen appliances, enormous kitchen counters, pantries, and large wine coolers are presented in every home-design magazine as the new "normal." These kitchens are often the centre of the home, with living spaces connected to them on all sides, presenting the food centre as the true centre of the home.

While this approach to kitchens does not necessarily mean that its inhabitants have become dedicated foodies and great cooks, it does signal a renewed appreciation for food and wine in North America. In an AU neighbourhood, while not every home has to have a showcase kitchen, the kitchens are significant in size and usefulness and are the centre of the home.

In contrast to the trophy kitchen, we have the hotplate option. The lack of kitchens in low-income housing, such as the single residence occupancy units often found in areas with a large homeless or low-income population, presents a key challenge for people to prepare foods (even if they are able to afford groceries). Private or shared kitchen facilities are essential for food security for people living in social or temporary housing.

Pie Competition in McLean Park, Vancouver BC
Photo: Janine de la Salle

Celebrations and Festivals for Food

The recent growth in attention and enthusiasm for food in popular culture has taken the historical country fair and created a plethora of food- and drink-related festivals and celebrations throughout the year in many communities. The proliferation of such events has become a key way for people to organize and network over food issues. The range of festivals and food events serves as a starting point for considering the types of food events that could be programmed into an agricultural urbanist community.

Slow Food

Although critiqued as a bourgeois movement lacking in appeal to the masses, one of the most significant food movements in the world, and in particular around the celebration of food, is the Slow Food[43] movement that emerged in the mid 1980s in Italy. As of 2009, the movement has over 85,000 members in 130 countries. The essence of the Slow Food movement is to use food as a means to slow down the pace of our lives and to reacquaint ourselves with our local food heritage and traditional methods of cultivation, cooking, and eating. This goal has lead to another emerging trend that the Slow Food movement calls *ecogastronomy*, which focuses on addressing the sustainability of the food system — a goal directly aligned with the purpose of AU.

A sampling of food and beveradge events from accrross North Amercia
Source: www.foodreferece.com

Summary

Agricultural Urbanism tries to support a more sustainable food system through planning and design and increase the profile and celebration of food in a community to enhance the quality of life of all who are there. This can be done through the physical design and programming of festivals and food-related events throughout the year. The nature of food is such that once a culture of celebrating food has been visibly established in a community, it will tend to reinforce itself and continue to grow, based on the power that food has in our lives and the life-affirming experience of celebrating food.

14. Food Security

Food security is a critical and complex issue in modern cities and one that dates back to the earliest times, for humans have perpetually struggled with the issue of hunger. Over the past centuries, hunger and food security have been a significant city-shaping force in terms of storage, sale, and defense in times of war, when the security of a nation depended on its planning for food and water. Cities and civilizations that found themselves surrounded by exhausted farmland sometimes failed entirely and were abandoned.

In modern society, the issue of food security has at least two dimensions: social justice and food security of the residents of any community, and the much larger issues of climate change, terrorism and geopolitical insecurity, threats to the world's agricultural water supplies, and constraints on other aspects of the global food production system, such as fertilizer or secure soils.

Community Food Security

Earlier in this book, some of the challenges facing the global food system were briefly explored. The 21st century challenges associated with changing water supplies, petroleum-based chemicals, fuel costs, and many others will cause a rethink of many aspects of the global food system. The world's water supply will become one of the most critical future food security issues — particularly as climate change alters the hydrological regimes around the world. Currently, only 7 percent of the arable land in Africa has access to irrigation water, and the Intergovernmental Panel on Climate Change (IPCC) noted that a small change in global temperature could reduce the yields of non-irrigated fields in Africa by 50 percent.[44]

The right to food is enshrined in the Universal Declaration of Human Rights and in international law; however, few countries have the right to sufficient food in their constitutions. Global hunger has many causes, including war, weather, reduced investment in agriculture in newly industrializing countries, global trade agreements, and more. Children are the most vulnerable, and malnutrition is

Blueberries from a community garden near Lillooet, BC
Photo: Claire de la Salle

considered the cause of most child mortality in the world.

The Food and Agriculture Organization of the United Nations (FAO) notes that world production of food must rise by 70 percent by 2050 to meet the needs of the projected world population of 9.1 billion. In October 2009, the FAO released a report noting that the number of people in the world without sufficient food has surpassed one billion.[45]

The challenges of the food supply for unindustrialized or newly industrializing countries will be formidable in the next fifty years. Rising prices for food hits the poor the hardest because they already spend 70 to 100 percent of their income on food. The rise in costs of petroleum-based fertilizers and pesticides as well as water, compounded by a rapid growth in demand for grain for biofuels, is already impacting the supply of food for the world's poorer populations. Since many industrializing countries have a food trade deficit and are now importing their food as they shift focus from a rural to an urban economy, there is a rash of countries and companies now purchasing farmland around the world to guarantee the basic supply of food that their country needs.[46] This is also true for countries whose populations are growing but have poor farmland. In early 2009, the wealthy desert nation of the United Arab Emirates entered into a deal to buy one million acres, 404,686 hectares, of farmland in Pakistan to secure some of the food supply of the Emirates.[47] The United Nations is instituting voluntary codes of conduct regarding this practice due to its potentially serious implications over the next century.

The shift to larger-scale agribusiness for the supply of food around the world has a negative impact on the food security of many smaller, rural communities. The FAO reports that most all of the world's food energy is now supplied by approximately one dozen industrial crops, and that 75 percent of the agricultural biodiversity was lost in the 20th century due to this shift to a few agribusiness industrial corporations. A global movement is emerging in response to these trends around the concept of "food sovereignty," which focuses on support for local, small-scale agriculture so that people in rural areas around the world can feed themselves.[48]

Food security

The term food security has several definitions and is typically partnered with its opposite, food insecurity.[49]

FOOD SECURITY

"Access by all people at all times to enough food for an active, healthy life. Food security includes at a minimum:

(1) The ready availability of nutritionally adequate and safe foods (approximately 2,000 kilocalories / day / capita), and

(2) An assured ability to acquire acceptable foods in socially acceptable ways (e.g., without resorting to emergency food supplies, scavenging, stealing, or other coping strategies)."

FOOD INSECURITY:

"Limited or uncertain availability of nutritionally adequate and safe foods or limited or uncertain ability to acquire acceptable foods in socially acceptable ways."

The concept of hunger and food insecurity is complex, and significant work is being done to address it both from a policy point of view as well as through pragmatic programs to supply the hungry with food. However, regardless of the significant work, a startlingly large number of people in North America are food insecure and regularly rely on food banks, soup kitchens, and other charity-based food sources.

When we consider who in our communities is at risk of food insecurity, the list is surprising. Based on statistics from www.hungerinamerica.org and www.foodbankscanada.ca's Hunger Count 2009:

- **In Canada.** 8.8 percent of Canadians or 2.7 million people will experience household food insecurity every year, and nearly 800,000 people use a food bank in Canada in any given month. 2.4 percent of Canadians are helped by food banks.

- **In the USA.** An estimated 49 million Americans are food insecure, often facing trade-offs of buying food and paying for rent, utilities, or medical care. Food banks and soup kitchens in the USA provide assistance to more than 25 million people per year.

- **Working poor.** Over one-third of those who access food banks and soup kitchens in the USA had jobs, and over two-thirds of those who used food banks and soup kitchens live below the poverty line, with an average income of less than $1,000 per month.

- **Children and single-parent families.** Over nine million children, nearly 13 percent of all children in the US, accessed food banks or soup kitchens in 2006. The USDA estimates that 16.7 million children in the USA lived in a state of food insecurity in 2008. Nearly 25 percent of all children in the USA are at risk of food insecurity, and 18.5 million children from low-income families receive food assistance in school each day. In Canada, 37 percent of those assisted through food banks are children.

Canadian food banks feed over 290,000 children every month.

- **Recipients of social assistance of all types, including persons with disabilities.** The number of people living below the poverty line in the US numbered 39.8 million in 2008. That translates to 12.5 percent of the country's population and 15 percent of all families with children under the age of eighteen.

- **Seniors.** Nearly three million seniors a year in America access food banks and soup kitchens and of those, nearly 30 percent had to choose regularly between buying food and paying for rent, utilities and medical care. In 2008, 2.3 million US households with seniors were food insecure.

- **Rural dwellers.** In the USA, 2.8 million rural households are food insecure, affecting over a million children.

These numbers are profoundly sobering. Studies in many cities show that those who are food insecure come from every neighbourhood.

These statistics become nearly surreal when compared to the amount of food in our countries that goes to waste. The US Environmental Protection Agency notes that almost half the food in the United States goes to waste.[50] Food-waste losses account for up to $100 billion USD per year, with $30–40 billion USD occurring within the commercial or retail sector (restaurants and convenience stores) and $20 billion USD from farming and food processing.

SMALL-TOWN LEADERSHIP IN FOOD SECURITY: THE ARMSTRONG FOOD EXCHANGE

A CASE STUDY BY JILL DE LA SALLE

The city of Armstrong is located 23 kilometres, 14.3 miles, North of Vernon, BC. It has a population of 5,000 and is surrounded by the township of Spallumcheen, a rural community that also numbers 5,000. In 2009, Armstrong received grant money to start up the Armstrong Food Initiative, which included a pilot food-exchange program to connect those with extra produce from their gardens and orchards to those in need of fresh fruits and vegetables.

Central to the success of the Armstrong Food Exchange was a fruit and vegetable distribution centre. Anyone with extra produce was invited to deliver it to the site between 9:30 and 10:30 each Monday morning. Anyone who wanted or needed free fresh produce could come between 10:30 and 12:30 to pick it up. The group was amazed by the number of people ready to participate in this program. Sources of surplus produce included:

- A local strawberry farm that allowed a picking team to go over the finished rows and glean the remaining fruit. The strawberries were delivered to local seniors' facilities and used in a community canning session where strawberry/rhubarb jam was made. Not only did each participant go home with a jar of jam, but positive connections were made between members of the community who didn't normally associate.

- Local residents who had more produce from their backyard than they could eat or preserve. One community member brought in a huge head of cabbage, and traded it for a smaller, more manageable one.

- Fruits and vegetables gleaned from local fields.

In the eight weeks that this pilot was running, approximately 2268 to 2722 kilos, 5,000 to 6,000 pounds of produce was shared among seventy to eighty different people. Also, local groups such as the food bank, seniors' centres, and special needs organizations became recipients of the exchange program.

The Armstrong Food Initiative was a tremendous success in 2009, with many willing and ready volunteers. The Initiative not only met hard objectives, such as creating garden boxes, presenting at the Interior Provincial Exhibition, and gleaning produce for community use, but also met soft ones, such as building connections between members of the community, discussing food sustainability, and increasing awareness.

Agricultural Urbanism and Food Security

Any community that is taking sustainable food systems seriously, including all AU neighbourhoods, needs to grapple with ways to increase the food security of all its residents. As previously noted, those facing food insecurity come from all age groups, walks of life, and neighbourhoods. There are several areas of planning and action that can be taken, including:

- **Partnerships and advocacy.** The nature of food insecurity is that it requires significant attention and networks of agencies working together. Through partnerships, the reality of food security can be monitored, and coordinated initiatives can be undertaken to both address its impacts as well as to lobby senior governments to adjust policies and provide resources to address the problems.

- **Locating food banks, warehouses, and community kitchens.** Seventy-four percent of the food distributed to the hungry is distributed from food banks or pantries.[51] Food banks and soup kitchens can face challenges depending on where they are located in a community. Lineups for those who access food banks can be 50-100 deep with line-ups stretching down the sidewalk for several hours at a time. It is important to plan carefully to support these institutions and to situate them so that they are both convenient for and respectful of those who access them but not in conflict with the surrounding areas. Waste food exchange groups require warehouses to store food diverted from the waste stream until it can be distributed to food agencies. The Vancouver-based Quest Food Exchange fills and empties its 6,000-square-foot, 557 square-metres, warehouse every day.

- **Operational support for food banks and kitchens.** In addition to physical facilities for food banks, additional work is needed for reliable fundraising and volunteers for food banks. In the USA, 66 percent of pantry programs and 40 percent of soup kitchens have no paid staff at all.[52] Securing a steady and reliable food stream is also important, as is building partnerships with various sources. The primary sources of food for food banks, pantries, kitchens, and shelters in the US include government grants, religious congregations, local merchant and farmer donations, local food drives, and food purchased by the agency. Many communities will have a Food Bank Day or regional initiatives to raise money and food for the food banks. In 2009, the Canadian Broadcasting Agency's (CBC) radio drive for the food bank raised over $500,000 CND in one day.

- **Waste food recovery program for local business.** Connecting food banks and other food-charity agencies with the significant streams of wasted food from grocery stores, restaurants, caterers and others can have a big impact. The Quest Food Exchange in Vancouver diverts 5.77 million pounds , 2.62 million kilos, of surplus food from landfills each year, with a value of $7.12 million CND, yet it captures only about one percent of the food that is being wasted in Vancouver.[53]

- **Gleaning programs.** *Gleaning* is the practice of harvesting food that otherwise might go to waste and channeling it to humanitarian agencies. Many homeowners have fruit trees or unused garden space that can be accessed for food for food banks or other organizations. In 2007 alone, volunteers associated with the Portland Fruit Tree Project in Oregon harvested 3,400 pounds, 1545 kilos, of fruit for food banks.[54]

- **CSA programs**. Charitable food distribution agencies can sometimes participate in a customized Community-Supported Agriculture (CSA) initiative and arrange for a local farmer to grow a range of produce or protein for them in advance.

- **Community gardens**. Planning and designing food production spaces in every neighbourhood is one way to address food insecurity. For several months of the year, gardeners can provide additional food for themselves, and many can produce food to give to food banks. The social relationships created through community gardens help increase food security in all areas.

- **Addressing food deserts**. City and community planning needs to address areas that are beginning to be known as food deserts — neighbourhood areas with no food stores. The centralization of the supermarket industry has left many neighbourhoods in North America with few or no food markets, requiring people to either travel long distances to access food or pay inflated prices for poor-quality food in convenience stores. It takes a concerted effort on the part of many agencies to draw food retailers into some of these areas, but benefits of doing so are significant. Planning and zoning for food markets and a diversity of restaurants are key to keeping a healthy food supply in all areas of a community.

- **Schools**. A program for schools needs to be addressed, given that many of those facing food insecurity are children. School behavior and academic performance require that children have sufficient food. In addition, the integration of food education into the curriculum and onto the school grounds offers many benefits.

- **City twinning for food**. Programs that connect cities in North America to those in unindustrialized or newly industrializing countries are few. Opportunities exist for those who want to "*twin*" cities or create other partnerships that specifically address food issues to help cities in less affluent countries increase their food security. The Federation of Canadian Municipalities has a municipal partnership program that twins cities in Canada with cities in other parts of the world to provide venues for knowledge transfer. Such a program could serve as a foundation for efforts to support food security and sustainability.

The issue of hunger and food security has been with humankind for thousands of years and will remain with us for the foreseeable future. The challenges the 21st century brings to the global food supply will trigger new attention to the resilience and scale of regional food systems to ensure that cities have secure food supplies. Many opportunities exist to build greater food security for cities and their residents and to increase the overall economy and quality of life at the same time.

Part III: Planning & Design for Agricultural Urbanism

Agricultural Urbanism is an approach for inviting food and agriculture back into our towns and cities. City builders, including planning and design professionals, local government, and community members need ideas and tools for addressing the question of how we can start to plan and design settlement areas and communities with food and agriculture systems in mind. These chapters focus on integrated infrastructure, urban/open-space design, human-scale agriculture, food hubs and precincts, and transition areas for agriculture and other land uses.

Urban infrastructure provides the pipes, pumps, wires, fleets and roads that support the function of a city, and are usually the responsibility of a local government or utility.

The majority of the standards that shape this infrastructure are based on simplistic, single-objective models that emerged in the resource rich mid 20th century, in response to the need to accommodate rapidly growing cities. In chapter 15 on infrastructure, Bud Fraser offers a new vision of urban infrastructure - one whose innovation is stimulated by the opportunities that an intense food system can offer in a city. The integration of natural systems into urban systems through an AU concept offers new ways of conceiving of the movement of energy, water and material, to the benefit of both the city and the regional food system.

One of the most important things all urban designers consider is the issue of scale – what size does everything have to be and how should it all be fit together.

Urban designers typically know little or nothing about the scale of farm design and likewise, farmers generally spend little time thinking about the complexity of the scale required to create a great plaza, building or street. However, AU provides the designer with the conundrum of needing to consider both. In chapter 16 on scale, Edward Porter combines his expertise in both urban design and farming to offer a framework and typology for the intersection of farm and urban space that assists designers to establish appropriate scales and patterns for AU projects.

Great urban design is always driven by a "program" – a clear plan for activity and experiences which the physical design is intended to accommodate. An AU approach to design adds a rich new program of many aspects of the food system to conventional urban design programs. In chapter 17 on urban design strategies a group of designers from HB Lanarc explore a wide range of programmatic and design opportunities for a diversity of urban spaces to assist the reader in identifying AU opportunities for their own city, neighborhood or project.

While urban designers today understand how to create acceptable places, it is not common to have a high level of vitality in a new place. This phenomenon is because most urban design is intended to be relatively generic to accommodate a range of uses and it takes time for people to occupy and possess a space for themselves. Some of the most vital places in any city in North America or the world have a very strong presence of food. In chapter 18 on food hubs and precincts, Janine de la Salle and Mark Holland outline a new approach to planning and design urban fabric using food as a focal point to drive economic development in the food industry and to offer a rare and exciting experience of many dimensions of the urban food system to many city dwellers.

Finally, where urban development areas meet rural agricultural areas, a wide range of potential conflicts and opportunities arise. In chapter 19 on transition zones, Janine de la Salle outlines frameworks and strategies for meeting multiple objectives of food, urban function and habitat through design.

DPZ Designer at work, Southlands Tsawwassen BC.
Photo: Bob Ransford

Integrated Infrastructure for Local Food and Agriculture BUD FRASER

Infrastructure systems underpin our urban society. These include systems for water supply, stormwater drainage, sewage management, transportation, and energy such as electrical and gas networks. One of the main roles of infrastructure is to move critical resources around and transform them for different uses or disposal, for example, transforming municipal wastewater into treated water, methane gas, and other residuals. These major resources include energy, water, and materials, even what we currently think of as waste. Types of infrastructure can also be thought of as a spectrum from constructed, technological systems (such as sewer piping and pump stations) through to natural, ecologically based systems like wetlands and forests, as well as combinations of these.

Food and agriculture systems require specialized infrastructure that includes irrigation, organic waste management (plant and animal wastes), and energy systems. Through integrating water, energy, and waste flows between the urban and more rural/agricultural, new efficiencies are possible. This chapter describes how agricultural and urban infrastructure systems may be linked to improve overall performance.

Integrated Systems Thinking

Traditional city building dictates that new development is first planned and designed, and then the infrastructure systems are designed to service it. A challenge with this approach is that the potential for integrated and more efficient infrastructure systems is not fully realized or even explored. Emerging

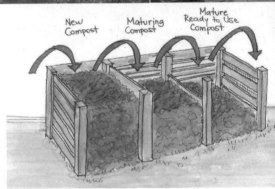

Integrated Infrastrucutre systems: Clockwise from top left: Bioswale (Photo: HB Lanarc); installing pipes for a district energy system (Photo: Revelstoke Community Energy Corporation); treatment system for water reuse (Photo: HB Lanarc); three bin compost system (Photo: HB Lanarc); rain garden (Photo: HB Lanarc)

approaches in community planning and property development are putting more emphasis on determining the infrastructure and resource management opportunities and taking these into account in the design. A more fully integrated design of systems (referred to under several names, including integrated infrastructure, integrated resource recovery, and others) can create new opportunities and change the cost/benefit equations significantly.

The ideas behind this approach are not new. Integrated systems can begin to mimic natural ecosystems and the inherent benefits of those systems, and have been used in many traditional farming systems. To be fully realized, however, they involve a departure from present-day conventional infrastructure planning and engineering.

PRINCIPLES OF INTEGRATED INFRASTRUCTURE DESIGN:

- Interconnect systems so that output from one system can be used as input to another, and treating all waste materials as resources.

- Generate value and revenue from these resources wherever possible.

- Achieve multiple benefits from each system or component wherever possible.

- Locate resource producers and users near each other to facilitate resource exchange.

Urban and Agricultural Resource Challenges

Development of towns and cities and large-scale food production well outside these centres creates **large material flows** over long distances in and out of both areas. This situation has evolved in part from economies of scale that are achieved in both realms. In both infrastructure and agricultural systems, over the last forty years or so the trend has been to create large, centralized operations, for example, city-scale, centralized wastewater treatment plants or very large hog-production operations that are optimized to provide a given level of service or production per dollar. In recent years, however, there has been recognition that the largest scale is not always the most optimal, especially when considering the lost opportunities (such as un-utilized waste materials and energy) and unaccounted for costs (such as the direct and indirect costs of energy and GHG emissions from long-distance transportation).

These material flows are largely **open loop**. For example, organic **biomass** (in the form of food) is grown on farms and shipped to the city. A portion of it is eaten and residuals are often land-filled, where they create GHG emissions. Through human waste, carbon and nutrients embodied in food products are also converted to **biosolids** (sludge) from wastewater treatment, which has different fates depending on the jurisdiction. These often include landfilling or incineration. Meanwhile, agricultural soil nutrients and carbon can become depleted and must be further augmented by other materials such as mined and synthetic fertilizers. In many cases, very little (if any) of the carbon is cycled back to the land. Some mined nutrients, such as phosphorous, are also becoming in shorter supply, and costs are expected to rise significantly in the future.

Current urban operations (such as transportation and building heating) and agriculture-related operations (such as fertilizer production, farm equipment, and greenhouse heating) are heavily dependent on fossil fuels, resulting in major greenhouse gas emissions from both sectors. Emissions also result from transporting food and waste (resources) over increasingly large distances. These large distances also decrease the opportunities to better manage our resources through **closed-loop** cycling.

Why Connect Urban With Rural Systems?

Juxtaposing urban environments and agricultural systems offers unique opportunities and can address some of the challenges described earlier. When food production is located adjacent to other uses, it opens up new possibilities for integrated resource management. Energy, water, and organic resources can be exchanged, transformed, and used in ways that benefit both the food growing area and the surrounding areas. This principle of local diversity has parallels in other sectors. For example, in urban **district energy systems**, interconnection of a diverse range of energy users can lead to a significant reduction in overall energy demand.

Agricultural land and infrastructure systems have the capability to transform and use resources where they are needed, taking advantage of the ecological infrastructure that growing systems provide. This soil-based, ecological machinery provides a variety of useful functions, in addition to food production, and can be integrated within a larger, more complex cycle. The ecological machinery (which at its core has a complex web of organisms— Please see Figure 15.1) can help recycle wastewater, transform organic waste into soil and food, help manage stormwater, and can even sequester carbon from the atmosphere. In some cases it can produce biomass for energy, recycling the carbon that plants captured from the atmosphere. In addition, mechanized growing systems or other food facilities can exchange energy beneficially with adjacent energy users.

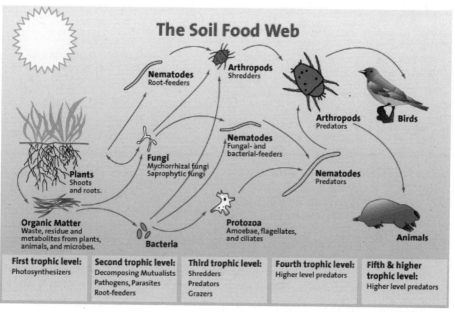

Figure 15.1 Soil food web
Source: Courtesy of Soil Foodweb Inc.

Food, Agriculture, and Infrastructure Resources and Flows

In conceptualizing what integrated infrastructure systems would look like, mapping the inputs and outputs of urban and rural water, energy, and waste management systems is a way to begin to identify ways to significantly increase efficiencies. Table 15.1 shows the water, material, & energy inputs & outputs for agricultural & urban resource flows.

Table 15.1 - Agricultural and Urban Resource Flows

	Agricultural Resource Flows	Urban Resource Flows
WATER INPUT	Primarily for crop irrigation but potentially for other uses; quality of water should be matched to use	Potable and non potable, though most municipalities only provide potable
WATER OUTPUT	Drainage or runoff of water, which may contain valuable (and sometimes problematic) nutrients	Wastewater (from residential and possibly other sectors), stormwater runoff (this typically contains pathogen organisms), carbon (e.g., expressed by **biological oxygen demand**), nutrients, and other potential contaminants including metals, depending on the sources connected to the collection system
MATERIAL INPUT	Material input – soil amendment (e.g., compost), fertilizer	Food
MATERIAL OUTPUT	Material outputs - plant-based residuals, animal manure, fish waste (aquaculture), and possibly animal-rendering residuals or mortalities	Material output, including landscaping debris, food residuals, wood waste, and paper products
ENERGY INPUT	Heating fuels for nurseries or in large quantities for glass-encased vegetable greenhouses or land-based aquaculture facilities	Vehicle fuels (typically gasoline and diesel)
	Fuels for farm machinery and transportation (typically diesel, gasoline, and propane)	Building heating and cooling
	Electricity; heating and cooling for food processing and storage	–
ENERGY OUTPUT	Energy is not typically exported from either urban or agricultural zones, but is provided from outside sources via the electricity and fuel distribution networks. However, using an integrated infrastructure model, there are a variety of ways to create energy outputs as described later.	

Using an integrated infrastructure approach, urban and agricultural needs may be met more efficiently, with a reduced reliance on fossil fuels and better use of all resources.

Integrated Infrastructure Strategies

Each project or site presents unique constraints and opportunities; there are no textbook solutions that will fit every case. In some situations, it may be possible only to implement limited aspects of a fully integrated design. This section presents some concepts of how urban and agricultural systems can potentially be integrated.

CYCLING OF ORGANIC RESOURCES

The proximity of agricultural areas to residential and commercial buildings creates the opportunity to close the loop of organic resources and support long-term sustainable agriculture. Given the unique challenges of managing organic waste such as food residuals, which include possible odours, space for processing and storage, and visual issues, agricultural land is usually better suited than urban land for these purposes. Many community gardens and farms, particularly those practising organic production, are already composting the residuals from their own operations. Compost has the capability to enhance soil quality and health, improve water retention, provide nutrients, buffer pH, and even suppress some plant diseases, which leads to increased food production, among other benefits, and is a key part of closed-loop systems.

The composting of agricultural residues can be augmented by co-composting with urban food residuals, as many agricultural residues can act as the bulking agent and carbon source that is needed for composting food waste. City landscaping residuals can also perform this role and be integrated with agricultural residues and/or food residuals.

One of the remarkable features of organic materials, unlike many other materials in the municipal solid waste stream, is the relative ease with which they can be converted into different forms. Discarded food can be fully converted into a useful soil amendment within several months with minimal input of energy or other resources. This can be done at virtually any scale, and does not necessarily require highly mechanized systems; it is in fact carried out by a huge array of micro-organisms, including bacteria and fungi. Mechanization, controls, and monitoring are used to handle materials at larger scales and to provide optimal conditions for the biological process, reducing composting times and assuring quality and product safety where feedstocks may contain pathogens (for example, manure or municipal biosolids/sewage sludge).

Composting systems can be small (worm bin or backyard composter) or large (static piles, windrows, or enclosed systems). The composting technology and scale need to be selected carefully based on location and site constraints, available feedstocks (materials for composting), operational preferences, and capital and operating cost considerations. For example, low-tech systems such as static piles can be relatively inexpensive to set up but can require significant ongoing effort to manage and monitor. An enclosed mechanical system, on the other hand, while relatively expensive, typically requires less operator time. Larger-scale composting systems, particularly those that compost food or animal waste, should be located at some distance from residential and commercial properties due to potential odours, noise from machinery, and poor aesthetics. Screening by hedgerows, trees, or other buildings is also appropriate.

Compost products may then be beneficially used to amend agricultural soils. Provided the feedstocks and process meet organic requirements, composting can be a mainstay for organic agriculture. Compost may also be used for landscaping purposes outside of the agricultural zone. Where compost is shipped off-site, revenue may potentially be generated from sales.

Top: Food waste composting using a Wright Environmental in-vessel system (Photo: Courtesy of UBC Waste Management); Windrow composting of combined farm and food residuals with a tractor-driven turner (Photo: Courtesy of Dean Dack, Classic Compost); Co-composting of biosolids and wood waste using aerated static piles (Photo: HB Lanarc)

SHARED AND DISTRICT ENERGY SYSTEMS

In district energy (DE) systems, heat (and possibly cooling) is distributed from centralized plants by circulating water (or low-pressure steam) through underground piping to multiple buildings. This shared system supplants a conventional scenario in which each building has a standalone heating system. Key parts of the system include the shared water-piping infrastructure and energy centres or heat plants that are connected to this infrastructure.

Interconnection of diverse types of buildings and facilities via district energy systems can significantly reduce overall energy consumption as well as peak energy requirements and system sizing. These reductions occur because of several factors. The diversity in energy loads means that the energy needs of different uses peak at different times, flattening the demand curve. The systems supplying heat can therefore be smaller in capacity. In systems with both heating and cooling loops, waste heat from one facility, such as a large refrigeration system, can be used to supply heat to another building. This reduces the demand for energy input from outside the system.

Urban DE systems may be connected to higher-density residential, commercial, and industrial buildings, as well as to recreational facilities such as ice rinks and pools. These buildings and facilities may be complemented in the agricultural sector by connections to heated greenhouses, heated aquaculture, or larger-scale food refrigeration systems such as cold storage. For example, heat rejected from large food-storage refrigeration systems could be used by greenhouses for space heating, by aquaculture for water heating, or for heating buildings via the shared DE infrastructure.

Feasibility considerations include proximity of all buildings and facilities, density/ building size, energy demand, diversity of

District Energy Centre in Vancouver, tucked in under a bridge.
Source: Courtesy of City of Vancouver

heating and cooling loads, the potential for combining with other underground utility installations, and availability of energy sources and **thermal storage** (such as **geoexchange** systems). Typically, the agricultural facilities mentioned are distant from other types of higher-density buildings; however, an AU approach considers that much closer proximities may be possible. In addition, since most DE systems cross property boundaries, an energy utility is required to operate the system. DE utilities may be private, public (for example, local government), or partnerships.

ALTERNATIVE ENERGY SOURCES FOR FOOD AND AGRICULTURE SYSTEMS

In addition to utilizing rejected heat from refrigeration, other alternative energy sources could also be integrated within urban and agricultural infrastructure systems. Ideally, these are renewable and/ or low-emissions energy sources. These are discussed in the following sections.

One example of an alternative energy source is the use of biomass to produce heat (and possibly electricity), either through **thermal conversion** (such as **combustion** or **gasification**), or **biogas digestion** and subsequent combustion. Agricultural

operations often result in large quantities of either plant residuals or manure. In theory, either of these can be used as feedstock for either technology (thermal conversion or digestion); however, technical and practical considerations will dictate the feasibility and selection of appropriate technology. These considerations include the suitability of the materials for a given technology (such as energy yield per tonne), what form of energy is most useful at the location (heat, electricity, or gas fuel), or other available materials from off-site that could be co-processed together with the agricultural feedstocks.

Anaerobic digestion producing biogas also produces wastewater and **digestate**, a wet, solid material that remains after digestion. Wastewater must be treated and disposed of or used appropriately; digestate may be composted or co-composted with other feedstocks. Biogas is typically combusted to provide heat, or both heat and electricity, which is also known as combined heat and power (**CHP**) or **cogeneration**. CHP can result in significant efficiency improvements, but requires additional implementation considerations, such as electricity user assessment and distribution infrastructure.

Organic residuals from agriculture or urban landscaping can potentially be converted to biofuels for vehicles and equipment, for use in both agricultural operations and urban transportation. In recent years, biofuel manufacturing technology has evolved rapidly, with commercial systems producing both ethanol and biodiesel. Potential biofuel feedstocks include agricultural biomass (crops or residuals), wood waste, and used cooking oil. An emerging technology is **algaculture**, the large-scale production of algae for conversion into biofuels.

There are many types and variations of biomass energy technology, with varying degrees of maturity.

These energy technologies often require considerable economies of scale for economic feasibility, due to high capital cost. As a result, smaller agricultural operations may not produce sufficient feedstock quantities to supply a larger-scale system. However, by integrating other feedstock streams, additional scale can potentially be obtained, and better feedstock mixes can be achieved. For example, an anaerobic digestion system producing biogas for heat and power can be supplied with some types of agricultural residuals (such as liquid manure) as well as source-separated organics from urban areas, including residential and commercial food waste and waste oil from restaurants.

In planning biomass energy systems, careful consideration should be given to the most appropriate use of organic resources. While combustion of these is typically considered to be greenhouse gas neutral, it does in fact result in emissions; this use should be balanced against other uses that may sequester some of the carbon, and against other potential energy sources that could address that need.

At an individual building level, as in an urban environment, solar thermal panels can be attached to or integrated into the south side of any building or structure with solar access and interconnected to buildings' hot-water systems or even district energy loops. These solar thermal systems can contribute energy for water heating or building space heating.

For electricity generation, wind turbines and solar photovoltaic systems can provide electricity either for on-site use (typically requiring energy storage), or for feed-in to electrical grids, depending on generating capacity and other factors. At present, these systems are typically less competitive on a cost-per- unit- of- energy basis than grid-supplied power, so may be most appropriate where grid power is not immediately available or where grid-supplied power is expensive and/or has a high greenhouse gas emissions factor.

Wastewater Treatment and Reuse

Residential and commercial wastewater can potentially provide a source of water for irrigation of agricultural crops.[55] In a conventional municipal scenario, wastewater collected from all building sectors is treated at centralized plants and discharged to adjacent water bodies. An integrated approach may be able to take advantage of smaller-scale, decentralized treatment systems, as these may be able to be located near an agricultural zone. In addition, decentralized systems can avoid much of the contamination from industrial and other sources that often occurs in large municipal systems through servicing a limited area that is primarily residential and does not include industrial wastewater.

Using reclaimed wastewater for irrigation requires an appropriate level of wastewater treatment and monitoring to ensure safe application and protection from health and environmental risks. Depending on the jurisdiction, multiple standards and regulations for water reuse apply, including those from both senior and local governments. Constituents of concern in reclaimed water for irrigation include pathogenic organisms, nutrients, and contaminants such as heavy metals or industrial chemicals.

One important note is that, generally, reclaimed wastewater is not accepted for organic production. In this case, other uses for reclaimed wastewater may include irrigation of landscaping, **groundwater recharge**, augmented stream flows, or non-potable building uses such as toilet flushing. When not being used for irrigation or other uses, treated wastewater must be discharged, either to land (an **infiltration area**) or surface water.

Wastewater treatment involves another set of systems that benefits from economies of scale, often making it more challenging to implement at smaller scales using a decentralized model. However, the economic case for this model can potentially be strengthened by using an integrated resource-recovery approach, where additional value can be generated through recovery and reuse of by-products such as wastewater heat and biosolids for composting or biogas production. Some systems can provide additional value such as a living machine or solar aquatics system, in which aquatic plants are used to treat the water in a greenhouse, potentially playing a technology demonstration and aesthetic role.

Conceptual designs where these strategies are integrated are illustrated in Figure 15.2, integrated infrastructure opportunities.

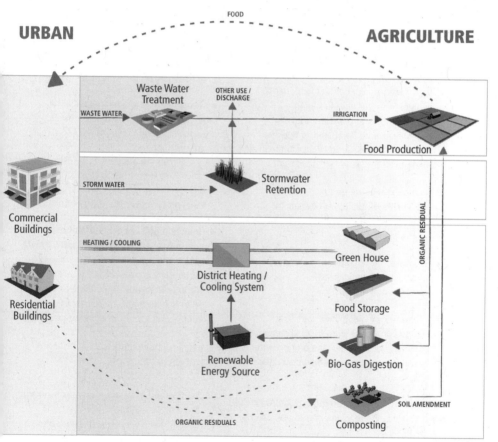

Figure 15.2 Integrated Infrastructure Opportunities
Source: HB Lanarc

Implementation: Challenges and Strategies

Despite the strong rationale for integrating aspects of agricultural and urban infrastructure systems, there exist a number of challenges to implementing these opportunities. Part of the challenge is that some of the concepts are moving into largely uncharted territory in the North American context. This means that some of the barriers and challenges will only be uncovered once the process of implementation is started.

Some of the primary challenges include:

- Regulatory requirements and issues at multiple levels, such as satisfying reclaimed water criteria for irrigation or processing urban organic residuals on land zoned as agricultural. Proposed designs may cut across multiple government departments or levels, and may require discussions between these to determine where regulatory responsibilities lie.

- High capital costs and attendant economies of scale, particularly for systems such as district energy and biogas digestion.

- Residuals management challenges, such as odour and vehicle traffic in proximity to residential areas.

- Integration of disciplines and new design paradigms outside of common practice; operational risks and potential issues associated with new or unproven technology.

To facilitate AU integrated infrastructure opportunities, the following strategies can be pursued:

- An integrated design and planning process, bringing together all relevant disciplines early in the process.

- Integrated resource-recovery principles:
  - Design and implement systems that meet multiple objectives wherever possible.
  - Treat all wastes as resources and generate value/revenue from them.
  - Find opportunities to interconnect infrastructure systems to facilitate the transfer of resources and flows between uses.

- Pilot projects to demonstrate integration and innovation at smaller scales or between specific systems.

- Government and stakeholder engagement early in the process to uncover barriers, maximize buy-in, and garner support.

- Innovative financing mechanisms and private-sector management solutions such as private utility partnerships.

- Selection of technologies that are appropriate for the context, and learning from experiences in other jurisdictions, particularly internationally where similar plans or innovative technologies have been implemented more extensively and operational experience has been gained.

CREATIVE INFRASTRUCTURE SOLUTIONS IN PRACTICE

Growing Power, an organization that develops community food systems, runs a greenhouse operation at its headquarters in urban Milwaukee, Wisconsin. The facility features about 20,000 plants and vegetables, thousands of fish, and a livestock inventory of chickens, goats, ducks, rabbits, and bees, in a space no larger than a small supermarket. It integrates a number of resource-management strategies including:

- Aquaponics systems that integrate elements of **hydroponics** and aquaculture, where fish waste becomes nutrients for plants.

- **Vermicomposting** (worms) and anaerobic digestion of organic residuals including brewer's grains, wood waste, pre-consumer food scraps, and coffee grounds, much of which is from off-site.

- Production of "**compost tea**" from the compost process, for plant application.

- Use of compost for soil amendment.

- Heating of two greenhouses using heat produced from composting.

Acting as a model for community food systems, the centre also provides a range of educational programs and a small retail store. It demonstrates a range of low-tech, integrated infrastructure and resource management methods and technologies that can be not only operated within an urban environment, but also integrated with resource management within the broader community.

Growing Power, an integrated urban farm and market in Michigan that includes aquaponics, composting and greenhouse growing – one of Growing Power's facilities. Photos: Courtesy of Rhodes Yepsen, BioCycle magazine

Bakerview EcoDairy/Nutriva Group is a group of integrated farming and commercial operations with innovative energy and resource management. The Nutriva Group, based in Abbotsford, BC, consists of three main business units that provide a wide range of products and services. When completed in early 2010, Bakerview EcoDairy will host: A Nutrifoods Farm Market, An eco-friendly dairy farm, Agri-tourism operations, and an R & D facility. Nutritech Solutions provides products and services to dairy, hog, poultry, and aquaculture commercial producers; Nutrifood Solutions develops specialty functional food products.

Bakerview Ecodairy (artists rendering)
Photo: Courtesy of Bill Vanderkooi, Nutriva Group

Bakerview EcoDairy not only integrates multiple commercial operations on-site, but is also located adjacent to other commercial and retail areas and is less than one kilometre, 0.62 miles, from residential areas. The farm is in the process of implementing a number of innovative infrastructure and resource-management projects. An anaerobic digester will process manure from fifty dairy cows as well as process locally produced whey and bakery by-products. Biogas produced will be used to generate electricity and hot water for use on the farm, digestate will be used as bedding for the cows, and wastewater will be converted to fertilizer. The EcoDairy will also incorporate features such as a green roof, rainwater collection, solar energy capture, and wind power generation.

Summary

By consciously planning and designing both the urban and agricultural infrastructure systems as one system, towns, cities, and regions will become more resilient over time and be better integrated with the natural systems that surround settlement areas. This section has given a broad overview of the opportunities and challenges involved in integrating urban and agricultural infrastructure systems. The evolution of 21st century approaches to infrastructure systems will require increased efficiencies in water, energy, and waste management; linking urban and agricultural systems will require increased efficiencies in water, energy, and waste management; linking urban and agricultural systems can contribute significantly. Towns, cities, and agricultural areas stand to benefit a great deal as a result of this shift.

Agricultural Urbanism & the Human Being: Intent, Program, & Scale EDWARD ROBBINS PORTER

This chapter brings together the larger planning rationale for a more integrated vocabulary of urbanism and agriculture, a means by which decision makers, designers, and planners can more readily understand the links between robust local food systems and the resiliency of local communities. Here we explore the fundamental physical characteristics of both urban and agricultural landscapes, with a focus on examining the links between the parallel urban and agricultural programs and scales.

The design detail of human-scale agriculture is grounded in the larger discourse on contemporary and innovative responses to urbanism, which shapes the very essence of being human and the formative experiences we wish to propagate.

Expanding the Urban Design Vocabulary

Agricultural Urbanism is admittedly a cumbersome term. And yet, despite years of exploring its larger intent and finer details, a better description has yet to reveal itself. In the end, this is of no consequence, as all of these "neo"-schools — from "new urbanism" and "new ruralism" to "neo-agrarianism" and "ecological urbanism" — are, in a word, convergent. So long as we steward our respective models in a manner that is additive and complimentary, our sum-total model of urbanism will grow healthier with each generation. More specifically, it should be noted that the tenets of AU are as informed by the writings of the neo-agrarians (Wendell Berry and Norman Wirzba) as they are the proponents of traditional neighbourhood design. In the end, we must be deliberate in the type of urbanism we propagate. Agricultural Urbanism reflects the most fundamental merger of urban form and culture with the noblest of professions: agriculture. We intend to evolve best practices as they pertain to urban design to respect our most fundamental communion with the land, represented in our local food systems.

Food & Agriculture: The New Urban Design Mandate

To state the obvious, urban designers seek to improve our most basic physical relationships to the world around us. For example, public squares, where community events such as farmers' markets, concerts, rallies, and festivals may occur, play a key role in fostering a sense of place and community. In the context of AU, we expand our lens to consider food and the myriad systems inherent in its production, procurement, and provision. While we urban designers have recently adopted a more holistic approach to considering economic, social, and environmental needs of current and future generations, deliberate attention to food has largely been overlooked and/or oversimplified to a narrow set of key issues such as farmland protection (gross acreage and capability) and urban agriculture (community gardens). Agricultural Urbanism attempts to bring greater focus to the full range of food system opportunities and expand the mandate for urban designers.

Agricultural Urbanism marries the aforementioned models of urbanism to working agricultural landscapes through a fundamental planning and design approach focused on compatible scale. Put more simply, **human-scaled agricultural systems** are dovetailed into pedestrian-friendly models of excellent urbanism.

Where City Meets Country: A Dysfunction of Scale

Both landscapes — that of sprawling, single-use residential suburb and the **monocropped quarter section** — only do one very specific thing. And therein lies the problem. As their relative programs have been specialized in the name of efficiency, their respective compatibility has been neglected. Moreover, from a physical design perspective, the characteristics of each have left the other seeking creative solutions to better buffer their adjacency.

Our present-day urban-agricultural edge continues to be defined by a decades-old dysfunction: suburban homes stand with their backs to an industrial agricultural hinterland, separated by little more than a perimeter fence and bramble. The best-case scenario looks like a neighbourhood bordered by a thick wall of plant material... also known as a buffer. A buffer is an object that prevents incompatible or antagonistic landscape characteristic from coming into contact or harming each other. In that sense, our current simplification of the urban-agricultural relationship is, in most cases, deemed incompatible. The physical world we live in is illustrative of the psychological disconnect among people, community, food, and agriculture.

And yet, in many cases today, while suburbia is being slowly retrofitted with more and more best practices in urban planning and design, its neighbour in agriculture has continued to follow the "bigger is better"

mantra of industrial agriculture. Even with urban populations at its doorstep, a for-profit agricultural operation rarely significantly benefits from neighbouring labour and markets.

It is no wonder that the models of traditional neighbourhood design — based on the fundamental building block of the human-scaled, walkable neighbourhood — have struggled to develop a meaningful and lasting relationship with these alienating, industrial landscapes. In the end, the current relationship between agriculture and the urban edge is marginally functional at best, with suburbanites enjoying and paying for the pastoral views of agricultural land.

Scale and Program: A Transect-Based Approach.

Beyond the greater rationale of why AU, we approach how. To begin, we borrow from the New Urbanists and the scientific rigour of the **transect**, a systematic way of considering context-appropriate design strategies (please refer to figure 16.1, the agricultural transect). The power of a transect-based methodology to physical design is that it provides an intelligent framework for the understanding of a given program across multiple scales and contexts.

Moreover, the New Urbanist understanding of the transect and the relationship between urban and rural landscapes creates a sort of **figure-ground relationship** between city and country. AU employs the transect as a basis for developing context-appropriate approaches to a more deliberate exploration of the role of the food and agriculture system in cities and how this role is supported by the practice of excellent urbanism. A common misunderstanding of AU results from an oversimplified scaling up of urban agriculture, where often-underutilized parcels of land are reprogrammed for the purpose of community amenities, education, or

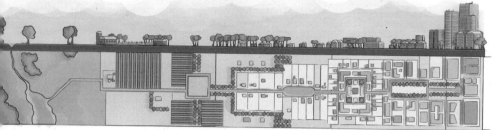

Figure 16.1: Agricultural Transect.
Source: HB Lanarc

food production. In this model, agricultural systems fit wherever they can — typically in remnant spaces, where the free hand of the market has yet to identify a higher and better use. In contrast, AU is an altogether re-informed model of urbanism that considers the health of the local food system — from land security and production of food to processing, marketing, and distribution — within every aspect of physical planning and design, across multiple scales.

Refitting the Pieces: The Quarter Section & The Five-Minute Walk

It is, perhaps, no coincidence that the most basic unit of pedestrian scaled planning efforts — the five-minute walking circle — encompasses approximately the same extent of the historical quarter sections granted to American and Canadian frontier farmers in the early 19th century. Consider for a moment that the scale of the homestead was, for all intents and purposes, the same relative scale as the neighbourhood of modern-day urban planning. In no way a coincidence, these parallels point to a most fundamental human need: at its most basic, our human experience requires an understanding of its surrounding landscape and of its general structure and function. While the re-birth of urbanism has made significant inroads in suburbia's hostile

takeover of the North American landscape, the topic of food — its production, processing, marketing, distribution, and ultimate composting — has been largely overlooked, because the procurement of a loaf of bread and a gallon of milk is only a five-minute walk away. AU threads the food system back into the fabric of urbanism, based on the application of an appropriate program at an appropriate scale.

As a means to better understand the parallel systems of agriculture and urban form at varying scales, the following demonstrates the relationship of program to scale from the more generalized planning unit of the *pedestrian-shed*/quarter section down to the individual yard/garden row.

COMPATIBLE SCALES: SUSTAINABLE AGRICULTURE & SUSTAINABLE URBANISM

Figure 16.2 begins to demonstrate the fundamental organizing structures of both urban and agricultural landscapes, based on program (function) and scale (form). While this list is in no way complete or comprehensive, it begins to relate spatial programs at similar scales in hopes of demonstrating a common language between the two land uses. Each of the program scales is dictated, for the most part, by a fundamental human need to organize and classify space.

Urban Program	Urban Unit		Scale	Agricultural Unit	Agricultural Program
Complete range of urban services: live, work & play: access to regional transportation network & park system	PEDESTRIAN-SHED		160+ acres (65+ hectares)	SECTION	Complete range of crops, including production at scale of grains, legume livestock & dairy; forestry & NTFP viab
Pedestrian-friendly mix of land uses & services, including neighbourhood-scale commercial, social gathering spaces	NEIGHBOUR-HOOD		40+ acres (16+ hectares)	QUARTER SECTION	Small scale grain & livestock productic specialty forestry products; fully diver "homestead"
Mix of housing types; pedestrian circulation to access larger neighbourhood sevices/amenities	BLOCK		5+ acres (2+ hectares)	FARM	Commercial orchard operation; scale affords wholesale market potential o variety of crops
Designated land use, defining neighbour-hood "function," open space	SITE / PARCEL		1+ acres (0.4+ hectares)	LARGE GARDEN / SMALL FARM	Mixed produce & small fruit productic small scale orchard; typical "farm uni
Residential / Commercial unit(s); access	LOT		1/8+ acres (0.05+ hectares)	GARDEN PLOT	Micro-share CSA; specialty crops
Open space / Recreation	YARD		400+ sqft (37+ sq m)	ROW	Kitchen garden

from regional planning to placemaking

from the human body to place

Figure 16.2 Urban & Agricultural Programs as Related by Unit and Scale
Source: Edward Porter

A GOOD FIT: HUMAN-SCALED AGRICULTURE & PLACEMAKING

By design, AU is organized around more pedestrian-scaled systems, as discussed, in the exploration of similar relative scales, comparing hierarchies of urban design with human-scaled agricultural production units. Perhaps more importantly, when specifically considering these human-scaled systems, individual components of each system are themselves scaled to a more fundamental daily experience. This section considers the individual production components of AU as a means to better understand how the principles and objectives of AU apply to the experiences of participants.

While the intent of AU is to articulate a more resilient form of urbanism in general, it is the layering of systems and programming, based on a fundamentally human-scaled relationship with productive landscapes, that affords AU such tremendous opportunities

for placemaking, perhaps the most tangible and enduring form of sustainable design.

The following provides a picture of the main characteristics of an AU-compatible, human-scaled agricultural operation that illuminates the programming and placemaking opportunities present in all aspects of the food system.

INPUT: LAND, LABOUR, CAPITAL

From a physical design perspective, the development of more localized food systems — and the more human-scaled production *farm unit* (see below) — serves to establish more opportunities for the layering of commercial, industrial, educational, and recreational programs in and around the farm. In that sense, the land input associated with the local food system is, by design, more flexible, given the availability of additional input of labour and capital. Additionally, localized food systems can more effectively substitute increased labour input (associated with non-industrial intensive production models) for land (associated with more extensive operations). Finally, in the context of small- to medium-scale organic farm operations, capital costs are minimized due to the decreased mechanization and reliance on chemical fertilizers. In any case, the fundamental approach of AU and the development of local systems and markets focus on the potential input to be principally acquired and provided for at the neighbourhood scale. Figure 16.3 Mediators of the Edge, provides an overview of these individual components.

OUTPUT (FOOD, NUTRITION, HEALTH)

Based on the more neighbourhood-scale associations of AU, the farm output considered here is developed beyond the more conventional context of yield per acre (Please refer to Figure 16.3 for a list of examples of farm output that supports a healthier neighbourhood and greater urban environment).

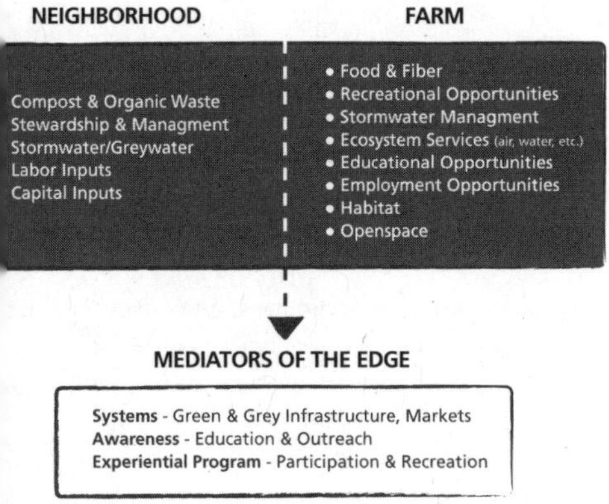

Figure 16.3: Mediators of the Edge
Source: Edward Porter, Masters Thesis 2006

COMPONENTS (PRODUCTION, PROCESSING, STORAGE, MARKETING AND DISTRIBUTION)

As noted in other sections of this book, human-scale agriculture has a unique set of components.

- **Production.** All production areas are based on a fundamental farm-unit building block, scaled up from two fundamental dimensions: the size of the human body (comfortable working positions) and the 100-foot, 30 meter, row, (the standard dimension for seed sales, also reflective of a widely acknowledged psychological threshold in planting, cultivating, harvesting):

    □ Assumes 18-inch, 46 cm, row spacing — required for plant habit and healthy root growth as well as to enable intercropping.

    □ Three rows within a 4-foot, 1.2 meter, width (based on dimension of bed shaper/linear distance between tractor tires).

    □ The 6-inch, 15 cm, walkway (compacted soil along tractor tire path).

    □ Long-term crop-rotation (eight-year ideal as per Eliot Coleman's The New Organic Grower, 1989).

    □ 100-foot, 30 meter, row length: harvest (experiential) threshold, seed sales standard.

    □ Farm unit: 3 acres, 1.2 hectare, of production within a 5-acre, 2 hectare, field space.

- Production during growing season provides for approximately thirty families/dwelling units per acre.

- **Processing.** Based on the typical farm unit, processing facilities can be accommodated at the block or neighbourhood scale, including the provision of more flexible facilities, such as community (commercial) kitchens. In addition to adding value to farm products through canning, pickling, drying, freezing, and more, the community kitchen can also provide significant social programming through the accommodation of community dinners, workshops, or other special events.

- **Storage.** Smaller farm unit scale facilitates smaller-scale production of value-added products for local market and, as a result, storage requirements can be more decentralized and smaller in scale. Where required, longer-term (post-processing) storage space can be shared among individual producers in more centralized locations associated with shared equipment storage, as desired.

- **Marketing and distribution.** Local distribution of farm produce and value-added products can be facilitated through a variety of avenues, including:

  □ Community-supported agriculture (CSA). Growers are supported through the purchase of farm shares, and participants in the program share in the risks and returns of the growing operation. Coordinated CSAs can be organized by distributors to feature a range of local and regional products.

  □ Direct sales and farmers' markets. Regular markets become part of the daily experience for both residents and visitors. Local growers are available to connect with customers and to sell produce and value-added products.

□ Farmgate sales and special events. Seasonal events and harvest cycles provide the opportunity for individual farms and gardens to host special events and directly market produce at the local or neighbourhood scale.

□ Restaurant-direct sales (and farm cafés). Providing direct sales of local farm products to local restaurateurs is another very effective way to support the economics of local agriculture, while elevating its cultural profile via the medium of local cuisine.

□ Wholesale supply to local and regional distributors. Not to be overlooked, wholesale production of farm products is an important component of a local food system, where individual growers can specialize at production of a slightly larger scale.

- **Waste and nutrient cycling.** At the neighbourhood scale, recycling of nutrients provides a significant link between the urban and agricultural realm. From organic waste to stormwater (often treated as a waste in urban environments), the local farm system acts as a "sink" and, more importantly, can utilize these products as input for farm production.

- **Boundaries and edges.** As previously mentioned, the boundaries of the local agricultural farm system are intentionally more blurred in the context of AU, in which the food system permeates every aspect of the urban experience. As a result, the more urban "experience of place" is rooted in productive agricultural landscapes. Very deliberately, the traditional boundaries of the food system permeate the built environment to encompass every aspect of daily life and, as a result, traditional edges between the urban environment and the larger working landscapes of agriculture merge to reveal new opportunities in programming and placemaking.

Back to the Basics of Land, Food, & Community

What lies at the centre of this discussion is a fundamental means through which to effectively address what Michael Ableman has termed the "crisis of participation" in local agriculture. By focusing efforts on the integration of the food and agriculture systems across all scales of our urban environment, we allow individuals to actively participate — and be more aware of their own participation — in their local food system, which has been deliberately planned and designed into the everyday urban experience. Through the elimination of buffers between urban and agricultural programs, the everyday practice of agriculture is seen within the context of livable urbanism. Conversely, the everyday convenience of urbanism can be enjoyed in the context of productive agriculture. At once, the best of both becomes accessible to all.

It should be stated for the sake of clarity that AU seeks a more humane form of urbanism. As we confront the challenges of the 21st century as professionals engaged in shaping the world around us — and that of future generations — we cannot afford to forsake our origins as an agricultural society any longer. Moreover, as designers of the built environment, we must always consider the most fundamental experiences that promote health, happiness, and the essence of being human. AU attempts to redouble our collective efforts to focus our attention on the most fundamental landscape experience of all: eating. And so, when considering the future of our collective urbanism, don't forget to think of how it tastes.

17. Urban and Open-Space Design for Food and Agriculture STEVEN CLARKE, JOAQUIN KARAKAS, KELSEY CRAMER, & MARK HOLLAND

Urban design is a critical part of the livability and functionality of our cities and as such, is a cornerstone of good urbanism. Urban design addresses the overall layout of our communities, the massing of buildings, architectural character, and the design of streets, plazas, parks, and other community open spaces, and more. Urban design establishes the physical character of urban environments in which we live and has a profound impact on our quality of life (Photo 17.1).

The integration of as many elements as possible of a sustainable food system into urban fabric and function is the purpose of AU. Agricultural Urbanism has significant implications and opportunities with respect to urban design. This section explores a

range of perspectives and opportunities for integrating the rich program of the urban food and agriculture system more significantly into urban design.

Urban design is the art of placemaking in the context of ensuring highly sustainable communities that are also highly desirable places in which to live. Urban design integrates and layers the many strands of community planning and design at all scales, from the building to street, neighbourhoods to cities. Urban design fundamentally shapes a community's identity and activity patterns, establishing the physical framework for how we engage with each other and the environment to meet our everyday needs.

Photo 17.1: Granville Island Market, Vancouver, Canada: an example of an urban redevelopment in the late 1970s of industrial land to city market.
Photo: Steve Clarke

As illustrated in this book, food and all that it encompasses is more than a requirement for survival: it is a deeply rooted passion that is at the centre of social, cultural, and spiritual practices. Food is both a means and an end in itself, and is fundamentally related to the identity and quality of life of individuals and the communities we live in.

Good urban design, when considered in the context of the goals of AU, acknowledges and embraces the many aspects of food and agriculture as central to fostering health, joy, and celebration in our lives and everyday activities. Furthermore, we use food as the platform from which to address other important elements of community ecology and livability, including physical, social, economic, cultural, and environmental health. Seen in this way, food and agriculture is a foundational layer upon which other elements of community life, including how and where we live, learn, work, play, and celebrate, can be interwoven through the physical planning, design, and programming of places.

Ensuring meaningful integration of food in the physical planning and design of communities requires attention to both the urban design process and its physical outcomes. Therefore, this chapter has two parts. The first part focuses on the urban design process and the second part explores the physical design characteristics of communities and a range of built-form and open-space typologies to identify opportunities for integrating food and agriculture into the everyday fabric and activities of communities.

Food, Agriculture and the Urban Design Process

The community planning and design process can be thought of as having two main streams: the *policy development process* and the design process. The policy development process focuses on

dealing with concepts and words to develop a vision and approach to a project. The *design development process* focuses on the physical form through design and engineering work. While these two process streams are inextricably linked and inform each other, pulling them apart enables identification of the range of opportunities available to integrate food and agriculture from policy frameworks to physical design plans.

THE POLICY DEVELOPMENT PROCESS

The policy development process involves establishing a regulatory and legislative framework that supports food and agriculture as an important goal and as a fundamental element of a plan or project. Rather than considering them as an afterthought, setting food and agriculture goals early in the process provides the best opportunity to be integrated into the broader planning and design objectives. For public institutions this can be accomplished at the local, regional, and provincial/state level. Private organizations and institutions can accomplish this by integrating food-related objectives and principles into their mission statements, mandate, and business plans to ensure that food-system issues are addressed as a core piece of their business practice.

Local governments are increasingly finding themselves on the front-lines of sustainable community planning in that land-use is paramount to any strategy for addressing climate change, affordable housing, economic development and food and agriculture, among others. For this reason, this section on planning and the following section on design focuses on local government level of policy development and community design. More dialogue, research, and strategic thinking is required to address sustainable food and agriculture in provincial and federal policy frameworks.

Food and agriculture can be integrated early on as a key element of local government policy frameworks through the following:

- **The community visioning process**, through which a community articulates its values and desired future to inform the development of strategic plans and other high-level policy frameworks and integrates sustainable food-system objectives into the foundation of its identity.

- **The master planning process**, which establishes the broad policy framework for land use, transportation, housing, economic development, and sustainable growth and development for the city as a whole, and through which food systems can be established as part of the overall urban plan.

- **The local area planning process**, which establishes a physical and detailed framework for development on a neighbourhood scale and through which food system elements can be optimized among many objectives in the form and function of any neighbourhood. Local area plans also encompass agricultural area plans, which guide agricultural land use and economic development.

- **Servicing and infrastructure planning**, including planning for energy, water, wastewater, and solid-waste management systems and the opportunities that exist to integrate food systems and the city's infrastructure systems.

- **Planning for climate change**, including addressing the impact of future weather, hydrology, and sea-level changes and their implications to farming, the city's food, long-term food supply, economics, and supporting infrastructure for the city or regional food system.

- **The design development process**, which focuses on implementing the broad policy framework and strategies that resulted from the policy development process at the scale of the neighbourhood or site, including considering opportunities and constraints for all elements of the food system in the early stages of design.

THE DESIGN PROCESS

There are a number of stages or tools for integrating food and agriculture into community plans and designs, including:

- **Community visioning.** This process involves the community working together to answer questions of who they are as a community, where they want to go to become more successful and sustainable, what design character they want for their community, and many other considerations. Inserting food and agricultural issues and opportunities purposely into this process encourages the community to consider its past and future food supply and economy and to weave food into its fabric of identity and character.

- **Site inventory and analysis.** This step in the urban design process focuses on identifying key opportunities and constraints that will fundamentally shape the development of a site or neighbourhood. Addressing food issues in that process creates an implicit priority for food and sets the foundation for integrating food systems into conceptual and detailed design.

- **Typology Development.** This step involves identifying a range of precedents, from historic to current projects, as well as possibly creating new patterns for various elements of a project to draw on in the subsequent stages of design. Bringing food-system types into the process creates a range of options for development, character, or form that supports various parts of a food system.

■ **Conceptual design.** This step involves articulating a fundamental concept, policy framework, and development program to drive the design, and then creating the overall design concept for the site or neighbourhood. These go to various levels of detail, but establishing food objectives as key elements of the development program will ensure food systems will be designed into the project.

■ **Design development.** This step is an iterative process where several versions of the site design are created over time to test and balance competing ideas, each time increasing the level of detail, refinement and response to various building and development codes and regulations. During this process, the real, practical elements of a food system will be secured in the design to ensure that they are built into the final project.

Food is a powerful element that can give a new sense of life and potential to the planning process, thereby attracting the attention and energy of many who otherwise may not feel connected to the process of designing a community. It also has not been an element in most conventional city planning and as such, most professionals in the design process are unfamiliar with food systems and are unaccustomed to responding to a program that includes food. Where food has been included in planning objectives, it has focused primarily on community gardens and spaces for farmers' markets; however, there is much more that needs to be considered in planning and urban design to capitalize on the opportunities that food and its social and economic dimensions offer a community.

On occasion, a project will have a broader policy framework related to food, but little of that typically makes it through to the design and site programming process. Focused attention is required to ensure food is addressed sufficiently in any urban design project. The following offers a range of perspectives, ideas, and opportunities for integrating support for the whole food system in design.

The Food City: Designing Food Into the Built Environment

The elements of a food system, as outlined in the introduction section, form the basis of the program of AU that need to be considered for every aspect of urban design. The elements of urban design into which food system objectives and programs can be integrated include:

■ Buildings of various types (residential, commercial, industrial, community).

■ Streets and transportation infrastructure of various types.

■ Parks and open spaces of various types and sizes.

■ Infrastructure systems (including energy, water, wastewater, solid waste, communications- Please see Chapter 15).

The following section offers a range of ideas and examples of how to incorporate opportunities for many aspects of the food system into each of the urban design elements.

BUILDINGS

Buildings are the fundamental mass that is manipulated in the urban design process to accommodate the activity program of the city, to give character to a city and its urban spaces, and to shape the nature of the experience of living in the city (Figure

17.1). Buildings are typically built one at a time by different owners and developers in accordance with their vision and a dialogue with a city planning department.

The process of urban design brings a different perspective where any specific building is considered in the context of the existing and desired character, function, and experience of the larger neighbourhood area. In new master-planned communities or in larger cities with clear visions and policies for how they want a neighbourhood to develop, the urban design process may precede the architectural work, and any specific building will need to demonstrate an appropriate fit with this overall vision for the area. Strategies for integrating food and agriculture into buildings are offered below.

Building programs to support food systems. The activity programs for the buildings in an agricultural urbanist project need to include a wide range of food-related functions and needs. These may involve buildings being designed outright for food uses such as a restaurant, chef school with industrial kitchens or food processing facility. Alternatively, adaptive reuse of a building may take place, such as fitting a café into an

Photo 17.2: Market Square, Winnipeg, Canada: one example of a historic ma building and district that can serve as an architectural precedent for Agricult Photo: Unknown

office building. Buildings with programs related to packaging, retailing or food education are quite common, however significant food production can also be designed into an urban building such as greenhouses on a roof or mushroom growing facility in a parkade. The building may also house key infrastructure elements such as energy supply systems, wastewater treatment systems, or solid-waste management systems. Once the food system strategy for a project or neighbourhood has been clearly articulated, designers can efficiently fit that program into the larger development vision and program for the area.

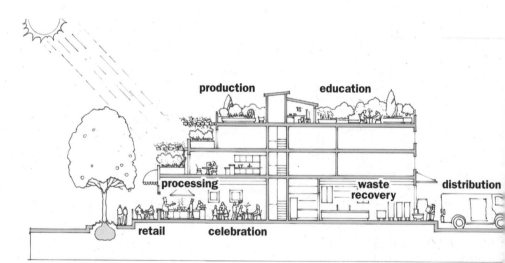

Figure 17.1: Agricultural Urbanism integrated with archite layered with the seven food system eler Illustration: Don Cr

Building design character. The physical character of a building may take on many forms, from strongly referencing architecture of the past (Photo 17.2), to being assertively contemporary, to engaging a style or character distinctly connected to a particular activity, such as a building influenced by existing barn architecture, regardless of its program. An agricultural urbanist project can adopt any physical form or character, although a rich history of food and agriculture buildings can form a strong foundation for influencing the design.

Building facade. The facade is where the building interfaces with both the natural elements and with the community at street level. The facade of any building needs to accommodate the food program, from views into a food store, processing facility or restaurant, as well as loading facilities. The building character will be expressed primarily through the surface materials and design details of the facade. In addition, more avant garde approaches to a building facade with respect to food can include growing food on the building walls – exterior or interior.

Rooftops. The rooftops of buildings has to shed rain and snow, but it is increasingly also a useful space in urban areas where they can become a significant opportunity for food production and social activities related to food. Rooftops can be designed to accommodate significant food gardens where appropriate or needed. Technical considerations regarding the building envelope and structure must be considered. For example, adding the weight of wet soil to the roof of an existing wood-frame garage may be found to be too expensive to retrofit its structure, while, designing a new concrete apartment building with planned rooftop gardens allows for the infrastructure of a food garden very little or no added costs (Photo 17.3).

Photo 17.3: Typical extensive green roof on new construction
Photo: Steve Clarke

Buildings are some of the most important elements in urban design for defining a community's function and character. Surrounding any building is the open space of a city, including its streets, plazas, parks, private gardens, and waterfronts. The interface between the external food program and that associated with any building is key for the overall system to function well.

STREETS, LANES, AND ROADS

Streets and roads are linear public corridors that facilitate vehicular transportation and the movement of people through cities. Roads are typically associated with transportation, whereas streets include vehicular and non-vehicular movement in the public realm. Lanes, alleys, and pedestrian-streets are examples of smaller-scale corridors that limit or prohibit the presence of automobiles (Photo 17.4). Streets can also be temporarily closed to create faux linear plazas for public use and enjoyment. Streets designed with boulevards, sidewalks, trees, and benches create a more inviting atmosphere for people. Bike lanes are also an important feature of well-designed streets. Arterial roads, collector roads,

Photo 17.4: Market in the Square, Duncan, Canada: an example of a street closure for a public market
Photo: Mark Holland

and highways are less conducive to public foot-traffic and would more typically be used for the transport of food and equipment in trucks.

A significant percentage of a typical community is devoted to roads and streets. In a city, this can be as high as 30 percent. A typical urban street comprises a given number of travel lanes, each around 3 meters (10 feet) wide, with parking potential on its edges. Sidewalks are often located on either side. Generally, a street is structured to direct stormwater to the edge where it is caught by a curb and channeled along the road edge until it reaches a catch basin that directs the water into the city's **stormwater conveyance system**. The landscape associated with a street can include a planted median in the middle of the street as well as street trees and boulevard areas adjacent the sidewalks, which is a useful device to provide some additional protection to the pedestrian from moving vehicular traffic.

An AU approach to street design includes exploring the following opportunities:

- **Connections to food**. Ideally, within a village, town, or city, one should live within a ten-minute walk of food retail. Retail opportunities for food along streets are endless and come in a variety of scales. From big-box supermarkets, to urban markets, to farmers' markets, to the corner store, each will shape the neighbourhood and street that they are part of. Big-box retail will typically be located along arterial streets and commercial strips where vehicular access is highly desirable by the retailer, while a weekly farmers' market may work on many scales because it is located at a neighbourhood amenity such as a park or community centre. Here, reliance on vehicular traffic for business is not the main goal, because neighbourhood residents have the option to walk to the event while others from outside the area may drive.

- **Eating and drinking everywhere**. A good agricultural urbanist street will provide many opportunities to eat and drink in the public realm as often as possible. This can include patios where restaurants can extend out onto the edge of the sidewalk, places to stop and eat take-out food alongside the sidewalk (Photo 17.5), or even a complete closure of the street periodically for a food event. An example is the Taste of Chicago, an event that started in 1980 as a one-day event on a three-block area of Michigan Avenue to celebrate America's Independence Day. This event has evolved into a two-week festival that sees millions of people participating in the celebration of global music, cultural activities, and most importantly, cuisine.

Photo 17.5: Street vendor
Photo: Mark Holland

- **Pedestrian-oriented.** The first priority is to make most streets in a city, first and foremost, for pedestrians. This includes providing a safe and appealing walking environment.

- **Presence of food and agriculture activity on street.** Street design needs to include a distinct program to make visible and celebrate food and agricultural activity in the community. This may include visibly locating along the street corridor places for producing food, processing food, storing equipment associated with agriculture and food businesses, selling food, celebrating food, and eating and drinking.

- **"Back of house is front of house."** In keeping with this central tenet of AU, street design should provide places to support the needs of the food businesses along the street, including storage of food and equipment, so long as a basic level of safety is maintained.

- **Productive edible landscapes.** Trees and shrubs are planted along most urban streets. Those that bear fruit or nuts can be used in some cases to increase the presence of food along the street (Photo 17.6). These types of plants must be carefully situated so that maintenance issues are not overlooked. Choosing appropriate plants is key. For instance, fruit trees may not mix well with parking areas for cars. In addition to permanent plantings in the street itself, container plantings are another way of introducing food into the urban landscape.

- **Signaling nearby agriculture.** Roads that connect with nearby rural areas present an opportunity for blending the rural and urban fabrics. The character and agricultural activities of the rural area can be consciously incorporated into design of various road elements at the interface between the city and the country, such as incorporating a grape arbour into a bus stop on a road that leads to wineries.

Photo 17.6: Grape vine hanging over a sidewalk in Holland
Photo: Kelsey Cramer

- **Transparency**. Urban design of the edge of streets should purposely include places to see food being processed, sold, and consumed, as well as to educate students in food. Extensive glazing in buildings along sidewalk edges adds significant interest to the public realm (Photo 17.7).

- **Habitat creation for pollinators and beneficial insects**. A careful selection of plants associated with the edible landscape agenda to provide habitat for insects and songbirds can increase biodiversity and pollination of nearby growing areas.

- **Stormwater management for agricultural irrigation**. Stormwater can be detained before it goes to urban storm sewers and percolated into the ground near trees and growing areas to keep the groundwater healthy. In some cases where space permits, stormwater can be harvested for direct irrigation, although it needs a sufficient measure of remediation to remove toxins in some cases.

Photo 17.8: Crown Street, Vancouver
Photo: Steve Clarke

- **Green streets**. In special situations, the entire model of the street can be completely revisited. As long as it can appropriately convey and park the necessary number of vehicles, the street can be redesigned to include community gardens, stormwater management swales, play areas, and other park-like elements. Where boulevards can be made big enough, they can even provide for small, linear, community garden plots. The most common examples of these are the Dutch woonerfs and British home-zones. Other examples include Seattle's SEA-Streets and Vancouver's Crown Street (Photo 17.8) or its country lane model.

- **Interpretive signage**. Interpretive signage can be included in many streets to tell the agricultural and food-related stories of the street and the area.

- **Farm equipment**. In a community with active agricultural and food production, the street or road may need to accommodate parking or turning radiuses for agricultural equipment. This is most visibly present in North America where historically, road right-of-ways were designed large enough to accommodate horse drawn carriages.

Photo 17.7: Café with a visible streetside kitchen and service to complement the indoor dining
Photo: Steve Clarke

Not all streets can be infused with an agricultural agenda, but many can. The more we make food and agriculture visible in our streets, the more we can claim multiple benefits from these key pieces of public infrastructure and land.

TRAILS, GREENWAYS, AND TRANSIT CORRIDORS

Trails and greenways are another form of urban open space that combines the program and agenda of both streets and parks. These can be standalone places or combined with transit or other corridors.

Greenways are defined as corridors of various widths linked together in a network.[56] These corridors can be urban or more natural in character. As urban spaces, they can resemble a street corridor dedicated to pedestrians, cyclists, and landscape. In more natural areas, trails of various widths and surfaces accommodate a diverse range of user groups. Nature trails, for example, are often surfaced with soft, natural material such as bark mulch, whereas multi-use or commuter trails are wider and surfaced with concrete or asphalt to allow for efficient movement through the landscape. Greenways can also preserve a contiguous stretch of landscape for ecological or cultural purposes. Farms can be included in greenways with the goal of protecting the cultural features of the area. In short, greenways have value for their multi-functionality and connectivity.

There are several types of transit corridors and many are conventional streets with a high volume of traffic, which offer limited opportunities for food-system objectives. However, for communities that have standalone corridors, such as for rapid transit lines or more conventional railway lines, there are many opportunities to use the often-vacant land alongside these corridors for various food-related activities.

Strategies for integrating food and agriculture into trails, greenways, and transit corridors include the following:

- **Linking food areas**. Greenways are linear corridors that link various areas within a community. They can be planned to connect directly to many food-related areas, including stores, restaurants, community gardens, or rural agricultural areas. Where specific areas such as food-oriented parks, food precincts, or other key food elements have been designed into a community, it is valuable to link them to as many greenways as possible.

- **Tourism opportunities**. Walking and cycling tours are immensely popular in regions where there is interest in local food, such as in California's wine country and Britain, France, and Italy. Planning a food-linked greenway network into a community can be integrated with marketing efforts to promote the community as a tourist destination. Themed tours, such as vineyard tours or urban-farm cycling tours, are a way to connect buyers with sellers (Photo 17.9).

- **Small-scale mobility**. Greenways need to accommodate pedestrians and cyclists where possible, and in areas with heavier food production, they may also need to support small farm machinery. Trails always require resting places, spots to stop and catch your breath for a moment or two. These could be areas that connect people with food. Examples include locating benches adjacent to fruiting shrubs or trees, or near a small kiosk selling fresh produce, to name a few.

- **Picnic spaces**. Greenways can offer many opportunities for urban workers to get away from the workplace to eat their lunch or snacks in a healthy environment. They can also be key places for families to picnic on a weekend during a walking or cycling outing.

- **Community gardens**. Greenways and transit corridors can offer community garden spaces in urban areas. Agreements and liability will need to be addressed with the corridor owners, but linear gardens can offer a great value, keep crime down, reduce unwanted garbage disposal, and make a transit corridor a seam that joins a community rather than a fence that divides it.

- **Productive landscapes**. Even more than streets, greenways and transit corridors offer a significant opportunity for urban orchards, vineyards, and other productive landscape designs. The risk of fruit damaging cars or disrupting heavily used sidewalks is lower and because of this, with the right management teams, significant food production can occur along a greenway network. Corridors of fruit or nut trees planted along the edge of trails not only delineate the path, but also cast shade for those exercising during the day.

- **Habitat network**. Greenways and transit corridors are critical to urban ecological health. Therefore, alongside the food program, habitat corridors, hedgerows, and other linear habitat forms need to be included in the greenway design. In communities where large wildlife such as bears co-exist, the integration of food into the greenway needs to be carefully addressed so as not to cause undue safety problems in certain seasons. In addition, for areas with a significant number of urban deer, the realistic agricultural productivity of a greenway may be diminished and deer fences may be required.

Photo 17.9: A cycling trail adjacent to a cluster of gardens in Holland
Photo: Kelsey Cramer

- **Public art**. Living walls, edible sculptures, farm equipment art can all be part of food and agriculture-inspired art that adds to the interest and liveliness of outdoor open spaces.

- **Interpretive signage**. Interpretive signage can be included along greenways and transit corridors to inform passersby of the agricultural elements of the area.

- **Stormwater management**. Greenways offer a significant opportunity to manage stormwater from streets, parking lots, and roofs in a way that can remove pollutants, provide urban habitat, offer a visual amenity to residents, and maintain the health of the area's groundwater. Using stormwater strategically can assist in offsetting irrigation needs for agricultural uses along a greenway.

Photo 17.10: Syntagmatos Square, Nafplio, Greece : an example of a plaza that serves as the town heart, with cafes and restaurants lining its edges
Photo: Steve Clarke

PLAZAS

Plazas are urban open spaces that were historically at the heart of a village (Photo 17.10). They formed the city square — an open area surrounded on all sides by buildings. Today, plazas can be large and prominent, truly forming a central city square, or they can be small and tucked away, creating pocket parks between buildings or intersections. Plazas are typically paved, may incorporate public art such as sculpture or fountains, and are often planted with trees and shrubs to offer shade and to provide visual interest. They provide venues for gathering, celebrating, and sometimes mourning. As such, plazas are destinations for a wide range of activities and experiences at any given time of day or year. The presence of food and food-related activities can add to the dynamic ambiance of any community's plaza. Here are some examples:

- **Restaurants and food stores**. Plazas throughout the world, particularly those in the old cities of Europe, are animated by both food stores and restaurants or cafés. Such plazas can offer significant benefits to a community, but creating them requires integration between the open space and the planning and design of buildings.

- **Farmers markets and festivals**. Plazas need to be designed to accommodate a wide range of markets and festivals throughout the year, through providing convenient access to electrical power, water, public washroom and waste facilities (Photo 17.11).

- **Temporary storage**. Consistent with the principle of making visible the food production process, stores and restaurants may be able to use small amounts of the plaza space to temporarily store raw foodstuffs or equipment, thereby increasing the authenticity of the plaza experience.

- **Views into food activity in buildings**. Buildings along the edge of a plaza should be designed with a high level of transparency (in the form of windows or balconies) to make internal food activities visible from the public realm.

- **Educational events**. Plazas are excellent places to perform live demonstrations of food-related activities. Food preparation, cooking, preserving, and pruning techniques are all examples of activities passersby can stop for a few moments to watch and learn. Food and wine tastings can also take place in plazas (Photo 17.12).

Photo 17.12: Herbs grown in seed trays set out in a plaza at a market for sale
Photo: Kelsey Cramer

Photo 17.11: Main and Terminal Farmers' Market, Vancouver BC.
Photo: Bob Ransford

PARKS

Parks come in various sizes and offer various amenities to people in the communities they serve. In general, parks are venues for recreation and nature conservation. They are public places that, like plazas, can become points of convergence for communities. Neighbourhood parks, community parks and regional parks are those that are most closely associated with urban centres. Types of parks include:

- **Neighbourhood Parks**. Often the smallest in size, but can be quite heavily frequented by local children and families. These parks usually provide non-programmed open space, playgrounds, picnic areas, and playing courts.

- **Community Parks**. Often offer activities similar to those of neighbourhood parks as well as an opportunity for nature appreciation. Community parks are usually larger than neighbourhood parks and can accommodate nature trails and the protection of natural features such as streams and forested areas. Often, there are some kinds of programmed sports facilities, such as baseball diamonds and tennis courts to name a few.

- **Regional Parks**. Frequently emphasize the protection of unique natural features and tend to offer more rural or rustic recreation opportunities, including waterfront activities. Unique features that often trigger the creation of a regional park can include natural, historic, or cultural elements worth protecting for public appreciation. For example, a local farm that has been given to the community by a pioneer family in the area could be showcased within a regional park. Finally, these parks are often larger and are meant to serve a greater population.

- **Provincial or State Parks**. Typically much larger than the other parks and usually situated outside of highly populated places with a natural conservation-oriented focus. There are examples of farms in these parks, although few are fully operational. Many have become heritage farms or homesteads but do not have functioning agricultural businesses.

- **National Parks**. Increasingly tourism, hospitality, and restaurant services are being offered in national parks, thereby providing an opportunity to showcase local food. One of the more famous in this regard is the Wickaninnish Inn on Vancouver Island, in Canada's Pacific Rim National Park, which is repeatedly voted one of the top boutique hotel experiences in North America. The inn's focus is on local farm and seafood.

Opportunities to incorporate a wide range of food and agriculture system elements into parks include:

- **Community gardens** (Photo 17.13). Community gardens are an important use for parks in many areas where higher-density residential brings many people to a neighbourhood, but also results in little land with sufficient access to sun for gardens. Typically a significant majority of people say they want to garden but, in reality, a much smaller percentage do. While the number of plots vary, a rule of thumb is garden plots should be provided for 30-50 percent of the population in a high density residential area.[57] Some cities have noted conflict between those who feel community gardens in parks are a

private use of public land and those who support community gardens. However, community gardens do not need to take up a lot of space in a conventional park and they offer a deep social connection to the park and ways to reduce crime and garbage. A good local community garden management association is needed. Community gardens become social assets that foster networks and build relationships. Gardeners usually share the food produced with each other and may donate excess to local food banks.

- **Demonstration gardens and education**. Parks offer significant opportunities for interpretive signage and demonstration gardens to provide educational opportunities to park users or schoolchildren. Composting facilities can be included in these gardens to provide not only places to manage the organic waste stream of a park and community garden, but also to provide education on composting to urban residents (Photo 17.14).

Photo 17.13: Community Garden
Photo: HB Lanarc

- **Farmers' markets and festivals.**
Parks are often the site of farmers'
markets or food festivals and
therefore need to provide space, water,
electricity, and public washrooms to
support these uses.

- **Areas for eating** (Photo 17.15). Parks
can provide small, private areas to
eat your weekday lunch or large, open
spaces to host a family reunion. In
more adventuresome directions,
Munich's Englisher Gardens offers a
summer long beer garden in its midst,

Photo 17.14: An interpretive element at an artisan cheese farm
Photo: Mark Holland

Photo 17.15: Picnic in a park
Photo: Mark Holland

completed by Oktoberfest celebrations
in the fall. These Gardens are a
significant economic success and offer a
memorable experience rarely accessible
in urban parks.

- **Restaurants and concessions.** Many
parks need an area for a seasonal or
temporary concession stand. In some
parks, a full restaurant can be included
to draw people into the park and to
assist in bringing in revenue to support
the maintenance of the park.

- **The edible landscape.** Parks offer
significant opportunity for orchards or
other productive landscapes, as well as
for more operative or educational farms.
Volunteer groups can manage gardens
in some cases and city staff can run a
small farm in others. Fruit or produce can
be given to local food banks. A majority
of the fruits and vegetables we enjoy
result from the relationship between
plants and animals. Animal pollinators
such as honey bees, ants, birds, and
butterflies are key in the process of
our enjoyment of food. Parks designed
with the intent to produce food should
most definitely include habitat for these
animals. Using edible planting, such as
fruit trees, creates important transition
zones where the park meets another
use, such as a residential edge. Working
or demonstration farms in urban parks
are emerging and include London's
Mudchute, Hackney City, and Deen City
Farms, Garden State Urban Farms in
New Jersey, and the widespread farming
program associated with Havana, Cuba.

- **Small scale local food processing.** If the
park has a farm-like setting or is in fact
an old farm, it may have on outbuilding
or two in which to process larger
quantities of food. Cheese, bread,
pies, jams, soups, and more could be
processed on site.

- **Habitat**. Like greenways, parks are part of the backbone of the urban habitat network and as such, need to have appropriate habitat areas integrated with other recreational and food uses.

- **Stormwater management**. In an urban environment, parks can offer stormwater overflow management areas for larger storms. Like greenways, parks offer an opportunity to use stormwater for agricultural and irrigation uses.

WATERFRONTS

Urban waterfronts are busy places (Photo 17.16). They serve as points of connection between the city and the rest of the world. Ports and piers see millions of people and products every year. Some waterfronts are developed with residential homes, while others are sited with industrial buildings. Many urban waterfronts are now being returned or developed for public park use with great success. Integrating the food agenda into an urban waterfront park can include:

- **Fishing piers**. Parks that have significant waterfront space can offer piers for fishing and crabbing (at ocean parks). These are places where people of all ages gather to fish, repeatedly casting and reeling in and engaging in a combination of the solo meditation of fishing and a fierce silent competition with their pier-mates.

- **Fisherman's wharfs and wet markets**. Public waterfront on rivers and oceans often includes areas that have been or continue to be commercial wharfs where fishing boats tie up and sell their catch straight off the boat (Photo 17.17). These wharfs offer something unique and rustic to the urbanite — a wharf promenade alongside boats of all types and ages with views into the eccentric living conditions of the families who own the boats.

Photo 17.16: The Granville Island Market is located along the Vancouver waterfront where it serves as a major hub for the city
Photo: Steve Clarke

Photo 17.17: Fisherman's wharfs are places where one can purchase fresh seafood from its source
Photo: Steve Clarke

Visitors experience a range of sales techniques from silent signs and bored children staffing the family stand to aggressive hucksters joking and chatting up large groups of tourists. The range of fish, prawns, squid, shellfish, and many other types of seafood piled in bins on a boat offers an unparalleled education on marine food.

Photo 17.18: Floating café in the heart of the city's harbor, Nanaimo BC
Photo: HB Lanarc

away. When the processing facility is visible, people can make the important connection between the company's sign and the label on a tin of fish in the local grocery store. There are many examples of how waterfront canneries or other food processing industries can be integrated into public parks and walkways. The Gulf of Georgia Cannery in Steveston, BC, a fully functioning cannery for nearly a century, was recently turned over to the municipality and redeveloped as an educational tourist destination full of equipment and stories of the region's historical economy.

- **Fishing charters and marine retail**. Marinas along public waterfront can offer fishing charters and other marine and food-related trips offering a bridge from a public area directly to the experience of fishing. Having a range of marine retail is also important to the viability of the waterfront industry and encourages people to consider the wide range of objects and activities that comprise the real waterfront economy.

- **Waterfront restaurants**. Waterfront parks and fisherman's wharfs offer a great opportunity to incorporate restaurants, from high-end seafood restaurants to small diners that cater to those who work on the waterfront (Photo 17.18). Small fresh fish-and-chip or seafood take-out restaurants that are floating or located next to a waterfront walkway are some of the most popular, and the restaurant-in-an-old-classic-boat is a common sight in many waterfront cities.

- **Art and signage**. A rich array of history, personalities, and activities form a part of any urban waterfront. Stories about these elements can be conveyed through art, heritage elements, and educational signage.

PRIVATE AND TRANSITIONAL SPACES

This section describes private spaces such as yards, gardens, patios, and balconies. The word transitional reflects the fact that while these spaces may be private, they are often viewed and appreciated by the public as they pass by. Residential properties are likely the most common place we think of, but private patios, balconies, and yards can also be found on properties in commercial, institutional, or industrial zones. These *transitional spaces* sometimes reflect the

- **Food processing industry**. Many public waterfront areas are also home to fish-processing and canning warehouses, which are either owned by the local government as park or heritage sites, or are privately owned, fully functioning industries. These areas need protection, as they are often a key part of history and the local economy. They offer great views into the processing activities as boats unload, crates are piled high everywhere, and trucks come in and out regularly hauling the products

personality of the site's caretaker and offer some unique and interesting ways to introduce food into the urban fabric (Photo 17.19). Transitional spaces can teach by example. Opportunities for promoting food visibly in the urban experience associated with private land include:

Photo 17.19: Garden
Photo: Mark Holland

- **Front-yard gardens**. North American front yards are typically highly manicured lawns and shrubs. A front yard devoted to growing food is rare and is often associated with families from other parts of the world. These front-yard gardens are rarely as "beautiful" as manicured ones, but they are far more interesting (Photo 17.20). They display a wide range of crops as they go through their stages, multiple ways of staking various plants, and vitality. In addition, they connect the usually mundane private landscape aesthetic with the promise of good food. A movement that allows urban farmers to garden in an underused part of your garden to grow food for charitable organizations is growing.

- **Boulevard gardens**. In neighbourhoods with space for only very small private gardens or where there is strong support from local government, boulevards along a sidewalk or in a traffic circle can become gardens. These are some of the most interesting and eccentric gardens in a city. In such gardens, it's not uncommon to see toddlers run from shrub to shrub, pointing at the bees and crouching down and playing with the dirt and mulch during midday walks with their parents. Vancouver has the Blooming Boulevards program that encourages people to garden in public boulevards. This program also holds lotteries for those who want to manage gardens inside neighbourhood traffic circles and holds an annual contest for the best one.

- **Balcony and patio gardens**. For higher density areas and multi-storey buildings, front yards may not often exist, and private open space is limited to small patios and balconies. These often can hold a rich array of food gardens in pots as well as outdoor BBQs and eating areas. Summer evenings in a city can become quite the soundscape of multiple BBQ parties on balconies and patios. Likewise, small sidewalk-edge seating areas associated with a townhouse can become a place where the owners, enjoying an evening glass of wine, will have more interaction with their neighbours than anywhere else.

- **Private garden stand**. Roadside stands selling produce in rural areas are relatively commonplace, offering a small stream of revenue for the gardener and a better form of engagement between farmers and travelling customers. One of the nice surprises of urban food is to come across a small garden stand at the sidewalk's edge selling a range of fresh produce from someone's urban or suburban garden. These garden stands often have a cooler full of fresh produce or vases of flowers, with a price list and a place to pay — on the honour system, of course. They can become a key destination in a community for people taking a walk to check on what is fresh every day. Although they are typically illegal and therefore temporary, few cities require them to be dismantled unless neighbours complain.

- **The BBQ**. Outdoor celebrations of food centered around BBQs are a staple of North American culture (Photo 17.21). In suburban areas, these occur in our backyards, typically away from street view. In a multifamily setting, however, they may occur in a courtyard in the centre of the building or even on the roof. These become an important annual ritual and maintain or build relationships in a city. On occasion, several neighbours may join together to hold a big summer feast with music and activities for children, creating a celebration on an otherwise quiet street. It is not unheard of for groups to get permission from city hall to close a street for such an event.

- **The Block Party**. Closing down streets in a residential, mixed use area and allowing eating, drinking and games to spill-out from private areas into public areas such as streets and parks, provides an important link between private and public spaces.

Photo 17.20: The front-yard garden
Photo: Keltie Craig

Sketching the Opportunities for Food

An opportunity exists for the designing of our cities to strengthen the relationship between people and food. This will be achieved by designing physical access to food through the context of the seven food system elements:

- Production

- Processing

- Distribution

- Retail

- Consumption + Celebration

- Waste Recovery

- Education

Photo 17.21: The Backyard BBQ
Photo: Janine de la Salle

It is important to design using all seven of these elements for a project. This integrated approach to design will make food the driving concept of the plan and eliminate the tack-on approach that typically happens. The following sketches illustrate the layered approach to designing a range of neighbourhood types using the concepts, strategies and opportunities presented earlier in this chapter.

HB Lanarc Design for Food Studio.
Photo: Janine de la Salle

Rural Areas

An example of a large rural property whose use is focused on food production, precessing and some marketing.

1. **Production:** Includes contiguous farmland for crops and other opportunities such as poultry and livestock.

2. **Processing:** Includes handling facilities include vegetable factories, slaughter houses, packaging factories and other farm facilities.

3. **Distribution:** Roads that accommodate equipment, such as tractor trailers and farm trucks to name a few. Food storage facilities include grain elevators and industrial refrigerators and freezers.

4. **Retail:** Farm market

5. **Consumption + Celebration:** Picnic area

6. **Waste Recovery:** Composting and specialized waste recovery facilities such as converting waste to livestock feed.

7. **Education:** Demonstration crops that includes interpretive elements related to production, processing and distribution of food. Other opportunities includes designing processing facilities with a "transparent view" for visitors to see how food is processed and packaged.

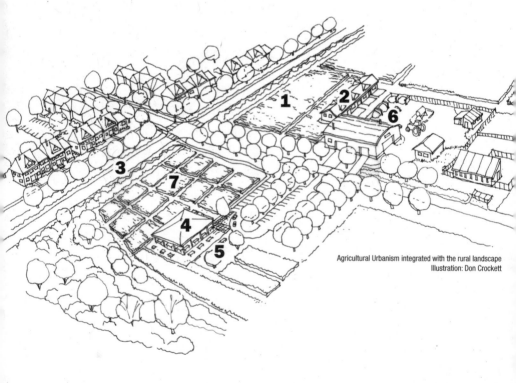

Agricultural Urbanism integrated with the rural landscape
Illustration: Don Crockett

Suburban Neighbourhood

This is an illustration showing a typical low-density residential street lined with single family homes with front and back yards in the early stages of being integrated with food systems. A large park is a community amenity space for residents (whose backyards are consumed by food production).

1. **Production:** A backyard vegetable garden allows for the personal production of food. Other design opportunities include:
   - Front, side and shared yard gardens
   - Planting along street medians and along boulevards
   - Retain and protect adjacent agricultural land.

2. **Processing:** The outdoor patio/summer kitchen provides a place to process food. This will supplement the typical indoor kitchen that every home has.

3. **Distribution:** Will typically be with the automobile. Providing a network of lanes, trails and sidewalks will also encourage walking or cycling to the corner store.

4. **Retail (not shown):** Neighbourhood grocery and corner store.

5. **Consumption + Celebration:** an outdoor patio/deck will serve as a place for gathering to eat and drink. Other options include:
   - Neighbourhood picnic areas located in the park
   - Open spaces where one can layout a blanket and eat and drink

6. **Waste Recovery:** Rainwater collection and composting is integrated with each household. A municipal collection and composting program will also play a role.

7. **Education:** It is surprising what you can learn from your neighbour – especially the avid gardener! Other neighbourhood sources for education include:
   - Schools
   - Grocery stores
   - Community kitchens

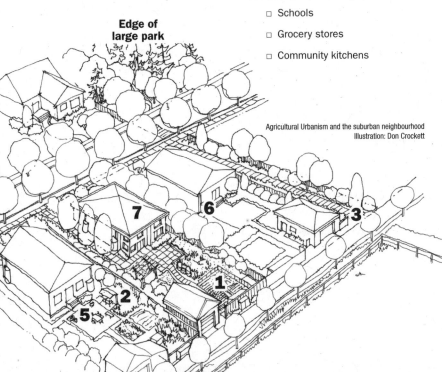

Edge of large park

Agricultural Urbanism and the suburban neighbourhood
Illustration: Don Crockett

Urban Village

A compact, mixed-use, urban node focused on a waterfront, commercial street and plazas, which is surrounded by multi-family residential buildings.

1. **Production:** Roof top gardens provide the opportunities for shared food production by residents. Other areas include:

   □ Window box gardens and balconies allow areas to grow food;

   □ Community gardens

   □ Locations for fruit bearing trees

   □ Parks and plazas

   □ Street medians and boulevards

   □ Allies

   □ Vacant lots

2. **Processing:** Takes place throughout the urban village:

   □ Restaurants and cafes

   □ Home kitchens

   □ Community kitchens

   □ Bakeries and deli's

   □ Small operator processing facilities and storage

3. **Distribution:** Local farm trucks visually connect the urban village to food harvesting and retailing activity. Other forms of moving food within the village include:

   □ Automobiles, bicycles and walking

   □ Storage facilities will include pantries and refrigerators

   □ Wholesale distribution and direct marketing

4. **Retail:** A fisherman's wharf offers a place to buy local seafood. Other retail opportunities include:

   □ Seasonal farmers market

   □ Street vendors

   □ Restaurants and cafes

   □ Neighbourhood grocer and corner store

5. **Consumption + Celebration:** Sidewalk cafes and restaurants have patios that line the waterfront, providing a hub of activity. Other places to celebrate food include:

   □ Street vendors near places to sit and eat comfortably

   □ Closing a street for a food festival

6. **Waste Recovery (not shown):**

   □ Municipal collection and composting program

   □ Rainwater collection

7. **Education:** A weekend farmer's market is a place where one can meet local growers and learn about food. Further examples are:

   □ Schools

   □ Community gardens

   □ Grocers, chefs and restaurants

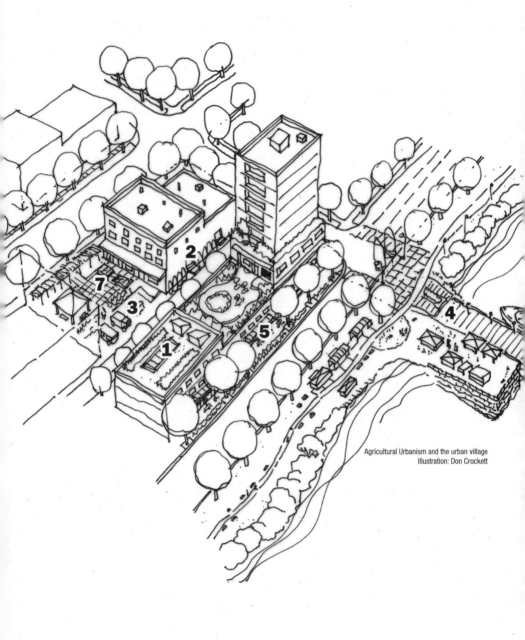

Agricultural Urbanism and the urban village
Illustration: Don Crockett

Inner-city Residential Neighbourhood

The drawing to the left depicts an example of a neighbourhood with mixed-use buildings, residential apartments, and towers with commercial uses at street level. Neighbourhood parks, pocket parks and plazas contribute to the open space.

1. **Production:** Window box gardens and balconies allow food production opportunities for individual units, while rooftops allow spaces for production opportunities such as greenhouses, chicken coups and apiaries.
   Other areas include:

   □ Community gardens

   □ Locations for fruit bearing trees

   □ Parks and plazas

   □ Street medians and boulevards

   □ Allies

   □ Vacant lots

2. **Processing:** Will take place in a variety of locations throughout this neighbourhood:

   □ Home kitchens

   □ Community kitchens

   □ Restaurants

   □ Coffee shops

   □ Bakeries

   □ Packaging facilities

3. **Distribution:** Food will be distributed through the network of streets and lanes. Storage facilities will include pantries and refrigerators

4. **Retail:** opportunities are at street level with restaurants and cafes. Other layers of retail include:

   □ Seasonal farmers market

   □ Street vendors

   □ Supermarket and grocery store

   □ Corner store

5. **Consumption + Celebration:** a vacant space over the weekend, such as a parking lot, is transformed into a special event such as a seasonal farmers market. Other areas include:

   □ Restaurants

   □ Sidewalk cafes

6. **Waste Recovery (not shown):**

   □ Municipal collection and composting program

   □ Rainwater collection

7. **Education:** a community garden presents a place to grow, share and learn about food. Other opportunities are:

   □ Schools

   □ Grocers, chefs and restaurants

   □ Farmer's market

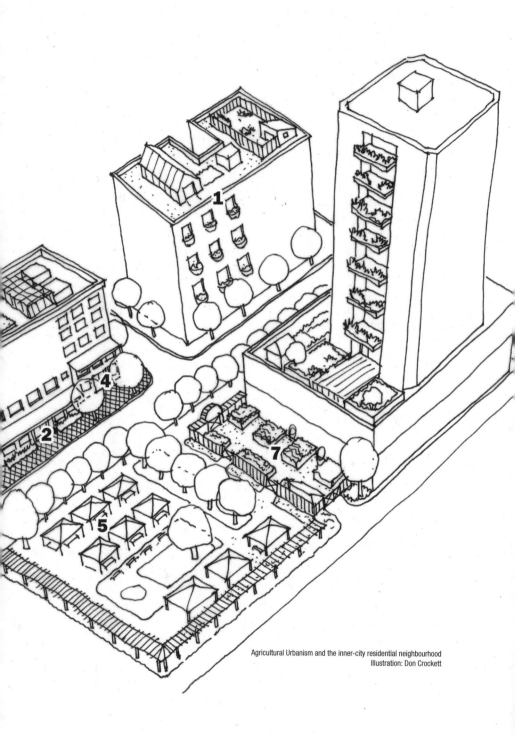

Agricultural Urbanism and the inner-city residential neighbourhood
Illustration: Don Crockett

Food and Agriculture Precinct

A food and agriculture precinct is a distinct area where the predominant activities are focused on food and agriculture. This precinct will include a permanent farmer's market building and plaza with the necessary space and infrastructure.

1. **Production:** A community garden provides an amenity for the precinct. The garden also provides locations for fruit bearing trees where maintenance issues are different from the urban plaza. Other areas for production include:

   □ Roof top gardens

   □ Plazas

   □ Street medians and boulevards

2. **Processing:** Will take place at many areas in the precinct:

   □ Market building

   □ Community kitchen

   □ Restaurants

   □ Coffee shops

   □ Bakeries

   □ Packaging facilities

   □ Small operator processing facilities and storage

3. **Distribution:** Although the precinct will be fed by the infrastructure of streets, a restaurant rooftop garden will provide fresh herbs for the chef at his doorstep.

4. **Retail:** There are areas for variety of both indoor and outdoor markets, along with restaurants, cafes and street vendors.

5. **Consumption + Celebration:** The market building, based on architectural precedent, is the focal point of the precinct – a hub of activity. From this, other opportunities radiate:

   □ Restaurants, cafes, street vendors and places to sit and eat

   □ Spaces for special events such as a seasonal outdoor farmer's market

6. **Waste Recovery:** This precinct will coordinate its own program of collection of rainwater, waste and composting with built-in facilities.

7. **Education:** A culinary school with formal programs and informal community programs will introduce and help people expand their knowledge on food. Other examples include:

   □ Community gardens

   □ Chefs and restaurants

   □ Market

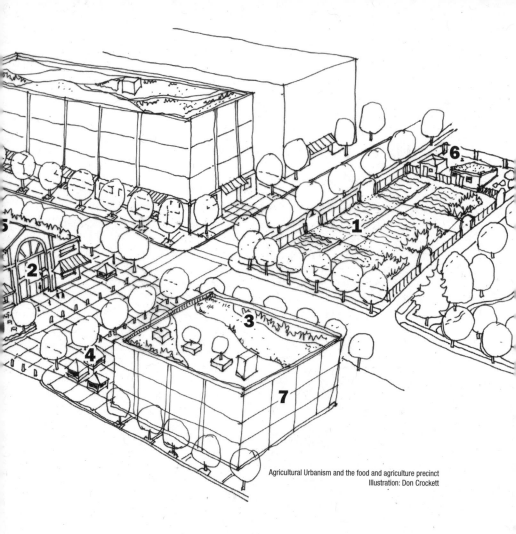

Agricultural Urbanism and the food and agriculture precinct
Illustration: Don Crockett

Summary

The design of our communities provides a range of food culture and industry-supporting systems and is therefore central to any AU neighbourhood. The ideas and policies that are created around food systems need to be included both in the urban design process and ultimately in its physical outcomes. There are many opportunities in any public space or building to promote food, and by doing so, we not only increase the viability and sustainability of local food systems, but also create special places that celebrate and support all aspects of food in a community, thereby increasing our quality of life.

18. Food Hubs and Precincts MARK HOLLAND & JANINE DE LA SALLE

Contemporary city planning focuses on creating an appropriate land-use structure for a city in order to provide the free market with enough flexibility to develop as it sees fit. Each individual business in the economy can operate anywhere in a city that it can find appropriate and affordable space — provided zoning permits its desired uses. At the same time as this high degree of flexibility is being preserved, the power of nodes or areas with a critical mass of a certain type of business or product is likewise being pursued. In

The Stop, Toronto ON
Photo: Janine de la Salle

many cases, a large company will serve as an anchor and attraction for customers, resulting in many smaller companies who sell similar products locating nearby. The results of this natural process can be seen in cities around the world. Many large cities have areas known for the best selection of fashion stores, automobile dealers, furniture stores, or others.

Interestingly, this nodal characteristic is not seen as often around food in our cities. This is partly because of the significant dominance of supermarket chains and their focus on capturing a very high percentage of a market for any given catchment area. The concept of food hubs or precincts is now emerging, however, as a way to create vital and animated nodes or destinations for food in a city. Food hubs or precincts are becoming a new movement toward sustainability in food and agriculture. Even though the idea of food hubs is far from novel, their resurgence in North American cities reflects the growing desire and need for increased public and business access to local food and agriculture.

Characteristics of Food Hubs or Precincts

A food hub or precinct is a place that brings together a wide spectrum of land uses, design strategies, and programs focused on food to increase access, visibility, and the experience of sustainable urban and regional food systems within a city. Each city's food hub would be unique, but the following are key aspects of a successful food hub or food precinct.

A diversity of food and beverage retail and wholesale. The presence of a diversity of retail outlets selling a wide variety of food and beverages as well as many other food-related goods, allows members of the community to meet their food needs and integrate a wide range of food experiences into their daily lives and ultimately into the fabric of the larger community. For a food precinct, this entails the presence of food stores, cafés, restaurants, and markets. These retail and food-service outlets can be of nearly any type, but they become most beneficial and exciting when they are owned by the producers of the food, including farmers, bakers, butchers, brewers, and others.

The processing and storage of food and beverages. The visible presence of processing or creation of food and drink is the foundation of an authentic food hub or precinct. Production can include many different things, including the visible growing, processing, creating, or packaging of food and drink. The presence of real production differentiates a true precinct from a shopping district, where production or manufacturing is visibly absent. Seeing a baker at work changes the relationship we have with the bread we buy. Seeing a butcher in his whites at work as we buy meat at the counter makes our purchase more valuable and important than if it were merely shrink-wrapped in a supermarket. Another aspect of this key element is our ability to interact informally with those involved in the production of our food. Sharing public space with food industry workers in their aprons and boots adds energy and authenticity to the food experience not found in a conventional food retail environment. In addition, the direct link between food processing and preparation and a restaurant generally means that the food will be fresher, taste better, and have a more interesting story. All food preparation and processing requires significant cold, dry, and frozen storage facilities.

Institutions and educational opportunities around food and beverages. The presence of key institutional or educational organizations and their facilities lends an important stabilizing quality to a food precinct. These institutions create an atmosphere of reflection, learning, research, teaching, and most importantly, the authentic energy and expression of students. The presence of institutions related to food and agriculture also provide an important employment node in the precinct, including white-collar professionals who can help support retail in the area during the workweek. Institutions and schools add a general intellectual dimension to a precinct, giving it a greater sense of itself than if it were merely food processing or retail. For a food hub or precinct, these uses might include chef schools, agricultural institutions, government departments, food companies, or others.

Architectural and landscape design that celebrates food. One of the most important aspects of a food hub or precinct is that it is visibly and physically designed and built around food. The buildings and landscapes in a food hub or precinct visibly express the activities and forms associated with food and drink and draw on the rich legacy of agricultural architecture — both rural and urban. It is important not to pursue this in a simplistic theme park manner or it will be experienced as shallow. However, the authentic activities and the local/historical architecture can be reflected in the buildings, street design, sidewalks, plazas, parks, and more. The reason character is important is that the precinct needs to distinguish itself from the rest of the community and deepen the experience of food. Each food hub or precinct needs to find its own appropriate expression of this character. One can imagine that a food precinct associated with a waterfront or fisherman's wharf could have sense of character quite different from a precinct located next to heritage granaries in a prairie city. Likewise, a precinct located in an area known for ranching might differ from one in the middle of fruit country. The landscape needs to be programmed and designed to support the widest range of food-related activities possible, including food production, retail activities, the storage of equipment, and support for food-related events.

Agriculturally influenced architecture, live-work
Source: Courtesy of DPZ, Designed by Lew Oliver

A diversity of programming around food. The final key element of a successful food precinct is that of programming community events throughout the year into the precinct. These events will regularly draw community members into the precinct and connect them to the activities and people involved in the food industry. This may include seasonal food festivals, farmers' markets, harvest events, and more. A wide range of stakeholders can be integrated into this programming. This dimension also suggests including facilities to support conferences or other learning experiences as well as plazas to support farmers markets' and other events.

Elements to Consider

The following paragraphs inventory the planning and design elements to consider in the development of a food hub or precinct, either as a new development or as the redevelopment/enhancement of an existing area:

Agriculturally influenced architecture, duplex with farm store
Source: Courtesy of DPZ, Designed by Lew Oliver

Retail stores of various sizes. Retail space needs to be provided for a range of businesses from larger markets (as in Vancouver's Granville Island) to permanent farmers' markets (indoor or outdoor), to supermarkets, to small boutique stores, to sidewalk food kiosks, and to portable vendor trailers. The widest range of retail options possible is desirable for a food precinct to support a diversity of food entrepreneurs. Non-food related retail will want to locate in the precinct as it becomes successful, and as long as long as food retail remains the dominant type of retail, this will not be a problem. Retail rents may need to be managed carefully to ensure that a successful precinct doesn't force out the small businesses that made it successful in the first place.

Restaurants. A range of spaces for cafés, restaurants, and pubs needs to be provided to create a social environment for people to gather and enjoy delicious foods. Encouraging these establishments to source as much food as they can from the producers and suppliers within the precinct will assist in deepening both the experience of the precinct as well as the commercial success of its tenants.

Storage and processing warehouses. Commercial storage and processing facilities of various sizes are needed to support the production businesses or for the storage of local farm products before they are sold. These spaces tend to be large and can create long blank walls to a street, which undermines urban vitality. Because of this, these warehouses or manufacturing spaces need to be located away from the street and integrate retail outlets along street edges, where possible. Alternatively, the buildings can be designed to be highly transparent, with windows allowing passersby to see into the workings of the food industry.

Commercial kitchens. Community kitchens and education facilities are excellent for supporting small-scale or new food entrepreneurs as well as providing opportunities for educational seminars on how to grow, process, prepare, and maximize fresh, healthy local food.

Cold storage at the Vancouver Food Bank
Photo: Janine de la Salle

Office and educational space. A diversity of office space needs to be available to support institutions, a variety of food-related organizations, and businesses associated with the local food and agriculture tenants and program of the precinct. In some cases, where promotion of sustainable food systems is a key agenda, space for a publicly accessible resource center may be included.

Outdoor market areas. Plazas and open space areas that can support farmers' markets and other events need to be centrally located in the food precinct, since they are the heart of the food experience.

Event facilities. Community event areas that can support a diversity of events and celebrations are needed.

Infrastructure. Space for management of organic waste is critical, as significant amounts will be created from the range and intensity of food activity in the precinct. In addition, innovative systems will be needed to reduce cost and emissions associated with the significant amounts of heat and water required for cooking. Significant amounts of wastewater will also be produced and can be treated and re-used in some cases.

Parking and logistics. A food precinct entails large numbers of people coming to work, learn, and shop, and appropriate parking will be required. In addition, the shipping in and out of goods will be significant and will require appropriate logistics facilities.

An additional consideration for the food precinct is the inclusion of residential areas within and immediately around the precinct. Living in a place with this much activity at different times of the day or night is not for everyone but, as an urban neighbourhood, a food precinct can offer a very high quality of life due to the significant presence of food and drink. The Fairview neighbourhood around Vancouver's Granville Island (with its food precinct) was recently voted as one of the best neighbourhoods in the world in which to live.

Perspectives and Considerations

Food hubs, in many different ways, broker rural food supply sources with urban demand through filling gaps in local food infrastructure. Based on North American trends such as the hollowing-out and centralization of the food processing infrastructure, focus on export marketing, and extinction of the small family farm, stakeholders in the local food sector are encouraging change.

What many local food hubs have in common is that they offer the necessary infrastructure to bring about market transformation and long-term regional food system resilience for producers, processors, buyers, and consumers, and combine it with a deep experience of food. For example, local food storage, processing, and direct sales facilities enable important economic opportunities that are not currently available to medium to small farm operations. Additionally, local food hubs can play a vital, leading role in local food system research and development, community education around food, supporting neighborhood food precincts, and reconnecting city-dwellers to agriculture.

Food Hubs and Precincts in Practice

The concept of a food hub is deeply rooted in the history of human settlements in which activities were focused in certain locations of the settlement and the architecture, organizations, and activities in these areas reflected these uses. The commonly referenced examples include small farming villages and the Greek Agora. Today in North America, there are a number of examples of food hubs and precincts operating as valued community places and local food-sector resource centres. Successful food hubs can have a wide or narrow range of functions that are designed to address sector needs within their specific contexts.

Granville Island in Vancouver BC is one of the more successful examples of a food precinct. Granville Island offers:

- An enormous food market selling every imaginable food, from fresh produce and meat, to refined and exotic foods.

- Many small restaurant outlets.

- Several breweries.

- Visible storage of food on the sidewalk and at street edges everywhere.

- Windows in buildings to allow customers to see into the workings of the Island's bakeries.

- The Pacific Culinary Institute located at the Island's entrance.

- Food events throughout the year.

Detroit's Eastern Market is an older example that started in the 1920s by providing an outlet for Michigan farmers to sell their products to retail, restaurant, and institutional buyers. More recently, Detroit's Eastern Market has transformed into a district encompassing warehouses and permanent stores that are open to buyers in the early morning and to the public later in the day.

The Stop in Toronto (www.thestop.org) is a community-operated repurposed facility (with LEED silver green building certification) that has urban agriculture, education, social services, waste recovery, and farmer-direct marketing functions. Specific program areas include:

- Community gardens.

- Permanent indoor farmers' market.

- High-quality teaching facilities including a community kitchen and outdoor wood-fired oven.

- Education programs for learners of all ages.

- Food bank and drop-in centre.

- Community advocacy and civic engagement resources.

- Artists' live work studios.

The Halifax Seaport Farmers' Market, a 3900 square-metre, 42,000-square-foot, facility scheduled to open the summer of 2010, focuses on increasing direct marketing opportunities for farmers and producers through a three-day-per week market and permanent retail shops owned and operated by market vendors. Other program and facility characteristics include:

- Education and extension services designed to help farmers scale up their operations and access available government resources.

- Permanent retail for vendors.

- Covered exterior for summer markets and community events.

- Community box office to support the arts and culture community in Halifax.

- Future plans to integrate a wholesale element, which will enable institutional and restaurant direct purchasing.

Preserves at the Duncan Farmer's Market.
Photo: Mark Holland

The Local FoodHub, in Ivy, Virginia, (www.localfoodhub.org) is a food wholesale distribution hub in a repurposed warehouse that moves local products to grocery stores, schools, senior facilities, and restaurants.

As a non-profit service organization, the Local FoodHub acts as a broker between producers and purchasers. Other functions include:

- Virtual and physical learning and education resources such as an off-site educational farm.

- Rentable refrigeration and freezer storage space.

- Liability and traceability coverage.

- Delivery and consolidation services.

- Processing facilities (still to be built).

- Coordination of donations to the charitable food sector.

- Planning support for growers.

An alternative version of a food hub is the Food Hub website in Portland Oregon (http://food-hub.org). The Food Hub is a resource for food buyers to purchase directly from producers or from mainstream wholesalers. The operation is owned and operated by EcoTrust, a non-profit organization (www.ecotrust.org). Revenue is generated through membership fees.

Food hubs and precincts are a key opportunity to advance the sustainable food system agenda in cities by concentrating a piece of the local food economy in one place to achieve a critical mass of vitality, experience, learning, and business activity. They can be created as new places, or retrofitted into existing areas, possibly with the intent of expanding and enhancing existing food areas that may have one or more elements of a food hub or precinct. These hubs or precincts can become some of the most valued places in a city because of the rich diversity of experience they offer everyone.

19. Thoughtful Transitions: Integrating Food & Agriculture in Cities JANINE DE LA SALLE

Planning and design for integrating food and agriculture in and around cities calls for new approaches to how transition zones are planned. Every bit of area in a town or city is contested space with multiple needs. In thinking through design-based strategies for how different uses may fit together, ideas and requirements for integrated planning and design emerge. This section provides a high-level analysis of treatments for different transition areas.

Transition areas are identified as points of integration between different land uses and programs such as: Agriculture, recreation, wildlife and habitat, residential, commercial, industrial, and institutional uses. Integrating these uses is an essential element of complete communities. Design elements such as landscape features, buildings and structures, required facilities (parking, etc.), signage, as well as dedicated spaces, edge

spaces, buffers, and circulation systems, are important opportunities for integration of these uses.

Integration Guidelines

The guiding principles listed below provide the general parameters for integration of food and agriculture with other uses in a town or city:

- Areas of intense integration should be treated appropriately. Where multiple uses or programs are overlapped such as agriculture, recreation, and wildlife, integration must be carefully designed as to ensure no one program is marginalized. For example, wildlife integration into a farming area consists of land stewardship, planting of hedgerows and riparian buffers that provide habitat for agriculture-friendly/

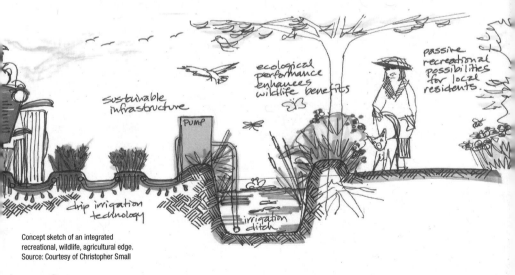

Concept sketch of an integrated recreational, wildlife, agricultural edge.
Source: Courtesy of Christopher Small

beneficial creatures...etc. Design elements should reflect a hierarchy of components ranging from those inviting interaction and full integration of uses to those areas that need more controlled use or priority of use to be successfully integrated.

- All design features should maximize the interaction of multiple uses and activities.

- Design elements should be flexible and cost-effective in order to adapt to evolving programs.

- All design elements should reflect and augment the aesthetic values of the town or city's history and vision.

Integration Techniques

Practitioners can take on several strategies for integrating food and agriculture in and around towns and cities. Applying these techniques requires collaboration between planners, landscape architects, architects, business owners, the community, and others.

- **Co-location**. Where possible, combine food and agriculture uses with other complimentary uses. For example, locate community gardens near children's play areas or food processing within retail areas.

- **Building form and function**. Use the form and character of buildings to not only support food and agriculture uses but also to create places that have a food and agriculture experience. Examples of this range from architecture that is agriculturally influenced to functional elements of the building.

- **Recreation**. More specific to urban and peri-urban farms, including passive recreation opportunities in agricultural

areas is a great way to increase the experience of agriculture for neighbours. The integration of recreation on farmland needs to respect farm operations. Through proper signage and landscape cues, people can experience the beauty of a farm without interrupting its operations. Also bringing people into a farm area through recreation opportunities also offers synergies with other uses such as having farm stands selling products as well as education and training opportunities.

- **Circulation and connectivity**. No farm is an island. By thoughtfully connecting trail systems across farming areas and to food retail areas, community gardens, culinary schools, and other amenities, we can make farms active places that are linked to other land uses in the community. Similarly, every part of the food and agriculture system should be connected to several other facilities and functions in a community.

- **Views**. People like to see fields and observe their food being made. Increasing views of agriculture and food system activities enhances the genuine experience of a place. Applications of this include vistas over farmland from homes, restaurants, or offices as well as the "back of house is front of house" principle, by which passersby can observe the cheese-making process or a canning class through a glass window.

- **Ecosystem planning**: In addition to agriculture, recreation, and food-system activities, the role of ecology in urban environments is a paramount consideration in planning and designing for the integration of food and agriculture. Examples of ecosystem planning include:

- Planting hedgerows to support species diversity and protect riparian areas.

- Grassland set-asides (areas set aside for habitat).

- Ley crops (crops planted on purpose for wildlife).

- Preserving and creating riparian areas to support wildlife as well as manage stormwater.

Interpretation and Signage

Interpretation and signage provide direction and inform visitors about the environment and its historical, cultural, or natural significance. Signage can be integrative, that is, not conventional signs but markers, working models, colours, physical barriers, or landscape features incorporated into the surrounding environment.

Signage from the University of British Columbia Farm
Photo: Janine de la Salle

An integrative approach to a park signage system incorporates signs or elements that perform multiple functions. The signage may provide effective information and direction for people, encourage learning experiences, help maintain an image of the area, and communicate area rules. Signage should:

- Meet specific needs and target certain areas, yet be kept to a minimum within the park.

- Be collaborative and coordinated across the study area.

- Demonstrate a sense of place and pride, and incorporate the history of a specific site.

- Be clear and accessible to all park users and be a recognizable element within the surrounding landscape or facilities.

- Where appropriate, incorporate a "sense of play."

TYPES OF SIGNAGE REQUIRED IN AGRICULTURAL AREAS IN OR NEAR CITIES:

- Informative and interpretive signs or elements.
- Regulatory signs.
- Warning and risk signs or barriers.
- Point-of-interest signs, markers or vantage points.
- Event notification and other temporary signs.
- Directional signs or markers.
- Trail markers.

Turnip greens going to market. Portugal
Photo: Odete Pinho

Part IV: Perspectives

As an emerging field, AU is rapidly evolving and constantly redefining itself. Part IV presents unique perspectives on the economic opportunity for urban agriculture, abating urban encroachment and promoting food and agriculture as key elements of urbanism, the public engagement opportunity around food, agriculture and community building, and personal insight into the meaning and power of food in our lives. The concluding chapter of this section and the book offers a path for foregrounding food and agriculture in our cities.

Context for Chapter 20

The romance of the idea of responding to the challenges of the 20th century food system by turning cities into farms has driven a significant rise in interest in urban agriculture in the past several decades. Many books have been written on how much food can be grown or raised on the smallest possible piece of land in an urban setting. For most all who have pursued serious gardening in urban environments or the designing of urban agriculture space into planned communities, the juxtaposition of the high cost of land and low price that fresh produce typically fetches becomes a juggernaut. Within the constraints of urban development and the cost of land and everything else in a city, how is it possible to make urban agriculture anything other than a personal hobby, especially when farmers in ideal circumstances still barely make ends meet? In this probing chapter, experienced businessman, journalist and food champion Peter Ladner explores a range of strategies and stories around making urban agriculture pay.

Growing money.
Photo: Janine de la Salle

Economic Potential of Urban Agriculture PETER LADNER

Mr. Ward Teulon has to time his compost deliveries carefully. The elevator of the Fresia condominium in the heart of downtown Vancouver can get crowded. "Don't be there at 4:30 or 5 p.m. when everyone's getting off work," he warns. Teulon, the self-dubbed "City Farm Boy" has to use the elevator to haul compost and soil up to one of his less-accessible gardens, sixty-five raised beds on a rooftop terrace, designed for building residents but now part of his urban farm network of gardens. An agrologist who grew up on a farm in Saskatchewan, Teulon is one of a growing number of entrepreneurs across North America ramping up community food production from a backyard hobby to a serious business — except he's building his serious business in backyards and on the Fresia rooftop.

The Next Generation of Urban Agriculture

When Teulon first got the call to come to the Fresia and take over the abandoned beds, they were overgrown with weeds and moss — a litter repository for residents who ventured out on the roof but didn't really have the time or the urge to do their own gardening. It sounded like a good idea when the building went up: add a gardening option to enrich the residents' lives, help build community, let them grow a few veggies. "They got the demographic wrong," says Teulon. "The single people in these 500-square-foot condos — many renters — aren't interested in gardening." So Teulon now uses those beds for growing carrots. "It works out well," he says. "The carrot flies don't get up that high so I get natural pest

control." The building owners appreciate Teulon's help in keeping the rooftop terrace in order. "People don't throw garbage in gardens," they say. And the carrots don't seem to mind the elevator music on the ride down to Teulon's van.

Teulon loves farming, but he wants to make it pay. Decent financial returns on agricultural goods are scarce in the lives of many commercial farmers these days. Farm debt in Canada is soaring, as are operating costs and total farm cash receipts, resulting in net farm incomes declining for decades and now hovering around zero.[58] In a recent survey of 1,303 Western Canadian farmers, 52 percent said they would be out of farming if farm incomes did not improve.[59]

Ward Tulon and the Fresia Rooftop Garden, Vancouver BC
Photo: Peter Ladner

A study of farming in the Kootenay region of British Columbia found that of the 1,394 census farms in the three Kootenay Regional Districts, the average capital value of land, livestock, and equipment was $1.3 million in East Kootenay; $746,000 in Kootenay Boundary; and $683,000 in Central Kootenay. Average farm receipts were $39,420 (East Kootenay); $59,801 (West Kootenay); and $53,388 (Central Kootenay), but (reported) net income was a measly $133; $1,680; and $5,422 respectively.[60]

Can urban and peri-urban farms and food-producers find new economic opportunities not available to their rural counterparts? It looks like they can. The key, ironically, is to keep it small and simple.

Growing food in an economically sustainable way is the first prerequisite for a sustainable economy, yet the business of growing food can be so laced with emotion, tradition, culture, passion, subsidies, and regulations that hard numbers seem to melt into the soil. How do you put a value on the satisfaction of working the farm that was cleared by your grandfather? Or knowing that everyone else in the country depends on you for their most basic need? You can't, but the dollars coming in still have to be greater than the dollars flowing out. Farmers and food producers have to survive economically, and new developments in urban agriculture are showing how that's possible on a scale quite different from the typical industrial farm.

As part of a larger movement to reinvent free-market globalism to deliver more (and more equitable) benefits to consumers and workers, the current local-food-first movement is working hard to prove that diverse, artisan-scale, locally focused urban agriculturalists can survive in today's economic environment — and feel good about what they do. It's not always easy to untangle the emotional high of buying from a needy nearby farmer and the need

for everyone to keep costs down and turn a profit. On the demand side, so-called locavores are also driven by a gnawing need to protect themselves from the risks of food imported from distant industrial farms, with growing numbers of people knowing those farms are highly dependent on fuel supplies threatened by peak oil price spikes, soils beset with salinization and erosion, dwindling water supplies, and the vulnerabilities of monocultures to disease and corporate control.

While national agricultural policy makers struggle with pro-farming legislation, seasonal tariffs, free-trade agreements, supply management, and farm-support subsidies to help struggling industrial farmers, today's urban farmers are discovering they have a lot of advantages over their rural counterparts. Working under the radar of big agriculture, urban farmers are building on the strengths of farming in a city.

ADVANTAGES TO THE URBAN FARMER :

- Access to cheap land.
- A variety of readily-accessible niche markets.
- Friendlier, warmer growing conditions.
- Easy access to water and organic waste.
- Plentiful opportunities for supplementary income.
- No need for hired labour.
- Minimal capital costs.

The Economic Advantages of Urban Agriculture

LAND

Ironically, one of the biggest barriers to rural farm success — the cost of land — is an asset for micro-scale urban farmers like Ward Teulon. His fifteen small plots are all free: "I don't pay cash for plots — my currency is vegetables," he says. Ward's plots pay for themselves through reduced yard-maintenance costs, more stimulating views from the land owner's kitchen windows, and social time when he comes to work in the owner's yard.

Other "free" land in cities is paid for by benefits that are unique to dense living areas and outside the metrics of conventional economics. Food gardens that replace abandoned brownfield sites in industrial cities under transformation make their neighbourhoods safer, cleaner, and more beautiful. Allen Street Community Garden in Somerville, Massachusetts, is a former contaminated residential property that was cleaned up and converted to a community garden by the city in 2007. It is now seen as an oasis for the residents of New England's most densely developed city, with a lineup of gardeners waiting for plots.[61]

Food gardens in place of lawns in public parks save the cost of mowing those areas, with city employees replaced by gardeners who are not usually paid by the city. A study in Philadelphia looked at the costs and benefits of farms within the city and estimated that turning ten 0.20 to 0.4 hectare, half- to one-acre, lawns into farms would save the city treasury $50,000 USD per year, based on seventeen annual mowings costing $200 USD each.[62]

Food gardens tied to feeding and engaging people in low-income neighbourhoods provide so many "soft-revenue" benefits that

many cities hand over land funded by city taxpayers. Alemany Farm in San Francisco is entirely funded by grants and volunteer labour, aside from some minimal funds from produce sales. The payback is jobs and better nutrition for the Alemany Housing Project's low-income residents.[63]

In Hartford, Connecticut, the cost of remediating remnant lead-laced soils on an old paint store site is being covered by Trinity College students, who are planting vegetation that will absorb the lead until levels are safe enough to plant vegetables.

NICHE MARKET DEMAND

Cities are hotbeds of niche markets and specialized marketplaces. Every financially successful urban farmer depends on selling high-value niche products to some combination of restaurants, farmers' markets, or passionate, dedicated customers. Selling direct is always cheaper — and more feasible in a denser urban area with plenty of options for customers. Selling at farmer's markets, for example, brings twice the return of selling to a wholesaler,[64] notwithstanding the extra hours, opportunity costs, and spoilage involved in sitting under a tent at a farmers' market on a sunny Saturday. Here, as everywhere, smart management is critical. Successful urban farmers find the best direct sales route, whether it be road-side stands, farmers' markets, direct home delivery, community-supported agriculture (CSA) programs, or food-buying clubs. In Saanich, BC, three young, small-scale farmers teamed up in a cooperative venture that meets their particular needs by selling through a combination of large-volume sales to restaurants, a direct-to-customer box program inspired by CSA projects, and farmers' market sales.[65]

For urban agriculturalists, customers are much closer and more plentiful than for country farmers. A big market of customers also has a better chance of including wealthy people who will pay more for local food for ethical and political reasons. Shorter distances from the garden to the customer also allow just-in-time picking, which makes it a lot easier to deliver enhanced flavour and freshness, which in turn helps urban farmers get good prices. The real price premium is for novelty products: Ward Teulon sells white and purple carrots for 50 cents each. Contrary to anecdotal impressions driven by products like Teulon's designer carrots, urban farmers selling at farmers' markets are competitive with other producers. Some studies show that the average prices at farmers' markets are below supermarket prices. A spring 2008 study by students of Professor Stacy Jones at Seattle University found that the average cost per pound of all organic produce at the Broadway Farmers' Market was $2.36 USD, compared to $2.98

USD at the QFC store, and $2.53 USD at Whole Foods. Two other studies comparing farmers markets' in the Seattle area came to the same conclusion: farmers' markets are cheaper (although most produce compared was organic, which is priced well above non-organic produce in grocery stores.)[66]

Any farmer who can line up future customers with money for a share of the crop through a CSA program has a big leg up. In a CSA, people buy annual shares in a farming operation in return for a weekly supply of fresh produce throughout the growing season. Not only is cash flow enhanced, but the customers are essentially providing insurance by sharing the risk that the crop might not be there as promised. Often CSA members come out to the farm and provide free labour and build rewarding community links. For many small urban producers like Ward Teulon, this is gold. CSAs are becoming more widespread: LocalHarvest.org claims to have the most comprehensive directory of CSA farms in the US, with over 2,500 listed in the database, including 557 CSAs that signed up within 2008, and another 300 in the first two months of 2009.

GROWING CONDITIONS

As Ward Teulon discovered with the lack of carrot flies on the Fresia rooftop garden, cities can provide more benign growing conditions: they're warmer, with fewer wild pests and built-in wind protection. The jury is out on whether the damage to crops and urban livestock from a city's rats, raccoons, dogs, squirrels, coyotes, and crows is greater than that of deer, bears, cougars, hares, voles, ground squirrels, eagles, and other predators that break into fields and pens in wilder areas. Community gardens are more prone to theft by humans than private gardens or rural fields, but individual-plot community gardens are not where you want to be if financial returns are a goal.

Sorting and packing for specialized markets at Saanich Organics
Photo: Courtesy of Saanich Organics, Robin Tunnicliffe
B.C. Institute for Cooperative Studies

ACCESS TO WATER AND ORGANIC WASTE

Cities also have built-in water systems and a wealth of distributed, backyard, organic-waste sources. Where water shortages are an issue, cities are rife with opportunities for collecting and diverting rainwater from gutters and downspouts into rain barrels and gardens. Cities also have a lot of other organic waste, which is increasingly being diverted from conventional waste streams and turned into compost, either in backyards or in central locations. On a larger scale, methane tapped from the Metro Vancouver landfill is used to heat nearby greenhouses in Delta, BC.

OPPORTUNITIES FOR SUPPLEMENTARY INCOME

Cities also have a wealth of fall-back income sources for the majority of farmers who have to supplement their incomes — or who have spouses or partners who supplement the family income. (Ward Teulon's wife is a lawyer.) Cities also are home to a wealth of credit and financing sources, including non-profit funders who invariably look more fondly on projects they can see close up.

Economic Challenges for Urban Agriculture

This isn't to say that farming in and around cities is easy. For those not able to get at free small plots, or who need more space, buying affordable sizeable plots on the edge of cities just for farming, when almost every other use provides a higher financial return, is next to impossible. The closer to the city centre, the higher the price of the land. Where farmland isn't protected, speculators typically drive up the price of suburban land, and then don't care a lot about whether it's in production or just waiting empty for a rezoning or a farmer who can somehow afford to buy it.

In trying to find the financial sweet spots in urban farming, it's important to distinguish between the direct and indirect financial rewards of food growing in our cities. In many cases, especially where there is grant funding or volunteer labour, the shortage of financial returns can be shrugged off in return for the social capital payback of building neighbourhood bonds, making streets safer, feeding low-income people, sourcing supplies for food banks, educating children about where food comes from, improving diets, and keeping people productive at prisons or senior centres. All of these goals are highly desirable rewards in themselves but difficult — and distracting —to quantify financially. In social enterprises whose primary focus isn't the bottom line, having multiple social and environmental goals dilutes operators' attention from strictly financial goals. But what if financial returns were essential for your vision of success — perhaps out of necessity?

Elements of Economically Successful Urban Agriculture

Exactly what does it take to be financially successful in today's hybrid world of AU? Wally Satzewich has one of the clearest answers. He's the founder of SPIN farming, an acronym for small plot intensive farming, specifically tailored to the high-end jewels of urban agriculture: free land, no capital, and labour-intensive, high-value plots.

Wally's Urban Market Garden in Saskatoon, Saskatchewan, is made up of twenty-five residential backyard sites rented from homeowners, with an aggregate size of about 0.2 hectares, half an acre. (Rents are nominal, sometimes traded for produce.) Individual plots range in size from 46 square meters to 279 square meters, 500 square feet to 3,000 square feet. He claims to be grossing over $50,000 a year, selling mainly at the Saskatoon Farmers' Market.

You can tell he's focused on revenue just by visiting his website at www.spinfarming. com. Right off the top of the home page, he's got instruction manuals to sell. Minimal mechanization and maximum fiscal discipline and planning are the hallmarks of the SPIN formula. SPIN emphasizes intensive relay growing, producing as many as three crops a year in a northern climate like Saskatoon's, and precise revenue target formulas. Satzewich would be the last to claim he's doing anything new, but he has managed to package and systematize his knowledge in a way reminiscent of a business franchise — except all he sells is knowledge. It works. According to one study, the most important factor in determining yields seems to be the management skills of the farmer.[67]

"We are producing ten to fifteen different crops and sell thousands of bunches of radishes and green onions and thousands of bags of salad greens and carrots each season," says Satzewich. "Our volumes are low compared to conventional farming, but we sell high-quality organic products at very high-end prices." SPIN's low-cost simplicity is stunning: "All we needed to buy was a van, a used rototiller, and an old Pepsi cooler we put in the garage," says Pauline Scobie, an Oak Bay, BC, SPIN practitioner. "We have our market right next door." She had to get around a municipal bylaw forbidding agriculture in the city, but that's another story.

There are two things all SPIN farmers have in common, says Satzewich: markets to support them and an entrepreneurial spirit. The entrepreneurial spirit is evidenced by the range of books and learning guides he sells online. Similarly, Ward Teulon supplements his farming income with garden tours, building raised beds, and garden consultations.

SPIN's claims of revenues were proven in a carefully monitored experiment on the

(donated) Somerton Tanks Farm property in Northeast Philadelphia. Backed by city and state funding to promote local economic agricultural development, the Institute for Innovations in Local Farming (IILP), and the Philadelphia Water Department, the

Small Plot Intensive Gardens In Saskatoon
Photo: Courtesy of www.spinfarming.com

Small Plot Intensive Farmer
Photo: Courtesy of www.spinfarming.com

0.2 hectare, half-acre, SPIN farm grossed $26,000 USD in its first year of operation. (Please see Table 20.1) After four years of refining the system, improving the soil and building the farm's reputation for quality produce, revenues were up to $68,000 USD. A follow-up economic feasibility study projected that revenues could reach $120,000 USD on less than 0.4 hectares, one acre, of growing space using the SPIN methods. Unfortunately, the plot was abandoned when the property was needed for other uses.

"A critical success factor is markets," points out Roxanne Christensen, president of The Institute for Innovations in Local Farming (IILF). "It is here that urbanization can be turned to the farmer's advantage because cities provide a variety of sales channels — farmers' markets, CSAs, restaurants, high-end specialty food stores — that are able to pay premium prices." Christensen says SPIN now has a network of more than 500 sub-acre farmers around the world who use these methods.

Grow Biointensive is another micro farming system (www.growbiointensive.org). It promises all the calories and nutrients for a complete diet for one person on a tenth of an acre of growing space. By 2005, 1,413 people from forty-six states and twenty-four countries were trained at Ecology Action workshops, taking the lessons to small gardens around the world.[68]

According to Ecology Action's Executive Director, John Jeavons, Grow Biointensive farming techniques can feed one person on a vegan diet (499 kilos, 1,100 pounds of vegetables) on 372 meters squared, 4,000 square feet of land.[69] Predicting economic returns from those yields would depend on the local market and the savvy and intent of the growers. Regardless of the financial outcomes, Grow Biointensive confirms the

SPIN farming claims that urban farming on small plots can be highly productive.

Beyond small entrepreneurs focused on income are some larger, not-for-profit urban farms that have managed to become significantly self-supporting. Fairview Gardens in Goleta, near Santa Barbara, California, is a 4.8-hectare (12.5-acre) organic market garden now surrounded by freeways, tract homes, and shopping malls.

Under the leadership of Michael Ableman, it became an international beacon for small-scale urban food production, agricultural preservation, farm-based education, and community-supported agriculture (CSA) while grossing more than $700,000 USD in 2005.[70] Fairview gardens has blossomed into the Center for Urban Agriculture, selling not only food, but books, videos, cooking and gardening classes, apprenticeships, DVDs, and membership in its CSA program.

Legendary community organizer and former professional basketball player Will Allen raises $500,000 USD worth of produce, meat and fish per year at his 0.8 hectare, 2-acre Growing Power complex in a low-income neighbourhood in Milwaukee, Wisconsin, with his bottom line boosted by 2,000 volunteers.[72]

For urban farmers focused on the bottom line, stepping up from sub-acre plots to more acreage can add new costs that can't be covered by the smaller increase in revenues. Wally Satzewich didn't start with small city plots, as Ward Teulon did. His first farm was a one-acre plot just outside Saskatoon. Thinking economies of scale, he then moved onto 20 acres on the South Saskatchewan River, where he and his partner, Gail Vandersteen, grew vegetables. After three years of fighting natural pests and paying the capital costs of more machinery, they realized they could do better growing multiple

Table 20.1 - Income & Expense History--2004-2006
Somerton Tanks Farm, Philadelphia[71]

Revenue:	2004	2005	2006
COMMUNITY SUPPORTED AGRICULTURE SHARES	$15,700	$23,800	$24,900
FARM MARKET REVENUES	$12,700	$19,600	$36,900
RESTAURANT/WHOLESALER SALES	$7,600	$6,500	$5,800
FARMSTAND SALES & OTHER	$2,800	$2,800	$400
TOTAL REVENUES	**$38,800**	**$52,700**	**$68,000**
Operating Expenses:			
GROWING SUPPLIES & IRRIGATION	$2,900	$3,500	$5,100
SALES SUPPLIES	$900	$1,700	$1,400
VEHICLE INSURANCE	$5,400	$5,000	$4,300
VEHICLE OPERATIONS & REPAIR	$1,600	$3,000	$3,000
EQUIPMENT PURCHASE & REPAIR	$1,800	$2,900	$1,900
MARKETING	$900	$200	$400
FARMER'S MARKET FEES	$1,000	$1,500	$2,300
EMPLOYEE LABOR--PART-TIME	$0	$10,200	$11,500
BUSINESS LIABILITY INSURANCE			$200
OTHER	$600	$0	$0
TOTAL NON-FARMER EXPENSES	$15,100	$28,000	$30,100
NET FARMERS WAGES	$32,400	$37,500	$39,700
TOTAL EXPENSES	**$47,500**	**$65,500**	**$69,800**

crops in the city. "People don't believe you can grow three crops a year in Saskatoon," Vandersteen reports on the spinfarming. com website. "They think it's too much work, but the truth is, this is much less work than mechanized, large-scale farming. We used to have a tractor to hill potatoes and cultivate, but we find it's more efficient to do things by hand. Other than a rototiller, all we need is a push-type seeder and a few hand tools."

Using Development Investment to Fund Urban Agriculture Operations

Beyond just getting around high capital costs for farmland, some developers, farmers, and foundation funders have teamed up to create new forms of farmland subdivision that generate new sources of funding for medium-sized plots on high-priced land near cities. Elsewhere in this book, AU describes approaches for using housing density on green fields to financially subsidize food production under a new economic model. Prairie Crossing, on a Chicago commuter rail line, is considered the foremost example in the US. It's a 274 hectare, 677 acre, development in the 2023 hectare, 5,000 acre, Liberty Prairie Reserve that includes 20 percent of the developed land for cluster housing and 59 hectares, 145 acres, for an organic farm. The rest is reserved for wild-habitat preservation.

In similar developments like Farmview in Makefield, Pennsylvania, and Qroe Farm Preservation Development in Massachusetts and Virginia, as much as 80 percent of the farmland and natural habitat is preserved as part of a housing development. Existing farmers can stay on the land, compensated by new owners who pre-purchase crops and cover taxes, lost development potential, and farm costs. Agricultural operating costs on these newly farmed lands can also be subsidized by educational enterprises (post-secondary farmer training, public courses, school tours), a source of income suited to lands near major population centres.

These "conservation developments" are envisioned to free a new generation of farmers from the current cost-price squeeze that's driving so many aging farmers out of business. Politically volatile and easily subverted into a token sweetener for urban sprawl onto farmland, this model has a powerful potential to marry homeowners' willingness to pay a premium for adjacent open space with an urban-edge farmer's need for new sources of funding.

According to Ed McMahon, senior fellow with the Urban Land Institute, these projects are still mostly boutique developments, but many developers are waking up to the attraction of providing an open-space amenity that generates cash flow even before any lots are sold.[73] "The only way these are going to go mainstream is if the developers can pencil out the numbers," he says. "Already we're seeing farmland going from being an amenity to being central to the development."

Selling these projects to a NIMBY public that would prefer to freeze any development on open farmland will depend a lot on the integrity of the farm-preservation component. Are the covenants on the land strong enough to secure the farmland forever? Will the business model keep the farm financially stable in tough times? These developments are too new to provide solid data on their durability.

Finding the Right Scale

Financially sustainable, human-scale, small organic farms close to cities have been around for a while. The Intervale Center in Burlington Vermont, the state's biggest compost operation, is part of a diverse organization that includes a CSA farm and the Intervale Small Farm Incubator. These are all part of a collection of thirteen independent organic farms that range in size from 0.4 to 26 hectares, one to 65 acres. The 20 hectare, 50-acre, CSA farm at the Intervale Center feeds 400 families, and the whole operation employs 60 people.

As noted in other chapters, finding the right scale of operation is an important factor in getting favourable financial results. Just as Wally Satzewich discovered that small-sized plots are financially feasible, a 1997 economic analysis of sustainable community food systems found that small-scale, on-farm processing can be more efficient because some of the work can be done by family labour in on-farm kitchens. But when quantities are too big to use hand-processed, low-overhead production methods, but not big enough to capture economies of scale, the profit margins disappear.[74]

Backyard chicken
Photo: Bob Ransford

The same study looked at chicken production and concluded that the profit per bird under homestead production is higher, although the net income at small volumes can't match that of higher-volume industrial chicken producers.

The challenge is finding the right volume for maximum revenue while keeping production costs at homestead levels. "The path to profitability for community-scale processors is to achieve a high margin on small production quantities as opposed to the industrial strategy of producing high quantities of low-margin products," says the study.

Public Policy to Support Economic Development in Urban Agriculture

The financial viability of agriculture in and around cities can be vastly enhanced by public policy changes. The biggest one is restricting conversion of farmland at cities' edges to higher-value, non-agricultural uses (residential, industrial, commercial). Ending that will drive out the speculative lift to farm real-estate prices. This can be done by greenbelt legislation, land trust purchases, or by methods like transferable density rights. Under transferable density, farmers whose land is deemed important for agriculture can sell the right to develop it to someone else. That person can then build to a higher density than would otherwise be permitted on urban properties where high-density development is desirable. When it works, transferable density protects farmland and compensates farmers for depressing the value of their land. Many farmers are reluctant to embrace that restriction, but in areas like Montgomery County, adjacent to Washington DC, transfer-development-right zoning has protected 16187 hectares, 40,000 acres, half the area's farmland preservation goal, without any public spending.[75]

Expediting approvals for projects such as the Jean-Talon Market in Montréal can help bridge the distribution gap between temporary, seasonal farmer's markets and the big grocery stores. The Jean-Talon market is noted as "the most important open-air market in North America"[76] and covers an entire city block that is open year-round selling produce in the core and specialty foods and restaurants on the outside. Farmers' markets are typically hamstrung by regulations that could be streamlined. City farmers have a long wish list of publicly funded initiatives that would boost their bottom line, including:

- Easy access to land in parks, school property, and vacant city lots.

- Free water.

- Distribution, storage, and processing hubs in neighbourhoods.

- Public institutional purchases of neighbourhood food.

- Free compost (preferably delivered) from city compost operations.

In addition to whatever cities, provinces, states, and regions do to grow the market for local food and make its production less costly, myriad outside forces point to a favourable future for urban farming. The biggest of these is a long-term rise in the price of petroleum, making imported industrial agriculture products more expensive. Every rise in the price of oil is another advantage for low-capital, low-fossil-fuel producers in a metropolitan area.

Using Technology to Overcome Barriers

Self-contained vertical farms (like the prototype commercial-scale Cornell University building that produces 1,245 heads of lettuce a day[77] and uses between 200 to 1,000 times less water than outdoor growing) will come closer to financial viability as the price of water and land increases. Will Allen at Growing Power in Milwaukee, Wisconsin, is using his 2008 $500,000 "genius grant" from the John D. and Catherine T. MacArthur Foundation to transform his urban farm "into a five-story vertical building [...] totally off the grid, with renewable energy, where people can come and learn, so they can go back to their communities around the world and grow healthy food," Allen, told the New York Times.[78]

Vertical farms are a natural extension of the evolution of human living spaces into denser, higher, more efficient buildings. One back-to-the-land prototype for self-contained homespun vertical farming is the legendary Solviva greenhouse pioneered by the indomitable Anna Edey at Martha's Vineyard in Massachusetts in the late 1970s.[79] To fill orders, Edey stacked four tiers of "growtubes" in her 279 square meter, 3,000-square-foot, solar-and-chicken-heated greenhouse complex, picking 41 kilos, 90 pounds (1,500 servings), of Solviva Salad a week at peak production. Even with eventual competition from bigger companies, she was able to get $10 USD for a pound of her fresh mixed greens.[80] Edey got her income up to $50,000 USD a year from her 279 square meter, 3,000-square-foot greenhouse, and 465-square-meter 5,000-square-foot outdoor garden, but was convinced that "if it had been run continuously with business-like consistency, the annual income from the greenhouse and the summer garden could have been well over $100,000 USD.[81]

That included the full-time attention of two main people: a production manager and a marketing/sales and business manager. Given salary costs alone, it's hard to see even her most optimistic scenario as financially viable.

Single-storey buildings with stacked plantings like the Valcent Verticrop system (www. valcent.net) are already in production. Valcent has a pilot commercial vertical farm at the Paignton Zoo in Devon, UK, designed to grow 11,200 plants at a time in a 37 square metre, 400 square foot green house, compared to 4332 plants in a conventional green house.[82]

While still mostly at the design stage, high-rise vertical farms, an evolution of "controlled environment agriculture," face formidable construction, energy, and operating costs as well as advanced technical know-how. On the upside, vertical farms offer some intriguing financial advantages for future commercial agriculture in an urban setting:

■ Year-round production.

■ More efficient use of a limited land base (0.2 hectares, one indoor acre, is generally equivalent to 1.6 to 2.4 hectares, 4 to 6 outdoor acres).[83]

■ No weather-related crop failures.

■ Dramatic reduction in fossil fuel costs due to tractors, ploughing, transportation, chemical fertilizers, and more.

■ Organic premium due to easier pest control.

■ Recycling water means low water use — estimated at 5 percent of outdoor crop water demand.

■ Energy sales from methane produced by compost.

■ Ability to include on-site processing: no agricultural runoff.

■ Proximity to employees and markets.

Not to be overlooked is the relentless expansion of online communications, which is making networking, ordering, farm maintenance, and selling a whole lot easier and cheaper with each passing month. Linking fruit trees on privately owned land, for example, with prospective urban farmers, is immensely improved with on-line tools.

Summary

Stripped of its defining social, health, and environmental benefits, urban agriculture in North America is struggling to match do-good community-building with a financially viable business model. While many would argue that the community benefits alone justify whatever subsidies are needed to make urban farming viable, finding a formula for standalone financial success would add a flood of entrepreneurial energy to the food mix. Grants and subsidies are getting harder to access as governments reel with deficits and foundation assets shrink. Heavily subsidized, environmentally-bankrupt, large-scale industrial farming doesn't provide many lessons for small-scale urban agriculturalists.

The best evidence is in the average North American city, where small-plot production with a minimum of labour and equipment can produce the best financial results, taking advantage of the unique economic advantages of growing food in city centres. Finding the best mix of building design and products in a controlled environment — basically building better greenhouses for plants and selected livestock — will lift AU to the next level. Urban agriculture may even achieve the financial viability that continues to elude all but a few industrialized farms.

21. Charter for Agricultural Urbanism JANINE DE LA SALLE & MARK HOLLAND

Tenets of Agricultural Urbanism:

In order for any site plan to be an AU project, it must rigorously and robustly adhere to the tenants of AU. AU projects must:

- Focus new development in existing areas where possible through infill and intensification strategies, to (re)develop compact, complete communities. Green field development should only considered where no other options are possible.

- Plan for success by developing a whole farm plan that addresses:

  □ How all elements of the food system (production to waste management) will be integrated into the site.

  □ The business feasibility of different types of agriculture, processing, storage, marketing, etc.

  □ Identifies guidelines and standards for farm practices and land management.

  □ The options for lease agreements with farmers.

  □ The governance and management systems that are needed to ensure the effective implementation of the agricultural urbanism agenda.

  □ The integration of wildlife and habitat with agriculture.

- Focus on human-scale agriculture that is highly food productive and exceeds the productivity of conventional farming.

- Plan for a mix of land use at all scales of planning and design to:

  □ Protect agricultural land under regulation, covenants, or other land-control mechanisms.

  □ Plan communities with land uses that support the full range of food and agriculture system elements.

- Increase land access for farmers through offering of graduated, long term leases with optional shorter-term trial periods. The lease agreement should be based on an affordable rate to encourage new farmers to participate.

- Forge partnerships to ensure the long-term viability of the farm program and maximize benefits to the broader community. At a minimum, these partners include:

  □ An organizational partner to manage the farming aspects of the site.

  □ An educational partner to promote on-site teaching and learning programs and awareness building and skills around agriculture and local food.

  □ An investment partner to finance the construction of facilities.

- Design and plan for a food precinct that becomes an essential component of the community experience.

- Design form and character of the urban aspects that provide for:
  - Urban agricultural opportunities.
  - Great open places for gathering and celebrating food.
  - Reflection of the agricultural character of the site.
  - Green building.
  - Prioritization of non-automotive transportation.

- Meet basic complete community standards including:
  - Be a minimum of sixteen units per acre and must bring the surrounding area up to a transit-supporting density.
  - Be complete, protect sensitive areas, provide housing choice, and support walkability to places of work, play, and learning.
  - Be transportation-oriented and provide alternatives to automotive transportation.
  - Have integrated infrastructure and green building systems.
  - Have a multi-use open space that accommodates community and ecological needs.
  - Provide community facilities and programs
  - Be an economic driver through providing a range of commercial spaces (live work, retail, office) and on-site jobs.

Context for Chapter 22

The battle between development and farms around the use of agricultural land is centuries old and has become a heated topic in the past several decades in cities across North America. There was a time when preserving land was all that was seen as necessary to preserve the food capacity of a region and this approach became synonymous with regional growth management and urban containment boundaries in many jurisdictions.

Agricultural land reserves of various types were established in many jurisdictions to preserve land, halt land speculation and hopefully preserve the farming legacy and capacity of fertile regions. The story of these land reserves varies between regions but all share the drama of pro and anti development lobbies battling it out in the city halls year after year. As the global food system became dominant and the business case for local agriculture began to suffer, much farmland became dormant and the opportunity and momentum to develop farmland into housing and malls grew.

In many cases, the land reserve boundaries have held and in many others they have fallen. Where the reserves and urban containment boundaries are holding, agriculture often continues in one form or another adjacent to suburban subdivisions. However, in many cases the stress of growing regions are putting significant development pressure on these agriculture lands causing the viability of many forms of farming to be lost and all too often replaced with equestrian estates, monster homes in the middle of hay fields or simply fallow land. Interestingly, in many cases, the prime actors in the removal of land from reserves are farmers themselves as a result of having come to their retirement age with no children interested in taking over the family farm and no younger farmers able to pay the price

to purchase their land. Facing the need to liquidate the land for financial security, farmers find themselves subdividing their farms or partnering with a development company to convert the land to other uses.

The conventional discourse around this conflict includes one perspective arguing vociferously that government intervention should stop the market in its tracks and lock down the land to preserve future agricultural capacity. Other voices express exasperation at the impacts to struggling elderly farmers who take the brunt of that approach and point out the compromised reality of those farms with their small parcels, nearby residential uses, high land prices and many other constraints, arguing therefore that development would be appropriate. Into this polemic, two professors, Patrick Condon and Kent Mullinix, have stepped to bring forward a 3rd option - one that allows the preservation of the majority of farmland while responding to both market forces and sustainability objectives. The following chapter explores the opportunity to harness the power of market forces to allow some development in order to both compensate farmers and to create a financial tool that local governments and land trusts can use to secure the remaining farmland for agriculture in perpetuity.

Agriculture on the Edge: Abating Urban Encroachment by Promoting Agriculture as an Integral Element of Urbanization PATRICK CONDON & KENT MULLINIX

The Vancouver area has unique characteristics, but many of them are shared with numerous other Canadian and American metropolitan areas. Most are surrounded by agricultural lands, in more or less danger of being consumed by sprawl. This is true for Vancouver. Most agricultural lands at the bleeding edges of metropolitan sprawl are influenced by the forces of land speculation. This also is true for Vancouver. Finally, most of the agricultural lands at the edges of most metropolitan areas are used to produce foods, not for a local markets, but for a national and often for a global market. This is true for Vancouver. In all of these ways Vancouver is a case study with problems and potential solutions that are applicable across the continent.

However, in some ways it is unique. On the policy side, agricultural lands in the Vancouver region are protected by legislation, said legislation prohibiting most agricultural parcels from further subdivision, and for uses other than agriculture. This policy framework, in addition to protecting farmland, has made battles at the edge particularly acute and protracted. The Vancouver situation is most akin to the Portland Oregon situation, where similar policy tools apply. The case study presented below provides strategies, rules, lessons, and potential ways to solve the food security crisis that are first and foremost applicable to Vancouver, but in many ways and aspects relevant to every single metropolitan area on the continent.

Context: Metro Vancouver and the Agricultural Land Reserve

Protecting agricultural land from urban encroachment is a worldwide issue. The discussion in this chapter is framed around the context of the Metro Vancouver region of British Columbia and the Agricultural Land Reserve (ALR). We believe that the issues and opportunities in this area are relevant and transferable to other areas that are experiencing growth and increased urban development pressure on farmland. Through a close examination of the BC context, we present more general, transferable ideas and solutions.

Metro Vancouver is located on the West Coast of BC and finds itself in a region with some of the best quality agricultural land in the country. With an anticipated doubling of the population in the next twenty to thirty years, much of these lands are increasingly under pressure for development.

In BC, agricultural land is protected under provincial legislation. The Land Commission Act was enacted on April 18, 1973, establishing the Agricultural Land Reserve that protected 4.7 million hectares, 11.6 million acres, of agricultural land in the province. The Government of BC worked with local governments to establish the boundaries of the reserve and local governments continue to play a pivotal role in upholding the ALR boundaries. The problems and opportunities around growth management, agricultural land protection, farming on farmland and farm vitality are discussed here in the context of Metro Vancouver and the ALR.

The Problem

Currently ALR-designated lands in southwest British Columbia, particularly those west of Abbotsford, are under threat from urban expansion and other non-agricultural uses. The strategy of relying exclusively on perilous regulatory tools (the ALR and Natural Area Buffers) to ensure land is available for food production and to provide a buffer between agricultural lands and urban lands has significant limitations, is politically polarizing, and fails to advance regional food security goals. Can we not also incorporate good land-use and urban design principles and practices that integrate food production and food security into the ALR, particularly at the urban-ALR interface, to enhance agriculture at the metropolitan edge and more effectively address this challenge?

Pursuant to the question posed, the intention of this chapter is to advance a much-needed dialogue, one that now seems polarized and paralyzed on all sides.

Much of the land originally designated to be within the ALR has been abandoned for agricultural purposes, either because it is too small for "industrial-scale" agriculture (the only form of farming recognized by ALR provision) or because it is being held on speculation. Five interrelated factors contribute to this dynamic, which is both counter-productive and threatening to the goals of preserving productive agricultural land and thus to providing some degree of regional food security:

1. Development pressures are mounting as nearly all of the easily developed sites outside of the ALR are either "built out" or planned for building. Developers and local politicians feel there is limited potential for development within existing urban zones (that is, they consider infill, intensification of existing neighbourhoods, or the wholesale reconstruction of existing urban areas

to be impractical at this time). Absent a substantial change in both the development community and the political culture, this proclivity will likely persist.

2. Most ALR lands near urbanized areas have been purchased for prices higher than justified (reaching $100,000 CND per 0.4 hectares, 1 acre, or more) by any form of conventional agriculture utilization. Thus ALR land is clearly being purchased by entities expressly to hold for speculative investment purposes, fully expecting the ALR to break down in the near future. What is more, land speculators are afforded a tax incentive, as agricultural lands are taxed on an advantageous scale with very easily satisfied agriculture production and demonstrated income generation requirements. This makes the cost of holding these lands much more affordable for land speculators.

3. Municipalities have been granted rights to review ALR exclusion requests first. Local municipal councils have proven more likely to allow exclusions than have provincial boards. Local politicians feel pressures to release lands more acutely than do distant provincial regulators, and therefore find it more difficult to deny an application from someone they may know, which may have political influence. Many concerned citizens are now convinced that municipal exclusions drive the system.

4. The majority of Lower Mainland agricultural lands (that are farmed) primarily produce crops for volatile, low-margin commodity markets in the global agri-food system. This provides increasingly marginal (and insufficient) return on investment. These lands are not farmed for high-value local/regional markets, which generally provide high return on investment. As a result, farms

continue to consolidate, fewer and fewer individuals and families farm, and young persons eschew farming/agriculture. Other ALR-designated holdings are used for low-intensity agriculture and produce low-value-per-acre crops such as Christmas trees or horses. These two factors significantly undermine efforts to actualize regional food security and to maintain agriculture sector economic vitality.

5. The interface between lands designated for agricultural use and the adjoining developed lands at the urban edge have become, in effect, a land-use battle zone. Those who live on the urban side of an arbitrary boundary affected by regulation often consider the practices of industrial-scale agribusiness as a threat to their quality of life. At the same time, they value the "protected agricultural lands" for little more than their aesthetic value as pastoral, open space. Meanwhile, those attempting to farm the lands on the agricultural side of the arbitrary boundary feel threatened by further urban encroachment, which brings with it the pressures of speculation on land values and operational conflicts that often arise with industrial-scale farm practices.

Singly and collectively these factors pose significant threats to the long-term preservation of regional agricultural lands and to the creation of a secure, regional agri-food system.

Certainly the problem requires rectifying, but in doing so we cannot ignore that most of the Provincial ALR land at greatest risk today is in fast-growing metropolitan regions and, under present circumstances, contributes very little to regional food security. They are lands protected solely by the regulations of the ALR, and not regulated for their agricultural productivity or

contribution to regional food security. To be fair, the ALR, a far-thinking and precedent-setting designation, has helped our region and urban settlement areas become more compact than many metropolitan centres in North America. The ALR has become a reasonably effective urban-growth-containment tool, while faltering in protecting food-producing land and failing to promote a robust agricultural sector, both original (and laudable) mandates of the ALR. Clearly, however, new measures are called for to ensure a sustainable, regional, agri-food system.

Options

The original intent of the ALR was to promote viable farming, not function as an urban growth boundary. If we all feel that it is, as presently administered, functioning satisfactorily and achieving that goal, then little action is required. If, conversely, we feel that the ALR policy is, in large part, falling short of promoting food security and a viable agriculture sector, and that the trajectory for the ALR is likely to be further compromised in fits and starts, one acre at a time, until very little is left, then more substantial and creative action may be justified.

We offer that such an action would somehow take all factors referred to above and recombine them to create economic and social opportunity to effectively address this persistent challenge. One seemingly radical but practical solution is summarized below. There may be many others, and we certainly hope so. The intention of this paper is to begin a much-needed dialogue and break us free from discourse that is paralyzed and polarized.

A Solution Proposed

What follows outlines six elements of a strategy to complement and strengthen the protection of farmland for farming. The strategy encompasses a new zoning designation, transfer of some urban-edge land value, lift to agriculture and the public sector, integration of local-scale, human-intensive agriculture with urban dwellers, promotion of a new and critically important agricultural and economic sector, and tangible contribution to regional food security.

The province, the region, and its member municipalities might allow a particular kind of development, to incorporate agriculture in a band of land (say, at least 500 meters, 1640 feet wide- please See Figure 22.1) at the interface between urban and agricultural or preservation lands. Such lands are be used for both urban and agricultural purposes in a deliberate and integrated fashion.

This new band could be rezoned for medium-density living on developed portions at, say, sixty dwelling units per net acre, allowing for significant return on investment. Assume sixty dwelling units per net acre (meaning the number of units per acre on just the development parcels) or forty dwelling units per acre gross (meaning the number of units per acre when roads are included in the calculus). At sixty dwelling units per net acre you would exceed ten dwelling units per "double gross" acre (which is the average density when open spaces and agricultural lands are also included in the calculation). Ten to fifteen dwelling units per double gross acre is usually considered the minimum

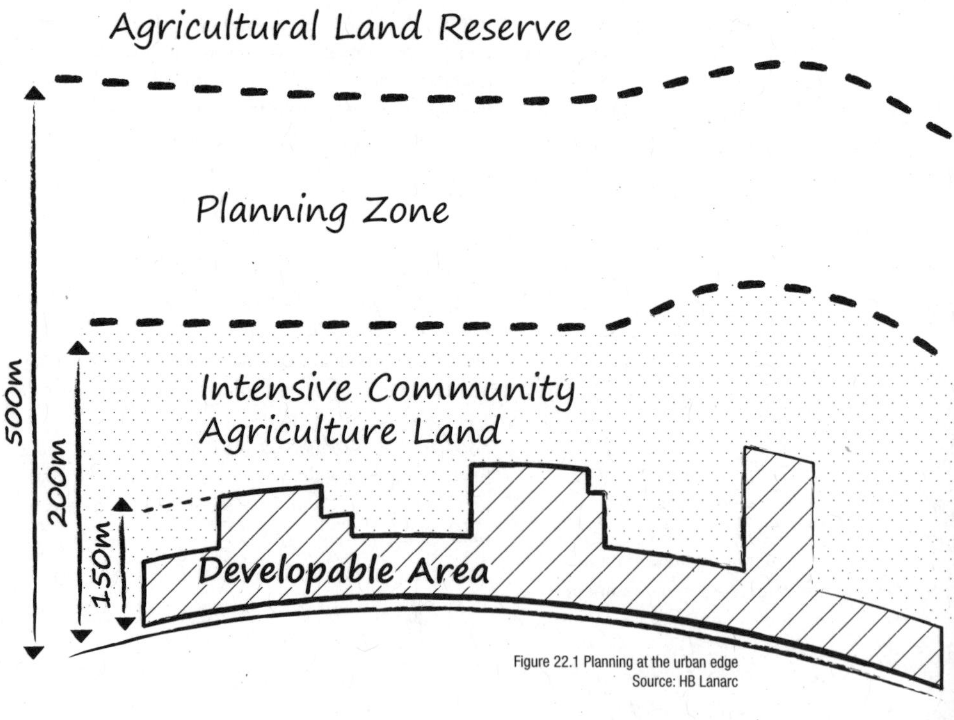

Figure 22.1 Planning at the urban edge
Source: HB Lanarc

density necessary to support viable transit service and local commercial services.

Protect, legally and in perpetuity (that is, via covenant or land trust consignment) two-thirds of this land exclusively for agriculture. It may be desirable that designated agriculture lands ultimately come under ownership of the associated municipality. If they do, we refer to this arrangement as Community Trust Farming.

Lease these agricultural lands to agricultural entrepreneurs and stipulate that the lands be farmed exclusively for local/ regional markets, thus contributing to the sustainability of our communities and to genuine, regional food security. Require that labour-intensive, high-value crops and value-added products (for example, organic, direct marketed) be produced and that labour-intensive highly productive and sustainable production practices be used as opposed to capital- and input-intensive industrial methods, such as pesticide use, fertilization, and mechanization.

Relegate the management of these lands to a non-governmental organization or organizations (NGOs), Community Development Corporation, community or resident association, or professional consulting agrologist for oversight under deed restrictions that would compel use as stated above.

Endow these lands with funds garnered at time of land sale to support local and sustainable agriculture in perpetuity. Through bylaws, local governments already exact a development cost charge from development projects as a means to finance public infrastructure and service requirements associated with municipal growth. Through this scheme, the local and regional agri-food system becomes an integral element of development. Thus, it seems reasonable that development cost charge structures could be modified and appropriately used to support

the creation and stewardship of community focused agri-food system components.

The Key

The economic basis for this concept is simple. When lands shift from agricultural to urban uses, land values increase substantially. This "lift" in value can be huge, ranging from $40,000 CND per 0.4 hectares, one acre, as agricultural lands to over $1 million CND per 0.4 hectares (one acre) depending on location and specific development capacity. Typically, the public act of allowing this to occur generates a huge shift in value to landowners and speculators and uncalculated subversion of many strongly held citizenry interests, including food security, curtailing urban sprawl/prevention of agricultural land loss, and having a viable agriculture sector.

The public sector, however, has the right and ability to change this dynamic by capturing a large portion of the value lift at the time of rezoning application and using it toward desired ends, which might be community trust farming or another mechanism supporting local food security. If one-half of the aforementioned value-shift were captured through development fees it would generate, for the sake of our discussion, up to or perhaps over $500,000 CND per 0.4 hectares, one acre. Using this figure, each 4 hectare, 10-acre, parcel would then provide $5 million CND to endow the activities of local agriculturists and community trust farming land management. Invested value capture would generate roughly $200,000 CND per annum (depending on contemporary interest rates) to support each 5 to 7 acres of labor-intensive and nutrition-rich agriculture operation held and operated in trust. It may also be that some of this captured value can be used to support regional agri-food system infrastructure and support, such as farmers' markets, incubator kitchens, research and education-support services.

Because intensive, ecologically sound, locally and regionally focused agriculture has difficulty competing economically in the current economic and global agricultural context, some level of support would be beneficial. However the payoff could be large.

Food products generated would, per stipulation, only be sold in local and regional markets, making healthy, wholesome, diverse, and affordable foods available to a larger number of citizens and putting in place an infrastructure requisite for local and regional food security. The increased nutritional content of sustainably cultivated food crops, a hidden and far-reaching economic benefit to consumers, is now documented. For example, organic fruits, vegetables, grains, and meats have been routinely found to contain significantly higher levels various vitamins, minerals, and antioxidants.[84,85]

A substantial and economically robust local and regional agri-food sector would result, one that supports entrepreneurship and small business, creates green jobs, and contributes to the regional economy. These potential economic and social benefits cannot be overstated. In addition to the straightforward benefits of regional economic diversification, most revenue generated from these farms would stay and circulate within the regional economy, multiplying in value and economic effect rather than quickly leaving to distant corporate headquarters, as is increasingly the case.[86] Concomitantly, the nature of a community's agriculture sector profoundly influences its social and economic character. Research indicates that communities dominated by smaller, family-owned farms and agriculturally related business, compared to ones dominated by consolidated, transnational agribusiness, have been found to have overall higher standards of living, lower crime and poverty rates, more retail trade and independent businesses, and more parks, schools, churches, newspapers, and citizen involvement in democratic processes.[87]

Research also indicates increasing consumer support for small-scale regional and local farming, sustainably produced food products, and a willingness to preferentially patronize such businesses while paying a premium.[88,89,90] In the US, farms smaller than 20 hectares (50 acres) that are human-intensive, local-scaled, direct market and those over 809 hectares (2,000 acres) (consolidated agribusiness) are the only ones prospering and increasing in number.[91] All others are in decline. In North America, organic foods is the only product category in retail food sales experiencing growth and in Canada, farmers' market sales exceed $1 billion annually. Indications are that consumers are now prepared to economically and politically support an agri-food system that is environmentally sound, promotes a sustainable and secure regional food system, and contributes to building economically vital and socially coherent communities. Per our scheme such an agri-food system complement would emerge without direct taxpayer support. Rather the support would come exclusively from capturing a portion of the value lift associated with rezoning.

What is more, the pattern of development could be configured such that the acreages closest to homes would be farmed in the most unobtrusive ways (that is, labour intensive, and chemical or noise free) to reduce potential conflicts between residents and farmers. As you move away from homes larger scale and more mechanized, conventional agriculture would be more suitable. Thus a range and appropriate complement of types of agricultural enterprise could be accommodated in a regional agri-food system. Additionally, in this new agriculture sector conventional farmers may find opportunity for economically advantageous diversification. Finally, even though projects might consume 25 to 40 percent of a site that may have been previously allocated to farming (in reality, now mostly uncultivated or leased to industrial farmers for low-yield or low-margin products), by requiring small-scale, labour-intensive farming on the remaining land, it is likely that its agricultural productivity, in terms of caloric output, nutritional value and regional economic contribution, will be many times greater than before.

Conclusion

As previously stated, we offer the above strictly as an idea to promote creative thinking to solve our growth management, food security, and agriculture land preservation conundrum. They are not three separate problems. They are one problem. We recognize that its acceptance may require a substantial paradigm shift. But we are reminded of Albert Einstein's sage advice, "The significant problems we face cannot be solved at the same level of thinking we were at when we created them." In this spirit, we invite the presentation of other ideas for solution.

Let there be no doubt: we are in crisis. [92,93] Inaction is not a viable or prudent option. Nor is recalcitrance, regardless of one's position. New and creative thinking, that befitting a sustainable 21st century and our progressive communities, is called for. And we must address this challenge collectively and collaboratively. In this spirit we have brought forth this idea and if it be found wanting, we will remain gratified that constructive and meaningful discourse ensues and that a viable solution is imminent as a result.

Andreas Duany presenting ideas to the public at the Southlands Charrette
Photo: Bob Ransford

Context for Chapter 23

In the first period of the emergence of Agricultural Urbanism (AU), examples of projects that have embraced a full scope of food system elements in their design are few and varied. Where they exist, the story of the community and its relationship to the land on which these projects exist or are proposed is a powerful factor. Because AU takes a different approach to development, especially where it engages agricultural land, based on considering all elements of a food system, the engagement of the community in exploring new ideas, envisioning new opportunities and having conversations with their neighbours about the issues is critical. These kinds of processes take time

to explore new perspectives, learn about issues, talk through concerns and fears, come up with new ideas, and ultimately create a story that can be compelling to local government officials and the media.

Bob Ransford is a seasoned communications and consultation strategist who has been on the front line of community discussions on sustainability for decades. In this section, he explores key issues around the public perceptions of AU issues and tells the story of the first stages of planning for an exciting AU-driven development in BC's Lower Mainland, in the heart of a small town in a growing region.

The Public Opportunity BOB RANSFORD

Many of us living in urban areas today are no more than two or three generations removed from a society and a way of life where local agriculture was woven through every part of daily life. Whether our close ancestors lived in a rural area where the farm was home or whether they lived in a city where everyone had a backyard garden and where the milkman stopped by daily with fresh products from the local dairy, agriculture and the local food system were evident to the masses. Local agriculture once impacted everyday living.

Local agriculture was also a durable and prominent strand that wove together the many active elements of the tapestry that makes a community — whether those were economic, social, educational, recreational, or environmental elements. People bought their food directly from the producer. Our community celebrations marked the changes in seasons and showcased the agricultural bounty. In fact, many of the annual summer and fall fairs that still exist today were organized as exhibitions to showcase the very best of what was grown on local farms or crafted by local food artisans. Community-based business and financial organizations, such as the livestock feed and farm supply cooperatives and local credit unions that were dominant in local commerce, were born out of a collective response to the needs of farmers. Community-based educational organizations and fraternal organizations, like 4-H and local farmers' institutes, extended the influence of local agriculture and permeated community life. Many of these elements were interrelated and together they formed the high-profile presence of local agriculture as a powerful force in community building.

AU has the potential to again be a powerful community builder, weaving local agriculture through many of the elements that physically, socially, and economically define today's urban communities.

This chapter will explore how citizens can be engaged and how they can participate in many parts of a sustainable and regional food system and its many stages of evolution, bringing local agriculture back into the lives of our communities.

Agricultural Urbanism Instigating and Activating Community Life

Agricultural Urbanism is an instigator and activator for community life. It is both the product of citizen engagement and the vehicle for citizen engagement at the community level. The re-birth of local agriculture in our urban areas depends on the active engagement of citizens in every element of the AU design paradigm.

There is no doubt that there is an increased public awareness of the many complex issues impacting food — how we produce it, access it, consume it, and even celebrate it. Concerns about global warming and peak oil have many rethinking the sustainability of global food systems so reliant on carbon-dependent transportation methods. Technological advances and the industrialization of agriculture have many concerned about not only food safety but also about food production's negative environmental impacts. Also, as our cities grow and become increasingly dense, many are looking for respite from urban pressures that exposure to agriculture's natural systems offers.

For these reasons and a number of others, local food security, the realities of sustainable urban and regional food systems, and the potential associated with local agriculture are topics of widespread discussion and action not just among community builders but also among citizens at large.

This speaks to the promise of successfully bringing food and local agriculture back into our lives as a strong influence in the form and character of our communities. That promise offers much for local civic engagement.

Human Scale and Local

As detailed in previous sections, the basic elements of a sustainable urban and regional food system revolve around agricultural activity that is both human scale and local. Inherent in both of these is community participation.

Human scale is just that — scaled to both rely upon and support the active and widespread participation of people.

Public participation opportunities exist at every stage in the evolution of AU in a community. In fact, the successful integration of AU requires public participation, ranging from decisions around planning to citizen involvement and action around implementation, public involvement in governance and public participation in all of the programs that flow from the integration of AU in a community, including the local economic, social, recreational, and educational activities that AU enables or reinforces.

Human-scale, or artisan, agriculture can touch people personally in that it provides opportunities for ordinary people to experience first-hand, understand, participate in, and benefit from the agricultural activity that produces much of their food.

This differs from conventional industrial-scale agriculture, which often has many of its elements invisible to the general public and whose reliance upon mechanization makes it impersonal.

A sustainable urban and regional food system strives to bring agricultural activity closer to consumers. By producing, processing, distributing, selling, celebrating, and teaching about food locally, each dimension of the food system becomes accessible to all citizens in a community. The local nature of AU means that all of the dimensions of our food system can weave through and help to bind together the rich tapestry of values, physical and cultural assets, and activities and aspirations that represent our communities, just as the local food system of earlier generations did.

Perhaps more than any other local activity or form-maker, AU can be a powerful instigator or activator for citizens to participate in their communities. The avenues of participation are many. Some of the key areas are outlined in the following paragraphs.

Heritage, Culture and Recreation

Our modern society is a mere few generations removed from an earlier era and past culture so influenced by agriculture. Therefore, opportunities exist for communities to honour and celebrate their heritage by re-connecting with agriculture and re-integrating agriculture into urban culture. In fact, that reconnection can reach back to understand, appreciate, celebrate, and even re-integrate many of the traditional practices of our First Nations peoples. They were the original, local hunter-gatherers and foragers, relying on the natural bounty of the lands they occupied. That re-integration might be as simple as having citizens organize community celebrations to mark the beginning and ends of the earth's seasons that coincide with the natural cycles of planting and harvest. Other ways of linking the agricultural past with the community's future can include integrating the agricultural story into local tourism offerings, including agricultural museums, various forms of agri-tourism, such as local farm-stay programs and farm-field dinners — local institutions and events that can be sustained by community participation and philanthropy (which are two more ways to build on the sense of community engagement).

Agricultural Urbanism can also be integrated with local recreation and leisure pursuits. Many people enjoy gardening as a main recreational pursuit, but opportunities also exist to integrate recreational activities with agriculture for those not interested in gardening, such as trail walking or cycling through productive farming areas where people can both enjoy the pastoral and scenic setting as well as observe active agricultural practices.

Local Economic Development

Agricultural Urbanism offers many opportunities to diversify a local economy and create new local economic opportunities at various scales that can employ local people and build new local enterprise to augment a community's trade and commerce. Opportunities exist to engage the public in various ways, whether as consumers connecting directly to producers, new entrepreneurs instigating new local enterprise, and workers employed in local agriculture-based industries, or merely as the indirect beneficiaries of increased local economic activity. Local human-scale agricultural production, processing, value-added processing, distribution, wholesale trade, and retail trade all provide opportunities to engage every economic level, from the smallest individual enterprise to small- to medium-sized local businesses and social enterprises. One example of new economic activity at a small scale in many communities today is the local farmers' markets, which have emerged as a new form

of retail market access for local farmers and food producers. Many communities can point to the recent phenomenal growth in the economic activity generated by local community-scale farmers' markets. Not only do local small-scale farmers benefit from this new retail activity, which is often organized as a community activity or social enterprise, the local economic impact is further multiplied to produce community-wide, direct and indirect positive economic impacts.

Education and Lifelong Learning

Linking economic development opportunities to educational and lifelong learning pursuits and connecting them to local agriculture reinforces sustained local economic development by ensuring that a community's population is able to acquire the skills and knowledge that can be applied in the activities that a commitment to AU spawns. That learning and teaching can start at the family level, where young people can be given an opportunity to understand very early on where their food comes from and how food is so closely linked to nature. Learning about food and agriculture can also be a key part of both the curriculum and general school life in our community's K to 12 school system. Learning can extend beyond the confines of the school and become an interactive community experience, where students and teachers participate in local food activities with citizens in the community, such as community-gardening, school-based produce markets, small-scale cooperative community food processing, and more.

In the educational area, there is also a huge opportunity to link local and regional food systems and agricultural urbanism to post-secondary education. Not only can teaching and learning at the post-secondary level ensure that we have qualified farmers and other food-sector specialists to sustain a local and regional food system, research carried out within the post-secondary education system can help evolve urban agriculture to ensure that it continues to meet the challenges of ever-present change and that it lives up to its potential as a community-building force.

In short, education founded on the opportunities of local AU becomes part of the community's life-blood and character.

Ecological and Environmental Stewardship

By linking people in a community to the natural systems that produce food locally, we can ensure greater understanding and awareness of the need to properly steward our precious ecosystems, especially when those ecosystems are threatened by the mounting impacts produced by urban intensification. Local resource recovery and re-use, such as household food waste composting and other domestic waste disposal, can be integral to AU and secure the natural inputs needed to sustain agricultural production on a land base. If people in a community can see and experience food being produced in a natural environment where the ecosystem is so obviously an integrated closed-loop system, community behaviour can be more easily and quickly influenced for the better. AU is perhaps the best way to activate behavioural change in the way citizens interact with and steward our shared environment and natural ecosystems.

Public Engagement in Planning Agricultural Urbanism

The public can be engaged at many levels in AU's evolution in a community. But the planning level is where public engagement is essential to the success of AU becoming the local urban design paradigm.

Agricultural Urbanism is an urban design paradigm that must be embraced in a community's future vision. Community

visioning engages the public in a process that identifies the values and the identity of a community and articulates those values and that identity in a declaration of what the future of the community will look like. If a community is to integrate AU, then the community's vision needs to speak to the values and identity that will be shaped by integrating agriculture into the fabric of the community.

Developing the community vision needs to be a participatory process that involves the public, identifying the multiple opportunities and multiple benefits AU offers.

Southlands Case Study

The Southlands community planning process proposed a new neighbourhood and a community-controlled farm in an existing suburban community, based on the principles of AU. This collaborative public planning process, facilitated by the property owner and driven by a group of community volunteers, culminated in a public design charrette that produced a master plan for the Southlands site.

Southlands is a 538-acre tract of land (over 2 square kilometers) surrounded by Tsawwassen, a community of approximately 23,000 in the municipality of Delta, British Columbia. Tsawwassen is largely a bedroom community of Vancouver, with 75 percent of its employed residents leaving for their livelihood. There is a lack of diversity in the local housing stock and Tsawwassen contains the highest percentage of single-family homes in Metro Vancouver. That housing stock appears mismatched with the current and emerging needs of the community's empty nesters — its largest population cohort.

The Southlands property, once referred to as the Spetifore lands, was removed from the British Columbia provincial government's Agricultural Land Reserve (ALR) in 1981 by application of the local government. The Agricultural Land Reserve is a provincial zone aimed at preserving farmland in which agriculture is recognized as the priority use, taking precedence over but not replacing local government bylaws. In Metro Vancouver, the ALR has served as a de facto urban-growth boundary. The provincial government justified the removal at the time by stating that development of the Spetifore lands would help alleviate the housing shortage that existed in Metro Vancouver at the time.

In 1989, a plan typical of suburban development of that era proposed a sprawling 2,000-home development and a golf course on Southlands, with little or no land preserved for agriculture. After a protracted community debate that involved the longest public hearing on a land-use proposal in Canadian history, the proposal was rejected by the local government. The current landowners, Century Group, acquired the property in 1990 after this failed development proposal.

The site is currently zoned for agricultural uses and is within Metro Vancouver's Green Zone, a regional government designation also designed to control urban sprawl. Portions of the property have been under various forms of low-intensity agricultural production. In order for soil-based crops to be viable, most of the site's soils require improvements, including costly drainage and irrigation.

For more than the last decade, the future of the property has remained uncertain and the division in public opinion on an appropriate land use has been a major undercurrent in the public and political life of the local community.

In October 2006, Century Group president, Sean Hodgins, presented a broad land-use vision to the community of Tsawwassen, with multi-use development on one-third of Southlands and two-thirds dedicated

for agriculture, recreation, and education uses. His vision aimed at achieving a more complete and sustainable Tsawwassen. He invited fellow residents to work together with him to discover how this might be possible.

THE SOUTHLANDS COMMUNITY PLANNING TEAM

Two dozen local citizens from all walks of life, all age groups, and all parts of the community responded to Hodgins's invitation. They volunteered to form the Southlands Community Planning Team and work with Southlands' landowner on formulating a plan. They worked for fifteen months to formulate a design brief.

Convening a planning process of this type can be a daunting task, with many interests represented at the table, a range of complex issues to consider, and an indefinite timeline. This planning process was all the more complex due to the uncertainty about the subsequent formal municipal process that might arise from any proposed plan. Early in this process, the political mood of the local government was not supportive of considering development plans for the Southlands. The community planning process not only had to take place independent of municipal expert and political involvement; it also had to culminate in a plan that would inspire enough grassroots community support to influence the political dynamics.

At the outset, the planning team identified their vision:

The Southlands Community Planning Team shall work towards a plan that integrates the Southlands into the existing South Delta community in a way that increases the sum of human happiness in our community.

Their collaborative planning process was built around a structure that led to clearly defined outcomes but was flexible enough to accommodate the ideas and direction of the volunteers serving on the planning team.

The Southlands Community Planning Team
Photo: Bob Ransford

The collaborative community planning process was based on a "discovery and deliberation" model. The planning team explored a list of key issues, beginning with a learning phase in which experts were brought in to explain concepts and provide background and options for direction. Then the planning team members deliberated, exchanged ideas, and worked toward a consensus on direction on each issue.

The key issues stemmed from the planning team's perception of strong community support to protect Southlands' ecologically sensitive areas and to maintain the agricultural heritage of the area. They defined other issues stemming from the public desire to enhance local quality of life by making Tsawwassen a more complete community. The issues they tackled included:

- The need for more recreation opportunities.

- Housing choice (aging in place for seniors).

- Housing affordability (young families).

- Transportation choice.

- Life-long learning opportunities.

- Small-scale farming opportunities.

- Connectivity of the regional park to the wider community.

- Creating a sense of place.

- Habitat creation and enhancement.

Many of the key topics were presented in the form of questions:

- What's missing in Tsawwassen?

- What could Southlands provide in terms of meeting community needs?

- What is the future of farming in Tsawwassen?

- What is the future of education and innovation in Tsawwassen?

- What is the future of housing in Tsawwassen — what type, form, density, character?

- How can we improve mobility and accessibility locally and regionally while growing?

- How do we protect and enhance our quality of life when developing Southlands?

- What are some important guides/rules to follow?

PLANNING FOR AGRICULTURAL URBANISM

Agriculture and integrating agriculture with urbanism were key topics for consideration. The planning team held a series of workshop-style meetings about every three weeks. Guest speakers provided information on various topics. The team also conducted a field trip to Portland, Oregon, to study on-the-ground examples of the new urbanism and local agriculture. The planning team's process was designed to accept and integrate the view of the wider community, so the team hosted a number of open houses to present ideas to the public and to invite feedback during the course of their fifteen months of work.

After a few months of learning and surveying the list of topics, the team decided that their main task was to formulate objectives and strategies in each of the topic areas to serve as a design guide for a later public design charrette that would culminate in a master plan for the site. The team broke into working committees to tackle individual topics.

Overarching all of the topics was a commitment to sustainable development. They organized their sustainable development objectives for Southlands under a framework titled "The Eight Pillars of a Sustainable Community Development,"[94]

A committee was assigned to formulate objectives and strategies in response to the specific question: What is the future of farming in Tsawwassen?

The agriculture committee understood the definition of AU to mean:

"An approach to integrating growth and development with preserving agricultural resources and enhancing elements of the food system. The cornerstone of AU is creating an urban environment that activates and sustains urban agriculture with important elements such as educational programs, small-scale processing opportunities and a farmers' market or other local sales conduits. AU offers an alternative to the practice of separating places where people live and where agricultural activities occur. Central to the concept of AU is the idea of integration not separation, transitions not buffers."

The committee started their detailed work on the agricultural future of Southlands by drafting a vision statement: "Sustainable agriculture managed by the community for the health and education of the community."

The committee then set out to explore the potential Southlands offered for a new type of agricultural activity — one that would be integrated with the surrounding community. After some research and consultation with farming and sustainability experts, they formulated the following objectives and strategies for their concept of AU for the Southlands.

Objective 1: Build community through interaction of people with the land

Strategy 1.1: Integrate footpaths and cycling trails within the agricultural areas.

Strategy 1.2: Establish community gardens and allotment plots.

Strategy 1.3: Establish a local farmers' market.

Objective 2: Promote small-scale sustainable agriculture.

Strategy 2.1: Set aside a minimum of one-third of the total land area for agricultural development.

Strategy 2.2: Manage organic soil.

Strategy 2.3: Produce organic food.

Strategy 2.4: Conserve soil, water, and other natural resources.

Strategy 2.5: Encourage community-supported agriculture (CSA) programs.

Objective 3: Protect the natural habitat for birds and wildlife.

Strategy 3.1: Plan and build wildlife corridors through developed areas.

Strategy 3.2: Establish hedgerows between crops and fields.

Strategy 3.3: Enhance biodiversity by improving and building ecosystems and habitat.

Objective 4: Create aesthetically pleasing viewscapes.

Strategy 4.1: Preserve existing 30 hectare, 75-acre forest.

Strategy 4.2: Plant trees, orchards, and hedgerows.

Strategy 4.3: Create and restore natural waterways.

Objective 5: Provide educational opportunities relating to sustainable food production.

Strategy 5.1: Support the establishment of programs for local schoolchildren.

Strategy 5.2: Establish a community kitchen.

Strategy 5.3: Consider an agricultural internship program.

The Committee also set a number of targets to measure how the strategies might be achieved in a master plan.

The larger community planning team endorsed the committee's objectives and strategies for agriculture on Southlands. The planning team also envisioned a unique physical form-maker that might flow from AU, where Southlands' planned urban area, created in a new neighbourhood, would intersect with the agricultural area through the creation of a food and agriculture precinct. The precinct was to be the nexus where agricultural activities could find economic and social realization within the community. The team challenged the charrette design team to include some or all of the following activities in the precinct:

■ A "centre of urban agriculture" education facility.

■ Light-processing facilities for value-added farm output.

■ A farmers' market.

■ A culinary school.

■ An urban commercial "high street" driven by food sales and fresh-food restaurants together with more traditional neighbourhood stores.

The team envisioned an architectural vernacular for the design of the buildings in the precinct that would reinforce the agricultural theme of the project.

Collectively, the Southlands Community Planning Team contributed more than 2,000 person-hours of volunteer work between February 2007 and May 2008 to a comprehensive design brief that not only activated the concept of AU, but also set a number of other objectives for the design of a new sustainable neighbourhood on Southlands, causing, in the words of the team's original mission statement, an increase in "the sum of human happiness in Tsawwassen."

A public design charrette was convened by Century Group between May 6th and May 13th, 2008. This intensive design workshop, led by Andrés Duany a founder of the Congress for the New Urbanism and one of the premiere town planners internationally, provided an innovative forum for the local community to be directly involved in the planning and with design work, which took place in public and where the public feedback was incorporated real-time as the design evolved. The Southlands Community Planning Team endorsed this approach and their design brief became the guide for the charrette's design work.

The charrette design team included Mark Holland and Janine de la Salle of Vancouver-based HB Lanarc, West Vancouver architect Richard Hulbert, and Chicago architect Doug Farr, as well as a team of over twenty architects, designers, engineers, and other specialists. Michael Ableman, an organic farmer and author from Salt Spring Island, British Columbia, is a farm specialist who helped with the details of sustainable community farming.

Mark Holland and Janine de la Salle at the
Southlands Charrette, Tsawwassen BC- 2008
Photo: Bob Ransford

The public participated in several ways, including taking part in three formal sessions over an eight-day period. These included an opening session, a mid-term review of draft plans, and the final presentation. At the end of each day, the design team also held spontaneous review sessions with members of the public who visited the design studio.

The charrette culminated in the presentation of three options for a Southlands master plan. All three options called for more than 81 hectares, 200 acres of land to be dedicated to community-controlled local agriculture. Approximately 40 percent of Southlands will be preserved forever for human-scale, local farming to provide Tsawwassen residents with access to nutritious, wholesome foods.

The agricultural land will be dedicated to the community and operated by a trust. Legal means will ensure that the Southlands agricultural land is used in perpetuity only for farming and agricultural education. The main objective of the community trust, which will be governed by local citizens, will be to make the Southlands farmland available to citizens for the kind of farming that enhances local food self-sufficiency and promotes community health and education. Farming will occur at various scales, including community gardens, public allotment gardens, and multi-acre farms growing produce for local markets. The Community Trust Farming proposal for Southlands is human-scale, local farming using high intensity, low-input, urban-friendly farming based on ecologically responsible farm practices. The trust will be able to lease land for local food production to farmers who might not otherwise have access to farmland, providing various terms of tenure and ensuring that the human-scale farming activities are both compatible with the surrounding community and support local food security.

The Community Land Trust will also make land available for agricultural education and research, inviting the participation of the Delta School District and other local organizations. Kwantlen Polytechnic University has also committed to establishing a Centre for Urban Agriculture on Southlands, providing a venue for teaching and learning. This educational facility will provide an opportunity to educate small-scale farmers in farm practices in a real farm setting and also allow applied research activities in the area of urban agriculture.

The Market Square, planned as the hub of the Southlands neighbourhood, will act as an important physical, cultural, and commercial link between farming activities and the Tsawwassen community. For example, celebrating and enjoying food plays a central role in building healthy communities. The Southlands Market Square will offer a range of facilities, including the Kwantlen Polytechnic University's Centre for Urban Agriculture, a Farmers' Market, a new Tsawwassen Arts and Cultural Centre, a culinary education kitchen, and a range of commercial outlets that support the goal of celebrating food. Live-work residences will also be located in the Market Square.

It was only through the direct and active involvement of a diverse group of local citizens and the cooperation of a willing and innovative land owner/developer that the broad vision for a multi-use development centred around agriculture could have been shaped into such a comprehensive and promising plan for Southlands — a plan that activates AU in a very real and meaningful way.

Seizing the Public Opportunity — Steps to Success

Lots of opportunities exist to engage citizens and allow them to participate in many parts of a sustainable and regional food system and during many stages in the evolution of that system, bringing local agriculture back into the lives of our communities. AU has the potential to be a powerful community builder, weaving local agriculture through many of the elements that physically, socially, and economically define urban communities today.

Some of the key steps to success in engaging citizens and encouraging their participation in a sustainable and regional food system are:

- **Engage citizens at the beginning.** Make the circle wide when brainstorming the possibilities and exploring the early opportunities. Don't limit creative thinking. The opportunities for local agriculture to touch everyone in some way are endless.

- **Look to the past.** Research and uncover the roots of local agriculture in your community. Remember, at one time most agriculture was local. Celebrate your agricultural heritage — Yesterday's stories inspire tomorrow's ideas.

- **Wear multiple hats.** Don't think of local agriculture as merely farming on farms by farmers. Farming is about science. Farming is a craft. Farming is about nature. Farming is about food. Farmers never stop learning. Farmers can be great teachers. Farming can be recreation. Farming is business and it is about economics. Farming can be fun.

- **Remember the land.** Land is not an infinite resource. What you take from the land you have to put back. Agriculture is about stewardship of nature's endowment — the land and what grows in and on top of the land. In metropolitan areas, many compete for land use, and good cities are planned around good ideas on how land use is allocated.

- **Build a big tent with open doors and flexible walls.** Once you start down the road of engaging and inviting the public to participate in building and evolving a sustainable and regional food system based on local agriculture, new people will want to be part of what was created, and new ideas and new possibilities will continue to germinate. Many will grow into breakthrough opportunities and expand the reach and community-building power of the system. Build a system that is resilient, flexible, and scalable. Ensure that public participation opportunities continue to exist as the food system evolves and that new people feel welcome to participate.

By weaving local agriculture through our daily lives and through the tapestry of our community, we are bringing us all closer together, tightening the bonds of citizenship and connecting all of us with the earth that sustains us.

Construction of the SOLE Food Urban Farm, Vancouver BC 2009
Photo: Janine de la Salle

Part V: Conclusion

24. A Path Forward: Next Steps in Agricultural Urbanism and Sustainable Food Systems MARK HOLLAND

Agricultural Urbanism is woven from the threads of many agriculture-related movements and perspectives on sustainable food systems with the intent of offering ideas and guidance in the planning and design of towns and cities in how to support more sustainable food systems. Progress in any area related to sustainable food and agriculture systems can further inform and develop AU. The steps forward can be organized into two levels: action at the regional or provincial/state level and action at the local or neighbourhood level.

Regional Scale Action

For a community wanting to promote AU and sustainable food systems, there are some fundamental areas of work to undertake.

A regional land-management strategy. Develop regional strategies that both allow appropriate economic development and preserve key landscapes, including resource lands, sensitive ecosystems, recreation areas, and a productive agricultural land base. These strategies need to include inventories, mapping, and guidelines on land use. Wherever possible, these need to be backed by regulatory power in the form of agricultural land reserves, regional growth strategies, and other tools. Each community will be starting from a different foundation for this work. Some will have extensive governance systems in place that may just need updating or refining to address the opportunities that AU poses. Other regions may have few plans or controls and will need to develop them over time.

Community master plans. Every community has a range of planning and regulatory documents. These can incorporate goals, guidelines, and strategies of AU to establish a strong foundation for promoting sustainable food systems within the community. At this scale, preferred locations for food hubs or precincts can be identified, along with strategies for integrating development and agriculture in key areas.

Provincial or state agricultural plans and agencies. Most provinces or states that have any significant amount of their economy or land base devoted to agriculture have a range of agricultural plans and government agencies devoted to agriculture. Unfortunately, these plans and agency mandates consistently fail to address "food" as their primary focus and instead tend to focus on commodity agriculture for export. While commodity exports are important to the economy, the failure to move the focus from agriculture to food results in many missed opportunities and the undermining of the local sustainable food agenda. Refining the focus and mandate of our agricultural plans and agencies is important to making progress on sustainable agricultural and economic development.

Sustainable agri-food policy and strategies. The promotion of sustainable food systems within cities requires an approach coordinated to many aspects of the city's economy, infrastructure, plans, and policies. The development of a food policy council can create a multi-stakeholder group of knowledgeable individuals representing both knowledge areas and key institutions working in the territory of food, who can work together to shape a path to increased sustainability in the food system. Because of the complexity of the issues and the need to choreograph many discussions on food, an effective initial focus of work in a city is to create a municipal sustainable food system strategy. This strategy can address many issues, identify and engage stakeholders, create partnerships, identify goals, and initiate projects. A strategy can also assist in establishing financial plans to support ongoing work.

Artisan and urban agriculture initiatives. As noted many times in this book, new and refined approaches to agriculture and food systems are needed to optimize value and food production in urban areas. Farmers practising conventional industrial approaches to farming may not be interested in the learning and restructuring required to develop profitable, artisan-agriculture businesses. On the other hand, many urban dwellers will benefit from education on how to effectively grow food in the challenging gardening environments of a city. A range of initiatives can be pursued to support both streams of work.

Urban-edge development strategies. Farmland at the edge of a city can frequently be an area of conflict between the dual goals of development and agriculture. Each community will have a different starting point for these conflicts. A range of opportunities can exist where development and farmland have to coexist, as discussed earlier in this book. AU as an approach to development can offer alternatives to permit development in some areas while maintaining or even enhancing the food economy in the community.

AU development guidelines. Where a community wants to promote food as a central part of their neighbourhoods or new developments, creating a set of design guidelines based on the principles and approaches of AU can greatly assist in establishing realistic expectations, identifying and addressing issues, and ensuring sustainable food-system objectives shape the design of new development.

Academic education and research. Incorporating research and concept development into the academic work being done on both agriculture and city planning and design will yield many benefits to a community. Academics and students have more resources and a greater capacity to research and develop innovative solutions in sustainable food systems than do most practitioners in planning, design or the food and agriculture industry. Projects that promote collaboration across institutions and permit universities and colleges to work with practitioners bring benefits to all.

This list serves merely as a starting point, and its suggestions can be followed in any sequence, depending on where each community is starting from, what resources are available, and what champions exist to lead the work.

For a Neighbourhood or Development Plan

Because AU is focused on action that can be taken at a city or neighbourhood scale, it is well suited to integration into the planning, design, and development process. The following outlines six suggested steps or areas of action that can be considered in a planning or development project:

Assessing sustainable food systems. The first step is to complete a preliminary or detailed assessment of the areas' food system, including its physical elements, stakeholders, culture, economic performance, and history. This assessment will establish key reference points for understanding the context and key opportunities for a project.

Establishing the concept, strategic goals, and principles. The next step is to develop a compelling concept for the food dimension of the project, recognizing that there will be many factors in a neighbourhood or development project to consider besides sustainable food systems. Strategic goals and performance targets can be created to focus the energy of all involved and to define what "success" would look like after completion.

Identifying and casting stakeholders and partners. The process of identifying key stakeholders and building partnerships will begin at the outset of a project and continue throughout the life of the project. There are many jurisdictions involved in any neighourhood or development project, and all who have direct impact on key elements of a sustainable food system need to be involved in the process in order for the project to succeed. As the planning, design, and economic development work proceeds, specific institutions or businesses may be identified as critical to the success of a project. These need to be approached and encouraged to participate (tenant casting) as early as possible, particularly if a food hub or precinct is central to the project.

Developing design strategies and guidelines. The sustainable food agenda can influence the design of buildings, open space, streets, infrastructure, and many other elements. Principles and guidelines will need to be established to ensure that sustainable-food objectives and elements are not missed as the project proceeds through the stages of design, engineering, and construction. All participants in the process must understand the goals and the intent of AU as applied to the project to ensure that they will hold themselves responsible for the project's performance. Many projects have developed innovative goals and concepts but did not establish appropriate systems to ensure that these objectives and opportunities were ultimately manifest in the final project.

Making operational and maintenance agreements. The success of an AU neighbourhood will involve many ongoing commitments and partnerships. Public spaces need to be maintained, and there may be any number of collaborative ownership arrangements of land, facilities, or equipment. Food precincts will need ongoing management to ensure that they respond to changes in market forces. A stewardship role or group can be set up to serve as a round table where all involved stakeholders can work together to address issues and pursue opportunities as they arise.

Communicating and celebrating. There are many dimensions to an AU community. To keep community members engaged, it is important to communicate and celebrate the many facets and activities that take place over the course of the year. The scope of communication needs to be relatively wide, as the success of some of the businesses involved will depend on the reputation, culture, and experience of the community. Ultimately, communication and celebration of sustainable food systems is part of the larger cultural shift that is needed to raise awareness, provide alternatives, and achieve sustainability.

There are many steps that can be taken at the larger or local scales to promote sustainable food systems. This section has outlined a few. However, each community will be starting from a different place and will need to shape its goals in response to local characteristics and stakeholders. Over time, we can expect to see a rich diversity of approaches and outcomes associated with AU as many cities, towns, and development projects embrace food as a core principle of their design and quality of life.

Conclusion

A significant number of the assumptions about society, our economy and our planet that dominated our decisions in the 20th century are now being seen as problematic as we begin the 21st century. The approach we have to both cities and our food and agriculture systems today are built upon those misguided assumptions. The 21st century is already beginning to force us to reorient and change our approach to city building, food, and agriculture towards a more equitable, prosperous and sustainable future.

The convergent and ongoing movements of urban agriculture, slow food, agroecological approaches to farming, local food, and many others are all threads in the fabric of healthier food and agriculture systems in a sustainable society.

Agricultural Urbanism is a framework and approach to more fully integrate these movements and many others into the planning and design of our metropolitan regions in a manner that not only makes the food and agriculture system more sustainable, but our cities better places to live.

Community Visioning, Smithers BC.
Photo: Janine de la Salle

This book has endeavoured to explore a wide range of issues and ideas around how we can begin to address all aspects of a sustainable food system in every element of city design. As the 21st century unfolds and brings changes in climate, energy, water, technology, the economy and many other dimensions of life, the opportunities for how we can bring food more visibly back into our urban experience will likewise evolve. Agricultural Urbanism offers a structure for identifying issues and opportunities as well as thoughts on actions that we can take to create both sustainable food and agriculture systems and sustainable cities.

Afterword: Reflections on My Love Affair with Food ROBERT BARRS

Antonio, my 86-year-old Italian neighbour has just brought me what looks like a handful of crushed, dried leaves. He gestures for me to hold out my hand and he tips the contents of his calloused mitt into mine. "What's this?" I ask him, puzzled, seeing that there are some rice-like seeds among the brown leaves. "Rapini," he replies, rolling the R in his pronounced Italian accent, still strong after decades in Canada. I have no idea if rapini is good to eat, or when or how it should be planted, but I gratefully accept his gift and wander back to pull weeds.

Some people excel at their work, others at love or poetry or sport. Antonio may excel at all these things, but I know only that he is a damned fine gardener. This season, his tomatoes grew taller, faster, and more abundantly than mine, his figs are sweeter, his grapes riper, his beans taller. And all of this gave him great satisfaction.

It is not that his garden is pretty. In fact, I am currently trying to grow bamboo as fast as I can to hide the eyesore he calls a fence — a pair of sliding glass doors fastened together with fencing wire. No, it's not pretty. But it is productive. Every square foot of that small East Vancouver lot that isn't occupied by house or driveway is dedicated to the growing of food. He finds it quite amusing that my wife and I plant ornamentals — a lilac tree here, an evergreen clematis around the front gate, hostas and black-eyed Susans in garden beds surrounded by a small lawn. To Antonio, these things are luxuries, wastes of time and space, unnecessary distractions from the primary purpose of production.

On this late October day, the air is pungent with the smell of rotting figs — there are far too many to eat or even give away, even though I dried some this year with a friend's dehydrator. So, we rake them along with the fallen leaves into the garden beds, sending drunken yellow jackets tumbling after them into the pile, trusting them to enrich next year's harvest. Incredibly, on the last day of October, there are still a few raspberries to pick. Wet, juicy, and soft to the touch, they are still delicious. The apples are already eaten — there was only a handful on our young trees — next year there will be plenty

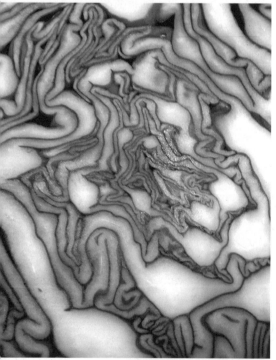

Cabbage.
Photo: Janine de la Salle

more. For now, the morning glory is winding its way up the trunks again, threatening to squeeze the life out of everything before winter draws nature's goodness down into the soil, protecting it for next year.

This year was a productive year in our small backyard garden. The sun shone often and sometimes fiercely, and yet there was still enough rain. We grew six varieties of tomatoes, two types of runner beans, never enough blueberries. It was a great year for Saskatoon berries, raspberries, figs, chard, lettuce, and radishes, and we had decent crops of spinach, rhubarb, herbs, green onions, snow peas and, yes, rrrapini. The strawberries didn't fare so well — too much shade from the bamboo, I think. Despite the heat, the eggplant never made it beyond knee-high. Despite a couple of failures, this year kept us in soft fruit and vegetables for many months while using only a fraction of a small lot. Certainly, we aren't self-sufficient, but it is surprising how much food came out of that cramped backyard.

This late October day seemed like a transition day — the real start of fall, when there is a noticeable change in the air. As I plucked the last raspberries and enjoyed some sweet grapes, I started thinking about my relationship with food in this very urban place that is Vancouver's east side. I started asking what can we do as individuals to influence this very large and complex food system that is the basis of so many livelihoods and has so much impact on the planet. What would help us become more responsible and engaged citizens when it comes to our food and agricultural system? And what would it take so I might be 86 and still growing much of my own food?

Reflections on a Love Affair With Food

The following are some things I try to be conscious about when buying and eating:

- Share seeds and compete for "best tomato" with my 86-year-old Italian neighbour while we sip last year's wine.

- Buy local, organic produce most of the time from a locally owned store that I walk to.

- Purchase free-range animal products when they are available and not exorbitantly priced, and prompt the store to stock them.

- Reduce my consumption of fish and meat (it helps that my wife is a vegetarian).

- Avoid unethical foods such as battery chicken eggs, veal, shark fin, farmed salmon, and fish from stocks that are threatened (seems to be many of them).

- Support local restaurateurs who are leading the way in the use of local, organic foods.

- Minimize the use of plastic bags and avoid foods that are over-packaged or unnecessarily packaged, figuring that the package won't add to the nutritional value much.

- Attend food celebrations and events.

- Fish cautiously for fish that I eat, following the regulations even though they are complex and frustrating sometimes.

- Write letters to the government about protecting threatened fish species and their habitat.

- Buy unloved vegetables not wanting them to go to waste.

- Attend farmers' markets because where else can you find purple potatoes and brandywine tomatoes?

- Buy from farmgate outlets when I can.

- Talk to my child about food and food ethics.

- Try to eat more slowly, but sometimes the food is too good to eat slowly.

- Remind my child to eat slowly and enjoy her food, but she reminds me that I eat fast.

- Love cheese in all its forms.

- My friend Jay says we should ban liquid cheese. I agree.

- Contemplate the magic that is photosynthesis, the only true productivity in the world.

Our Food Culture

If we define culture as the expression of a set of values, beliefs, and practices through which we understand and define our relationship with the world, then we can see that our relationship with food is inextricably part of our culture. In fact, the word "culture" comes from the Latin cultura, which stems from colere, meaning "to cultivate." This etymological relationship highlights the profound relationship between food and culture. It is easy to see how the Italian, Chinese, or French cultures are largely defined by their relationship with food. In North America, perhaps because we are immersed in it, or perhaps because we have so alienated ourselves from the essence and source of our food, it is somehow harder to see and understand the importance of food to our culture.

Obvious or not, our relationship with food is not only a large part of our culture, but our food culture also defines our relationship to the natural world. With the exception of northern families for whom wild food and foraging are still important sources of food, for most of us this means the agri-food system.

If we want to ensure a more sustainable relationship with food and indeed with the planet, we must cultivate a new food culture. Not only must we expose and celebrate aspects of the food system in a revitalized public realm. But we must also start to appreciate food more — not only for its taste and beauty (undoubtedly essential), but also for how it was grown, how it was killed, by whom and for whom it was prepared, and how its waste will be dealt with.

Chefs, farmers, planners, politicians, designers, and citizens – we all have a role to play in shaping and participating in this new food culture. Every decision that we make about what, where, and how to eat is part of that contribution. Local governments are playing an increasingly important role in facilitating those decisions by providing opportunities for education, celebration, spaces to grow and learn, and sometimes materials and equipment.

This new food culture, which is already gaining ground in many parts of the continent, will help reinforce who we are and what our values are. Hopefully, we will no longer merely be unconscious consumers, we will be fully aware tasters, revelling in the experience of soil and sunlight, appreciating the magic of photosynthesis, and training another generation in the politics and practicalities of food.

As the warmth of the October afternoon recedes, Antonio jolts me out of my daydreaming with a hearty Italian greeting. This time he hands me a glass of his homemade wine, and we sit enjoying his fine vintage — are those notes of blackberry, hints of lychee, or overtones of backyard tomato and fig, perhaps?

About the Editors and Contributors

SAAB Story

It was a typical cold and wet Vancouver winter morning as Mark and I steered down Oak Street in a SAAB, out to the Southlands site for a meeting with the community planning team. We were discussing the Southlands project, a private residential development that would see two-thirds of the 538-acre site protected for agriculture and wildlife habitat.

We knew we were working on something special, something new– a way to address the increasing growth pressure in our region while capturing all of the economic, ecological, and social value of building strong, local-food systems. The world-renowned team of Duany Playter-Zyberk (DPZ), founders of the New Urbanism movement was coming in a few short weeks to run an intensive design workshop to produce the first plans for the site. We realized that we needed to harness the design power of this team and direct it toward planning a site that truly and genuinely integrated agriculture, recreation, wildlife, and residential development. So, we asked ourselves, what exactly is the backbone for Southlands? What will make it special and stand out from those development projects that do not consider putting over 200 acres of farmland in trust and connecting urbanism to agriculture? As the SAAB approached the turn-off onto 56th Street, we had an a-ha! moment: the term "Agricultural Urbanism" landed in our laps, and we knew it was the right name for this new approach. Since then, AU has taken on a life of its own and has been used in other DPZ projects, has become the centrepiece of master's thesis work, has been beaten up at regional discussions on how to plan for the edge, and more.

Many people have contributed to the evolution of the concept, and we're sure that it will continue to be a collaborative effort in exploring new strategies for planning for sustainable food and agriculture systems for cities.

Janine de la Salle

HB Lanarc | Director of Food and Agriculture Systems Planning: BA, MA

Janine was born and raised in Armstrong, a small agricultural town in the interior of BC. After working on an organic farm and a trip to Cuba, Janine became part of the legions of people studying urban agriculture and searching for ideas and solutions for how to bring these systems into the North American context.

Janine is now one of Western Canada's leading professionals in the theory and practice of sustainable food and agriculture systems and is the Director of the Food and Agriculture System Planning practice at HB Lanarc Consultants. With a master of arts in international development in food security and urban agriculture and years of experience in the non-profit and private sectors, Janine brings food security and sustainability into focus for decision-makers. Janine works with communities, non-profit organizations, local governments, and developers to create food and agriculture system strategies, planning and design opportunities for food, and progressive food policy. She teaches and speaks about sustainable food and agriculture systems and is a long-standing member of the Vancouver Food Policy Council. In recognition of this work Janine has recently been awarded the CIP President's award for Young Planners (2010).

Mark Holland

HB Lanarc | Principal   Senior Planner: BLArch, MSc, MCIP, LEED

A member of a homesteading family, Mark Holland grew up in a log cabin in the woods. He learned about food at an early age, working with his parents through the seasons to grow and preserve the majority of what they ate each year. As a youth, he worked both in his grandparents' organic garden and in the industrial dairy, chicken, and hay farms in the British Columbian farming valley where he lived. Because of his many years of education and travel, as well as to his memories of an aching back from years of rock picking, weeding, haying, and harvesting fruit and vegetables, he is now an urbanite and a respectful champion of local food and farmers.

Mark is a LEED accredited professional planner who holds degrees in both landscape architecture and community and regional planning. He is also cofounder of HB Lanarc Consultants, one of Canada's leading sustainable development planning and community design firms. His consulting work has focused on integrating sustainability principles into both local government and the mainstream development industry to assist teams in finding cost-effective ways of developing in a more sustainable manner.

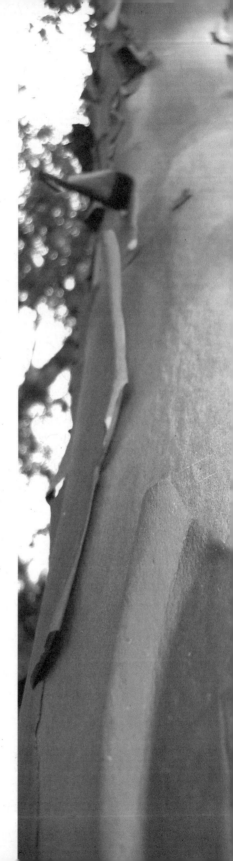

Mark has served as both a city planner and the founder and first manager of the city of Vancouver's sustainability office. His current work with local government focuses on city-wide sustainable development strategies for both small and large cities across North America, including introducing them to comprehensive sustainable food system agendas. Mark is known for moving forward planning and development innovations such as sustainable urban food systems, and has been a leader in frameworks and pragmatic applications of sustainability since the 1990s.

Mark was recognized for his leadership in the planning profession and awarded 2010 Planner of the Year by the Planning Institute of BC

About HB Lanarc

HB Lanarc is a leading planning and design firm that works to create complete, attractive, ecologically resilient, and prosperous communities in British Columbia and across North America. Our mission is to produce planning and design solutions for a sustainable future. HB Lanarc approaches sustainability through a pragmatic, idealist perspective, balancing the desired future with practical strategies for achieving these goals.

To bring about the shift towards sustainable communities, HB Lanarc has a full-service "green solutions" workshop, staffed with dozens of planners, landscape architects, and related professionals in fields as diverse as community engagement, sustainable buildings, renewable energy, greenhouse gas reduction, food systems, public policy, and information technology. The company supports projects from the earliest visioning stages through to construction drawings, with sustainable values and practices hard-wired into every step.

Visit us at www.hblanarc.ca

Contributors
(in alphabetical order)

Robert Barrs
HB Lanarc Senior Planner: BSc, MSc, MCIP, LEED

Rob Barrs is co-founder & principal of HB Lanarc Consultants Ltd., a planning and design consulting firm that focuses on sustainable communities. He is a LEED® accredited planner, a member of the Canadian Institute of Planners, and holds degrees in both Geology/Geophysics and Community & Regional Planning. Rob's passion is to help accelerate the transition to highly livable, sustainable communities. As such, he works closely with communities, development teams, governments and NGOs to identify practical, implementable solutions to the challenges facing these organizations. His experience as a planning consultant has included extensive work leading multidisciplinary teams through complex projects including official community plans, neighbourhood plans, sustainability strategies and sustainable development projects. Rob's research and writing has covered a broad range of topics including high performance buildings, tax strategies for

greening municipalities, and environmental stewardship. He recently led studies in residential intensification best practices, transit-oriented development, green building incentives and eco-industrial networking. Rob served on the board of directors of Smart Growth BC from 2001 to 2007 and was chair of the board from 2006 to 2007. He is currently the lead consultant and project manager for the National Capital Region's Choosing our Future process that will lead to a long term sustainability and resilience plan for the region.

Steven Clarke
HB Lanarc, Senior Landscape Architect, Adjunct Professor, UBC: CSLA, BCSLA, MLArch, BEnvD

Steven rejoined HB Lanarc with over sixteen years' experience in private practice as a landscape architect. He has worked in offices in Winnipeg, Nanaimo, and Vancouver, where he gained local and international design experience during collaboration and project management on multidisciplinary teams.

Steven's current focus is on sustainable landscape design and construction. His experience includes designing for urban trees, stormwater management, and using green roofs and living wall technologies. His previous research includes infrastructure and the ways in which it is designed into the built environment.

In 2005, Steven joined the Landscape Architecture Program at the University of British Columbia where he is an adjunct professor. In 2008, he received recognition from the University of British Columbia SEEDS program for his contribution to the Landscape Architecture Design/Build project, located on campus.

Patrick Condon
University of British Columbia Professor,
LANDSCAPE ARCHITECTURE: B.Sc. M.L.A
[University of Massachusetts] ASLA

Professor Patrick Condon has over twenty-five years' experience in sustainable urban design, first as a professional city planner and then as a teacher and researcher. He started his academic career in 1985 at the University of Minnesota, moving to the University of British Columbia in 1992, acting first as the director of the Landscape Architecture program and later as the James Taylor Chair in Landscape and Livable Environments.

In that capacity, he has worked to advance sustainable urban design in scores of jurisdictions, both in Canada and abroad. He has lectured widely and is the author of several books, most recently Design Charrettes for Sustainable Communities, 2008, and Seven Rules for Sustainable Communities, 2010, both published by Island Press.

He has successfully focused attention on how to make systemic change in the way cities are built and operated, notably in his East Clayton project in Surrey, BC, which precipitated a number of systemic changes in all parts of that city. Among these systemic changes was the implementation of an infiltration storm drainage standard and a blanket allowance for secondary suites.

He is currently focused on the Sustainability by Design project, a vision for a sustainable Vancouver Region of four million people, in the hopes that similar changes might be implemented at the regional scale.

He is now a senior researcher with the UBC Design Centre for Sustainability, an urban design think tank that evolved from the original efforts of the Chair and now employs over a dozen researchers.

Kelsey Cramer

HB Lanarc Landscape Designer: BA, MLA

Kelsey's experience comes from the fields of biology and restoration ecology. She has worked for both academic and public sectors in restoration-based research and invasive-species management. Her experience, which includes volunteer participation in community restoration initiatives, led her to pursue a master's degree in landscape architecture with the goal of designing opportunities for people in the urban realm to engage with nature.

Her definition of nature includes the processes of growing and recycling food. Working with HB Lanarc, she has gained experience on a diverse range of projects, including water conservation, parks and trails planning, and site-scale design.

Don Crockett

HB Lanarc, Principal, Landscape Architect | M. Land. Arch., B. Env. Studies, BCSLA, CSLA

Don is a registered landscape architect with nearly 20 years experience in private consulting and municipal settings, with an emphasis on Parks, Landscape, and Urban Design. Don has developed exceptional computer and graphic skills to provide visualizations of complex planning and design scenarios, either in computer generated photo-realism, or more traditional hand drawn renderings to creatively convey design and planning scenarios. Don has provided detail design and visualization services for ALRT transportation and urban design projects in Richmond and Coquitlam.

Based in HB Lanarc's Port Moody and Vancouver Offices, Don has been providing planning and design services to municipalities in the Lower Mainland and various locations throughout the province

Jill de la Salle
Community Activist

Jill is a community activist in Armstrong, BC. As a retired teacher of thirty years, Jill is an active community member working with others to build trail systems and improve recreation opportunities in and around Armstrong. Recently, Jill collaborated with other community members in setting up the Armstrong Food Initiative that has established a community garden and food exchange in the town. For the past several years, Jill and her husband, Harvey, have worked with gleaners, reclaiming waste harvest from farms and cleaning and processing the vegetables into soup stock for people in need.

Patricia Fleming
Executive Director, Delta Earthwise Society

Patricia Fleming is Executive Director of the Earthwise Society, a not-for-profit organization promoting sustainability through education. Fleming holds professional degrees in Landscape Architecture (BLA) and Community Planning (MA). Before her involvement with Earthwise, Fleming taught Landscape Design at Kwantlen University College and worked for many years in the private sector designing gardens based on the principles of ecology. Fleming has designed a number of public demonstration gardens including the award winning Brown Street Earthwise Garden, the McKitrick Garden in North Delta, and the Boundary Bay Earthwise Garden in Tsawwassen. In recent years, Fleming has taken a leadership role in implementing the Earthwise Farm, an organic demonstration farm at the Boundary Bay Earthwise Garden site. The Earthwise Farm involves students of all ages in learning about food from field to table. Fleming sees her involvement with Earthwise as a chance to make a positive contribution to the community.

Bud Fraser
HB Lanarc, Senior Engineer: MSc, Peng

Bud has eighteen years of combined engineering, project management, and research experience in Canada, Europe, and Asia. With a background in electrical engineering, Bud engineered communication systems for MDI/Motorola in many locations worldwide from 1988 to 1994, including some of the first wireless data networks.

Since 1997, Bud has focused his work on environmental and sustainability projects, developing and implementing innovative waste management technology, and integrating technical aspects such as biological processes with information technology. His role at HB Lanarc focuses on strategic and integrated technical approaches to buildings, infrastructure systems, and resources that include water, wastewater, solid waste, and energy, with a strong project management component. Most recently, Bud has been involved in the development of green buildings, energy and infrastructure workshops, and strategies for developers and municipalities.

Joaquin Karakas
HB Lanarc, Planner, Urban Designer: BA, MA, MCIP

Joaquin is an urban design planner with over three years of professional urban design and planning experience, including project management, the preparation of detailed site and concept plans, the development of urban design guidelines, housing research, policy and typology development, and public event and design workshop facilitation.

Joaquin has worked with a variety of clients in a range of contexts from large urban centres, to transforming suburban centres, to small, rural, resource- and tourism-based communities. Joaquin is a full member of the Canadian Institute of Planners and a current member of the Vancouver City Planning Commission.

Peter Ladner
Simon Fraser University, Associate

Peter Ladner is a former politician and business owner who is currently a fellow at the Simon Fraser University Centre for Dialogue. He was first elected to Vancouver City Council in 2002 and re-elected in 2005. He ran unsuccessfully for mayor as the NPA candidate in 2008. As a city councillor, he was the city budget chair, sat on the TransLink Board, and was vice chair of the Metro Vancouver board of mayors and councillors from around the Lower Mainland.

Peter has been publisher, president, and part owner of the Business in Vancouver Media Group, which he co-founded by establishing the award-winning Business in Vancouver weekly newspaper in 1989. In 1999 he was a finalist in the Ernst & Young Entrepreneur of the Year awards in his business category. He has more than thirty-five years of journalistic experience in print, radio, and television and is a frequent speaker on business and community issues.

His community and business experience includes participation in the Vancouver City Planning Commission and the Capital Campaign for the Vancouver Public Library and the Central Valley Greenway. He has also served on the boards of Leadership Vancouver, International Centre for Sustainable Cities, The UBC Alumni

Association, New Media BC, the Forum for Women Entrepreneurs, Jumpstart Dance Company, and the Association of Area Business Publications. He is the honorary chair of the Subaru Vancouver International Half-Iron and Sprint Triathlon and a member of the national board of Natural Step Canada.

Peter is a fourth-generation British Columbian. The town of Ladner is named after his great-grandfather. He lives in Kitsilano with his wife, Erica and they have four children. He is a long-time commuter cyclist as well as a keen runner, skier, kayaker, and singer. He is a former age-group record holder for the 50-kilometre Knee-Knackering North Shore Trail Run.

Edward Porter
EKISTICS Urban Designer, Project Manager

Edward is an Urban Designer and Project Manager with EKISTICS Town Planning, a Vancouver, BC-based multi-disciplinary planning & design firm. His Master's thesis in Landscape Architecture at the University of British Columbia's Faculty of Agricultural Sciences explored design opportunities presented by the deliberate integration of liveable neighbourhoods and working agricultural landscapes.

Born and raised in Columbia, Tennessee, Edward's interest in AU has grown from his own childhood experiences, witnessing the loss of productive agricultural land – and the culture of local food systems – at the hand of poorly-planned urban and suburban growth.

An early career in land conservation and program development with the Nature Conservancy in Arlington, Virginia introduced many of the collaborative and design-based approaches to capacity-building and land protection he later explored in the context of agricultural conservation. More specifically, the successful approach of the USAID Parks in Peril program inspired his pragmatic exploration of urbanization and its responsibility to leverage social and economic investment in the stewardship of local food systems.

In addition to hands-on experience in habitat restoration-based farm planning and management on his family's farm in Williamsport, Tennessee, Edward completed the organic farming pilot internship at the University of British Columbia' Centre for Sustainable Food Systems during the summer of 2006 and, more recently spent the 2009 growing season as an intern with Michael Ableman at Foxglove Farm on Salt Spring Island, BC. Returning to his urban design career, Edward continues to engage colleagues and clients in the fundamental questions of AU.

Kent Mullinix
Institute for Sustainable Horticulture, Kwantlen Polytechnic University

Kent Mullinix joined the Institute for Sustainable Horticulture (ISH) at Kwantlen University in British Columbia, Canada, in 2007. He is the director of Sustainable Agriculture and Food Security and is engaged in research and development to advance sustainable agricultural practice and agri-food systems. Before joining ISH, Kent held the Endowed Joint Chair in Pomology and was an associate professor in the Department of Horticulture and Landscape Architecture at Washington State University. He was concurrently the director of agriculture programs at Wenatchee Valley College. Kent was a horticulture research specialist (fruit and nut crops) for the universities of Missouri, Minnesota, and Kentucky. His specific areas of scholarly interest and work include development of sustainable crop production methods, development of sustainable bio-regional agri-food systems (including urban and peri-urban agriculture), agriculture education programming, and family-based agriculture revitalization as a critical element of sustainable agriculture and community.

Kent has developed many technical, workforce and undergraduate education programs and is currently leading the development of a curriculum for a BSc program in sustainable agri-food systems at Kwantlen University. He has developed and taught many agriculture courses, including plant science, soil management, ecologically based pest management, pomology, world trends in sustainable agriculture and food systems. He was also the founding director of the Institute for Rural Innovation and Stewardship (IRIS) in North Central Washington, the objective of which is to advance family-based agriculture, predicated upon environmental stewardship and community sustainability. Mullinix has authored numerous scientific, technical, educational, and lay publications and is frequently invited to speak on topics related to sustainable agri-food systems and deciduous tree fruit production.

Kent has lived and worked on a diversified family farm in central Missouri, and has owned and operated a pear orchard on the eastern slopes of the Cascade Mountains. Kent lives with his spouse of 31 years, Shauna, daughter Noelle and son Nathan in Vancouver, BC.

Bob Ransford
Counterpoint Communications

Bob Ransford is a public affairs and urban design consultant specializing in navigating the complex public processes surrounding urban development and land-use challenges. At Counterpoint Communications, he strives to combine effective public process, smart land-use principles and leading-edge urban design to add extra value to urban development projects. For a number of years he has written a regular, bi-weekly column on urban development and housing issues for the Vancouver Sun daily newspaper.

Growing up in the Vancouver suburb of Richmond, British Columbia, Bob worked in his family's small-scale market garden and helped sell the bounty of their harvest at a roadside stand.

He has been closely involved as a consultant to Century Group in their planning of the Southlands neighbourhood in Tsawwassen, British Columbia — a plan that fully embraces the principles of AU.

He is a former commissioner on the City of Vancouver's Planning Commission and has sat on the city's urban design panel. He is currently the president of Smart Growth BC, the country's leading advocacy organization championing compact, green, and diverse communities as a cornerstone of sustainability.

Bob also has a long record of volunteer service in the community, having sat on a number of boards of non-profit organizations, including that of Vancouver Farmers' Markets.

Appendices

Appendix A: Design Ideas and Considerations for Urban Agriculture

This appendix details design ideas and considerations for a range of urban spaces from rooftops to parks.

ROOFTOPS

In its most basic form, green roofs are rooftops that have some form of substrate (that is, soil or growing medium) and some type of plant life. Within the category of green roofs there are intensive (rooftop gardens) and extensive (green roofs). The main difference between the two is access. Low or no-access green roofs are mostly extensive, not intended for use and have limited access, and have a thin layer of lightweight soil approximately 8 to 25 centimetres, 3 to 10 inches, deep and use self-contained plantings such as sedums. Extensive rooftops are also referred to as eco-roofs, living roofs, green roofs, or sod or grass roofs.[95]

DIFFERENCES BETWEEN EXTENSIVE AND INTENSIVE GREEN ROOFS [96]

Extensive, non-agricultural green roofs are generally designed for:

- Stormwater management.

- Improved microclimate.

- Wildlife habitat for butterflies, birds, and insects.

- Energy-efficiency.

- Aesthetics (views from units above roof).

- LEED for New Construction credits.

Intensive agricultural green roofs (rooftop gardens) are designed for:

- Food production.

- Active recreation.

- Re-using waste (compost, stormwater).

- Educational and social opportunities.

- LEED for Neighbourhood Development credits

Intensive green roofs have soil depths ranging from 25 to 100 centimetres (10 to 40 inches) and can be designed to support a wide range of plantings, including shrubs, perennials, vines, and trees. There are also extreme cases of soil depths on intensive green roofs that push the range to 150 centimetres (60 inches). See table A1 for more information on soil depths and plant types.

Rooftops provide a range of urban agriculture opportunities, from beds of soil covering most of the roof installed at the time of construction to simple containers added after a building has been completed. Variations on green roofs include:[97]

- Semi-intensive roofs are lightweight rooftop gardens, soil depth of 10 to 80 centimetres, 4 to 31 inches, similar to extensive roofs but requiring more maintenance and irrigation.

- Intensive roofs are traditional rooftop gardens that use deeper layers of soil 35 to one 100 centimetres ,40 to 44 inches, and support shrubs and trees.

- Building roof decks with gardens are commonly seen in mixed-use and terraced developments. A single building may possess multiple roofing elevations and, as a result, have several different roof decks.

- Courtyard roof decks with gardens are often located over a parkade or commercial space. The courtyard is generally surrounded by residential or commercial suites and is accessed either from the deck by stairs, elevator, or escalator, or from adjacent spaces or buildings.

■ Garage roof decks with gardens are common in both commercial and multifamily developments.

■ Promenade roof decks are passageways that often provide an alternative to an interior corridor. They can be found connecting buildings or partially bound by them.

Table A1 describes design ideas and considerations for urban agriculture on intensive rooftops.

Table A1 Rooftops: Design Ideas and Considerations

Design Idea	Design Considerations
INTENSIVE GREEN ROOF FOR GARDENS	Cover the entire roof with soil deep enough to plant a successful food garden. This area can be given a basic design structure and then left flexible so that strata councils can manage its development into a productive landscape.
RAISED BEDS	Raised beds in any space that is on a roof or slab, either as a large flexible area or as individual beds. Raised beds can be designed to be universally accessible. These beds could be theme-based, with plantings specific to a culinary purpose such as a tea or pasta garden.
HERB GARDEN	Large or small herb garden on the roof or elsewhere to provide fresh herbs for residents. Herbs are already often included in ornamental landscapes.
ESPALIERED TREES	Opportunities to grow small *espaliered* fruit trees on the roof to complement existing railings and structures.
ARBOUR WITH VINES	Arbours with fruit-producing vines on the roof or integrated into residential units.
PERGOLA (TO COVER MECHANICALS)	Trellis structures with vines, shrubs, or trees to cover any mechanical structures on the roof.
COLD FRAMES	Cold frames to extend the growing season for the gardening community. Cold frames are essentially miniature greenhouses that provide a warmer micro-climate in cooler conditions and help to extend the growing season.

Design Idea	Design Considerations
EXTENSIVE GREEN ROOF	Extensive green roof designed for a range of plants to enhance a healthy site ecosystem and to provide a flower and seed base for bees and birds.
BEEHIVES	Space for beehives on roofs, especially on extensive green roofs where human access is limited. (For information on apiculture by-laws and resources, see the resource list.)
SMALL GREENHOUSE	Small structures on the roof, such as a small greenhouse, possibly integrated into the side of an elevator penthouse.
ROOF STEWARD STUDIO PLAN	Small studio space on the roof, which can be rented to a building resident at a lower rent in exchange for care of the rooftop garden (a roof steward).
GLASS ROOF (FULL ROOF COVERAGE)	Large greenhouse covering a significant amount of the roof that can be used by residents and even businesses (such as restaurants in a mixed-use building).
SUPPORT ELEMENTS	Support systems for the rooftop garden including a tool shed, a composting area for garden waste, and water for the gardens.
THEMED GARDENS	Consider planting communal edible garden beds that have themes such as a pasta garden that grows tomatoes, basil, garlic, and onions or a tea garden that grows a variety of plants that can be used to make tea. You could even grow a miniature vineyard to make wine.

BALCONIES

Balcony space can be optimized for urban agriculture in a number of ways. Because urban agriculture space will mostly consist of planters and containers, good-quality lightweight soil and adequate drainage is essential. The dimensions of planters, containers, and window boxes are highly variable and depend on the dimensions of the balcony and the type of plants to be grown there. For minimum container diameters by plant type, see Table A2. Loading capacity for intensive green roofs should be addressed at the building design stage.

Balconies.
Source: Drawing by Lees and Associates

Table A2 - Balconies

Design Idea	Design Considerations
PLANTERS AND CONTAINERS	Integration of large planters and containers into the design of balconies.
RAILINGS AND WINDOW BOXES	Integration of railings or window boxes into the building, ensuring their design is in keeping with the character of the building.
GREEN RAILINGS	Innovative designs for balcony railings to support vines or espaliered plants.
GARDENING SUPPORT ELEMENTS	Provision of balcony-scale support systems for gardening, including a hose bib, small composters (possibly custom-built), and possibly a small cabinet to hold tools.
VERTICAL STRUCTURES TO JOIN BALCONIES	Integrated structures such as latticework to vertically connect balconies. These structures could support vines and espaliered plants. Consider a vertical column of small glass structures to provide greenhouses for gardening.

AROUND BUILDINGS

There is a significant amount of underused space around buildings as well as in private yards and patios. Urban agriculture opportunities for these areas consist mostly of vertical growing, containers, espaliers, and arbours. Concentrate on east-, west-, and south-facing walls in order to maximize solar exposure (assuming no shade).

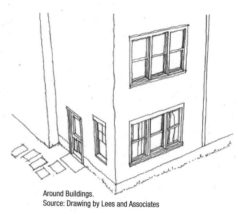

Around Buildings.
Source: Drawing by Lees and Associates

Table A3 - Around Buildings

Design Idea	Design Considerations
LIVING/GREEN WALL OR FENCE	Living wall with planting medium provided in a vertical context to create a wall of plants, either against the side of a building or as a freestanding fence or wall in the garden.
TIERED/STEPPED WALL	Stepped series of planting beds associated with a wall to support a wide range of agriculturally productive plants.
LEDGE ON WALL	Ledges on exterior walls to support planters containing edibles and ornamentals. Also consider trellis structures on the wall or a chain-link fence panel with clip-on shelves to support fruiting vines such as squash.
ESPALIER FRUIT/NUT TREES	A formal element in the garden comprised of espaliered fruit or nut trees against a wall, trellis, or fence.
TRELLIS	Trellis structures against or adjacent to walls, supporting vines or espaliered trees. Trellis structures can also be used as freestanding elements associated with fences, arbours, or gates.
ARBOURS	Arbour or pergola structure as a standalone structure or associated with a wall that can support vines or espaliered trees.
GREEN HOUSE	Hothouse or glasshouse structure associated with a building, or as a standalone structure, as in a conservatory, to support intensive gardening as well as other uses. In highly aggressive approaches to AU, multi-storey glasshouses could be offered with a relatively small ground footprint immediately adjacent or integrated into a building design.

Design Idea	Design Considerations
CONTAINERS	Large containers filled with a combination of productive and ornamental plants. A container garden offers significant flexibility to future gardeners.
BUILT- IN PLANTERS	Built-in planters integrated into the semi-public realm; e.g., buildings, patios, and landscape designs, and filled with food-productive plants. Also consider building large planters in the private realm so that residents may garden.
HERB AND VEGETABLE PLOTS	On residential building projects, consider garden plots (raised or at grade) for active food gardening by residents.
HANGING BASKETS	Food productive hanging baskets (seasonal or permanent).
PUBLIC ART & ORNAMENTAL STRUCTURES	Integrating of fruit-bearing vines or plants into ornamental or artistic structures in garden spaces.
NATIVE AND ASIAN MUSHROOM BED	For innovative and well-managed gardens, consider shade gardens that support a mushroom bed.
WINDOW BOXES	Window boxes that fit the building's character.
SUPPORT ELEMENTS	Compost areas, a tool shed support for significant garden areas, and hose bibs around the gardens. Also consider gardener needs such as the turning radius of wheelbarrows.
BUILT-IN OBELISKS	Attractive, built-in structures to support edible climbing plants.

INSIDE BUILDINGS: ATRIUMS, WALLS, ENTRANCEWAYS, & LOBBIES

In addition to the many opportunities on and around buildings, there are also opportunities to support productive landscapes and food production inside buildings.

Atrium
Source: Drawing by Lees and Associates

Table A4 - Inside Buildings: Atriums, Walls, Entranceways, & Lobbies

Design Idea	Design Considerations
HANGING GARDENS	Large hanging baskets can support a surprising amount of food productive plants.
INDOOR LIVING WALLS	Consider indoor living walls.
CONTAINERS	Container gardening indoors is a conventional practice with strong roots in productive landscapes. Examples include conservatories and citrus trees in containers.
KITCHEN HERB GARDEN	A kitchen garden space can be easily provided within units to offer an opportunity to grow fresh herbs. These areas can also provide places to start plants for outdoor gardens to extend the growing season.
ATRIUMS	Atriums in a residential unit can offer a range of opportunities akin to a small glasshouse or conservatory to support gardening.

COURTYARDS AND POCKET PARKS

Courtyards and pocket parks offer good opportunities for integrating urban agriculture. While courtyards are often constrained in terms of solar exposure are already heavily programmed, urban agriculture can be systematically designed and built within these parameters. Below are some ideas on how urban agriculture can be integrated into courtyards.

Table A5 - Courtyards & Pocket Parks

Design Idea	Design Considerations
EDIBLE LANDSCAPING	Consider edible plants such as fruit-bearing shrubs or herbs to add interest around the edge.
FRUIT TREES	Consider fruit trees and espaliered dwarf varieties for easy maintenance and harvesting.
RAISED BEDS AND CONTAINER GARDENS	Consider raised beds and containers planted with edibles.
GREEN WALLS/FENCES	Consider climbing structures along walls for fruit-bearing vines to grow on.
ARBOURS AND PERGOLAS	In social spaces and/or children's play areas, consider arbours and pergolas that support fruiting vines such as squash or grapes.

PARKS

Urban agriculture in the public realm, specifically in parks, represents significant opportunity for increasing the profile of urban agriculture, enhancing educational aspects of urban agriculture, and creating a neighbourhood food resource. Park areas are a major contributor to the amount of urban green space in a city and are used by a diverse cross-section of society, making them a valuable community resource for urban agriculture.

Park space is often highly contested by the public in terms of uses and programming. As public amenities, parks need to meet the needs of local residents and of the broader neighbourhood and community. Urban agriculture, therefore, needs to be integrated in a way that complements and enhances other planned uses of park space, such as formal garden beds. Urban agriculture also has to be integrated with a spirit of flexibility and adoptability in that urban agriculture opportunities need to be created, such as garden beds or planters for adoption, for future use by the residents.

In-ground planting in towns and cities must be carefully assessed in advance, because soils in cities vary greatly and may contain contaminants such as heavy metals and unsafe bacteria. Clearly, this represents a real barrier to the in-ground planting in parks. One solution is to use raised beds with clean soil from a composting centre. Considering that urban agriculture must occur in safe conditions (denoted by where appropriate in table A6), a short list of strategies for urban agriculture in parks is offered here:

- Gardening that uses clean soil in containers and planters.

- Creating raised beds with clean soil and an impermeable layer separating clean from existing soils.

- Replacing existing soil in strategic locations for the planting of food-producing species.

Table A6 - Parks

Design Idea	Design Considerations
FRUIT TREES	Plan an orchard of fruit trees set back from roads and main pedestrian ways to reduce problems associated with falling fruit. Species selection should consider rare and heritage varieties.
EDIBLE LANDSCAPING	Integrate food-productive plants with other landscaping; i.e., borders and in large plant beds (where appropriate).
URBAN AGRICULTURE IN UNDER-PROGRAMMED AREAS	Planning urban agriculture into under-programmed park areas such as neutral zones along sidewalks, playing fields, and fencing.
TIERED GARDEN	Tiered garden planted with food-productive plants in areas where the topography makes other uses challenging.
ARBOURS	Arbours planted with vines around resting areas.
GREEN FENCES	Fencing that enables climbing food-productive plants to create green fencing (where appropriate).
CLIMBING VINES	Climbing plants such as grapevines to conceal unsightly structures.
MEDICINAL HERB GARDEN	Plant a medicinal herb garden next to or integrated with social areas (where appropriate).
RAISED BEDS ALONG SIDEWALKS	Create interest along sidewalk areas by building raised beds planted with small shrubs, ground cover, and low perennials. Be sure to allow for the opening of car doors.
UNDERSTOREY CROPS AND EDIBLE GROUND COVER	Plant shade-tolerant, edible groundcover in and around groves of trees either in containers or in ground (where appropriate).

Design Idea	Design Considerations
LIVING ART	Use food-productive plants to create public art. Consider locating art pieces near social areas.
ESPALIER ON BUILDINGS	Espaliers on park buildings.
STRAW-BALE OR COB STRUCTURE	Cob or straw-bale structure to store tools or provide a focus for a social area.
MICROCLIMATE PLANTINGS AGAINST STRUCTURES	Take advantage of microclimate conditions against building structures and planting heat-loving plants like tomatoes either in containers or in ground (where appropriate).
CHILDREN'S GARDEN/ INTERGENERATIONAL GARDEN	Near play areas, consider a garden with edible plants kids can harvest. Also consider a "roots and shoots" intergenerational garden to provide opportunities for seniors to mix with youth and children.
PLANTERS ON WHEELS	Containers on wheels that are easily moveable and adaptive to new arrangements.
CUTTING GARDEN	Building a cutting garden where perennials, herbs, and medicinal plants are available to the neighbourhood. Make sure you label these plants.
HABITAT CREATION	Bird habitat, by installing birdhouses atop espalier supports or arbours.
ALLOTTED PLOTS	Personal-use plots.
HAMMOCKS	Locations for hammocks to provide resting areas for tired gardeners.

PLAZAS AND PUBLIC SQUARES

Plazas are often central areas where a number of different activities occur. They have an important role in creating social space and can be ideal venues for outdoor community events such as festivals and farmers' markets. As plazas are generally hardscape, urban agriculture should be intentionally designed into this space. While actual food production in a hardscape environment is limited, urban agriculture in plazas would be highly visible by the public and provide an excellent "education by exposure" forum.

Plazas and squares that are designed to hold farmers' markets and community celebrations create awareness around urban agriculture and rural agriculture and local foods, promote the urban agriculture program, and even sell foods that have been grown in the neighbourhood. Structural landscapes should be compatible with the needs of farmers' markets.

Plazas and squares are highly visible areas to integrate urban agriculture and businesses that are located next to the plaza may benefit. For example, businesses could adopt an urban agriculture program and take the lead in growing culinary herbs in containers or rooftops for use in their establishments.

Table A7 - Plazas & Public Squares

Design Idea	Design Considerations
FRUIT TREES	Plant a stand of soft-fruit trees in the plaza next to sitting areas.
CONTAINERS OR STEPPED BEDS	Edible garden centerpiece or attraction featuring plantings in containers or stepped beds.
ARBOURS/PERGOLAS	Arbours and pergolas can support fruiting vines and provide shade. Consider them around entranceways or sitting areas.
BERRY SHRUBS	Berry shrubs, such as blueberry, as edge plantings.
HERB GARDEN	A herb garden containing both edible herbs as well as ornamentals and aromatics that attract beneficial insects.
URBAN AGRICULTURE PUBLIC ART	Urban agriculture-oriented public art pieces in this hub of community activity.

STREETS

Generally considered the public realm, streetscapes are a central aspect of the functionality and aesthetics of a community. Urban agriculture in streetscapes creates interest in the space. Design should consider flexible spaces and the many uses of streets by pedestrians, drivers, and pets.

Table A8 - Streets

Design Idea	Design Considerations
ARBOURS ALONG OR OVER SIDEWALKS	Natural canopy over the sidewalk using arbours supporting vines.
LOW SHRUBS IN ROUNDABOUTS	Low-lying shrubs in roundabouts that have good light exposure.
PORTABLE GROW BIN	Portable grow bins that can be moved around and parked in car parking spots.
RAISED BEDS ON BOULEVARDS	Raised beds on boulevards for growing a wide variety of edibles and ornamentals. Consider raised-bed garden plots on the back boulevard or adjacent to property lines.
FRUIT-BEARING GROUNDCOVER	Fruit-bearing ground cover not necessarily for human consumption but to create interest along the sidewalk and potentially attract beneficial insects.
CONTAINER BEDS AROUND BASE OF TREES	To lower the health risk associated with pets and low-lying vegetation consider containers of edible plants around the base of trees.
ARBOUR OVER BUS STOPS	To create interest at pedestrian nodes, consider integrating living components such as arbours over bus stops.
LARGE CONTAINERS	Install large container beds for edibles and ornamentals along streets, in corner bulges, and in roundabouts.
PARTIALLY BURIED POTS	Where ground planting is not an option, consider partially burying containers and planters.
SWALE PLANTING	Plant moisture-loving plants such as mint or cranberry in swales and wet areas.

SCHOOLS AND COMMUNITY CENTRES

In school and in the community, hands-on education about preparing soils and planting, maintaining, and harvesting a variety of food plants is invaluable.

Table A9 - Schools & Community Centres

Design Idea	Design Considerations
TRELLIS	Trellis with vines to create shade and interest.
HERITAGE FRUIT ORCHARD	Heritage fruit orchard near school grounds and a social/study space within the orchard.
GREEN ROOF	Intensive or extensive green roof with a strong educational component.
GREENHOUSE ON ROOF OR OFF MAIN BUILDING STRUCTURE	Greenhouse associated with either the roof or the side of the structure.
CHECKERBOARD GARDEN	Checkerboard garden with trample-hardy groundcover such as thyme.
EDIBLE OR LIVING HEDGING AND FENCING	Shrubbery and other green fences to contain and create interest.
CONTAINERS	Containers of edible plants.
SCHOOL FOOD GARDEN	School food garden to be cared for by students and members of the community.

COMMUNITY DEMONSTRATION GARDEN

A community demonstration garden (CDG) is a way to showcase urban agriculture opportunities and to provide an educational resource for the community on urban agriculture methods and techniques. While it is important for a CDG to be designed with an urban agriculture program in mind, it is equally important that some flexibility be built into the design to allow the neighbourhood to establish a sense of connection to the garden. Design components should create structure around urban agriculture but also leave room for innovation by residents and community groups. Key components for the initial design of the CDG may include:

- Demonstration of urban agriculture opportunities relevant to the area (e.g., container and vertical gardening in high-density locations).

- Demonstration of urban agriculture techniques and practices, such as year-round harvest management, composting, and espaliers.

- Signage with information about the garden as well as upcoming special events, workshops, and other activities.

- Support structures that use recycled materials, solar power, rainwater, and (potentially) grey water.

- Social space.

Table A10 - Community Demonstration Garden

Design Idea	Design Considerations
GARDEN BEDS	A variety of garden beds like raised, mounded, and container beds. Also consider other aspects of the garden beds such as: Raised beds with an edge that can also provide seating. Pre-fab, recycled-plastic, amoeba-shaped beds with clear lids to be turned into cold frames.
INDIVIDUAL PLOTS	Individual garden plots for use by organizations.
MEDICINAL HERB GARDEN	Garden area that showcases medicinal herbs that have historical significance.
FRUIT OR NUT ORCHARDS	Variety of fruiting trees, including rare or heritage varieties.
VINEYARD	Small vineyard that could become a centre point for community celebration and wine-making.
PERIMETER OF HERBS	Perennial herb shrubs as a border and to provide cutting opportunities.
THREE-STAGE COMPOSTING	Compost facility to recycle organic matter and nutrients from garden trimmings. Also consider building the compost facility to also absorb household organic matter.
POTTING BENCH	Potting area associated with the compost.
PLACES TO SIT	Social, resting, and teaching spaces in the garden, providing something for everyone: ■ Stumps and stools. ■ Bales of straw. ■ Seating in fences. ■ Kissing nooks. ■ Logs. ■ Benches around the base of large trees.

Design Idea	Design Considerations
PLACE TO INFORMALLY SELL PRODUCE	Produce stand in or near the garden for selling surplus vegetables, fruits, and herbs. Establish an honour system and donate funds raised to the CDG for maintaining the garden.
ARBOURS	Consider arbours and vines at entranceways.
OUTDOOR COOKING FACILITY	Consider an outdoor cooking area with a freestanding adobe oven, BBQ, food preparation area, and feast table.
FEAST TABLE	Consider a large feast table near the main garden structure to provide an informal meeting area and dining table.
GARDEN FURNITURE	Garden furniture such as a feast table.
LONG COLD FRAME	Long cold frame as an architectural divider and to extend the growing season.
GREENHOUSE	Green house.
PUBLIC ART	Water features and sculptures.
SIGNAGE	Wide range of signage for the garden including: ■ Sign boards at the entrance that present the garden and post upcoming events. ■ Signage for stations on a self-guided tour. ■ Signs that tell what is in bloom and what needs to be done, or provide random facts, recipes, and more. ■ Community-scale posting boards ■ Plant, interpretive, and way-finding signs. ■ Educational scavenger-hunt signs. ■ Organic gardening info. ■ Food choices.
OUTDOOR CLASSROOM	Components for an outdoor classroom area, such as a weather-resistant chalk board and seating.
LIGHTING	Lighting that is not too invasive (e.g., low lighting on walkway) but that is safe, solar-powered, and strategically located around plants and features of interest.

Design Idea	Design Considerations
GATES	Several points of entry to the garden, such as a main entrance, garden-gnome gate, and secret gate. Characteristics of the gates and entranceways include: ■ Artistic, refined, and beautiful. ■ Using interesting natural materials such as driftwood. ■ Unlocked.
MAIN ENTRANCE	Main entrance with multiple features such as an information board, informal sales kiosk with lock box, self-guided tour sheets, arbour with vines, and bike rack.
FENCES	A variety of fencing to define the edge of the CDC: ■ Structures that divide spaces. ■ Made of living material such as edible hedging or espaliered trees. ■ A kissing nook. ■ Transparent fencing or wind block. ■ Mixed plants and structures. ■ Kid-friendly fences with a story on each picket.
BENCH AND STOOLS	Bench and stools to sit on while drinking coffee.
SURFACE MATERIALS	Consider compact crushed gravel or woodchips for walkways.
PLANT TO ATTRACT BIRDS AND INSECTS	Consider plantings that attract birds and insects such as bees and dragonflies.
GREEN SUPPORT BUILDING/GARDEN SHED	Consider a "green building" multiple-function structure for use as a tool-storage, processing, and learning facility. Also consider: ■ Demonstration balconies built into it. ■ Office space. ■ Composting toilet. ■ Green roof. ■ Size of about 37 to 46 square-meters, 400 to 500 square feet. ■ Garage door on one side. ■ Railings to demonstrate vertical-growing opportunities. ■ Interior communication boards. ■ Sink for washing vegetables. ■ Large, flat roof. ■ Rainwater capture.

Appendix B:

Platinum Certification for the Southeast False Creek Neighbourhood Development,
VANCOUVER BC

Southeast False Creek is described as "the greenest neighbourhood in North America", according to Tim Cole, Chair of the Board of Directors from the U.S. Green Building Council. In February 2010, SEFC was awarded more points than any other development worldwide, Southeast False Creek received the highest Platinum certification under the US Green Building Council's, LEED for Neighbourhood Development.

The Southeast False Creek neighbourhood rests on 80 acres of former industrial lands, situated on one of Vancouver's last remaining downtown waterfront sites. The development includes residential, live/work, retail, and office uses, as well as public amenities. When the entire site is completed, the Southeast False Creek neighbourhood will become home to an estimated 16,000 residents. This is a highly dense urban neighbourhood with 148 dwelling units/acre. Even with this high density, the site manages to include food growing and access to local food in the following ways:

- At least 30% of residences are required to have 24 square feet of access to growing spaces;

- Much of the growing spaces are accommodated through green roofs on the site;

- The site includes 24,000 square feet of a community demonstration garden;

- The neighbourhood is within a 10 minute walking distance from Thorton Park Farmers Market, which operates every Wednesday from June to October;

- The public plaza on the site, is designed to accommodate a future farmers' market, with water and electrical fixtures installed to accommodate this future use.

HB Lanarc and many other firms were involved in the planning and design of various elements of the neigbourhood. Specifically HB Lanarc has lead the two-phase urban agriculture strategy for the development.

PHASE 1: URBAN AGRICULTURE STRATEGY (2002)
The Strategy provided conceptual design guidance that has since informed many facets of the public and private realm. Crucially, it:

- Made the case for a designated demonstration garden to facilitate agricultural education

- Advocated for growing on rooftops and interstitial spaces within the development

- Outlined key management and community governance considerations to ensure that the potential of allotted growing space is maximized

PHASE 2: DESIGNING URBAN AGRICULTURE OPPORTUNITIES FOR SOUTHEAST FALSE CREEK (2009)

This document honed the priorities outlined in the Urban Agriculture Strategy. It provides:

- Design considerations – outlining requirements specific to various urban agriculture localities, including:
  - ☐ Rooftops; Balconies; Inside buildings; Courtyards; Parks; Plazas; Waterfront; Streets; Community Demonstration Garden – including programming opportunities

- Technical requirements – outlining growing, building structural and health considerations for these localities

- Management Strategies for urban agriculture applications in the public and private realm

- Designing Urban Agriculture Opportunities emphasizes:

- The layering of agricultural uses with other uses, including park spaces and other amenities. The goal is to create synergy between these issues, and reinforce urban agriculture as an appropriate component of a high density neighbourhood.

- Consider all growing opportunities, capitalizing on interstitial spaces

- Hardwiring urban agriculture opportunities into neighbourhoods right from construction – by providing suitable infrastructure and growing spaces.

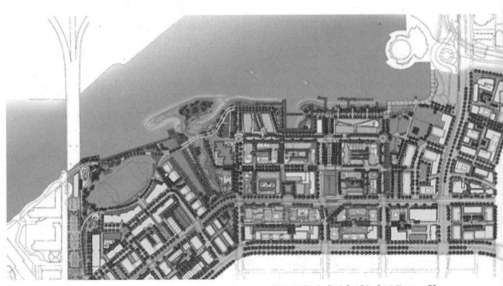

Illustrative Plan for South East False Creek, Vancouver BC.
Source: Courtesy of the City of Vancouver

Glossary

Anaerobic digestion – Is a process where in microorganisms break down biodegradable material in the absence of oxygen. Anaerobic digestion produces a methane-based biogas which is captured and used as a renewable energy source while at the same time reducing materials going into landfill sites. The by product of anaerobic digestion, the digestate, is nutrient rich and can be used for fertilizer.

100-mile diet – A eating regime that exclusively or predominantly includes food produced and/or raised within 100 miles of the point of consumption.

Agrarian – Relating to rural matters, a way of life that is connected to rural/agricultural areas.

Agribusiness human resources models – Federal programs designed to attract workers from outside the country to work in the agriculture sectors commonly as labourers.

Agricultural Urbanism – An emerging planning, policy, and design framework for integrating a wide range of sustainable food and agriculture system elements into a community at a site-, neighbourhood-, or on a city-wide scale. In short, it is a way of building a place around food.

Agricultural urbanist – An term used to describe a place such as a street or neighbourhood that has been planned and designed with an agricultural urbanism approach.

Algaculture – The large-scale production of algae for conversion into biofuels.

Anaerobically – A process that does not require oxygen, typically referring to metabolic processes.

Animal husbandry – The raising of domesticated farm animals.

Aquaponics – A closed system (e.g. Water tank) containing plants and aquatic animals that share a symbiotic relationship, providing food and cleaning functions.

Artisan agriculture – The type of agriculture that is compatible in and around cities.

Artisan food – Niche market, high-quality, whole foods hand prepared by experts often with fresh local and rare ingredients.

Biogas digestion – See anaerobic digestion.

Biological oxygen demand – BOD- Is a process for measuring the absorption rate of dissolved oxygen by the biological organisms in a body of water. BOD is often used to determine water quality in wastewater treatment plants.

Biomass – A source for alternative energy, is plant fibre used to produce power and/or heat.

Biosolids – They are nutrient-rich organic materials resulting from the treatment of domestic sewage in a treatment facility. When treated and processed, these residuals can be recycled and applied as fertilizer to improve and maintain productive soils and stimulate plant growth. (Canadian Water and Wastewater Association).

Biotechnology - Application of science or engineering to the use of living organisms or their parts or products, in natural or modified form. Covers a broad range of processes, from fermentation (e.g., use of yeast to make bread rise) to modern methods such as genetic engineering. (Parliament of Canada).

British Columbia's Agricultural Land Reserve – A provincial zone in which agriculture is recognized and protected as the priority use. Farming is encouraged and non-agricultural uses are controlled. (BC Climate Action Toolkit)

Buffer – A strip of land, fence, or border of trees, etc., between one use and another, which may or may not have trees and shrubs planted for screening purposes, designed to set apart one use area from another. An appropriate buffer may vary depending on uses, districts, size, etc., and shall be determined by the appropriate local board. (PD, Pomfret Township, N.Y.)

Carbon capture – Also referred to as carbon sequestration, a natural process whereby atmospheric carbon is transferred to a carbon storage reservoir such as soils, forests or oceans. May contribute to reducing atmospheric carbon dioxide concentrations. (Adapted from the Parliament of Canada).

Chemicalization – The process of adding synthetic chemicals. Often used to refer to the petroleum-based fertilizers, herbicides, and pesticides used in industrial agriculture.

CHP – Refers to "Combined Heat and Power" and is the simultaneous production of power and usable heat, that can improve efficiency from about 35 to 55%, to 80% compared to conventional power plants. These systems may be fueled by natural gas or biofuels (e.g., wood waste) and range in size from individual buildings to district energy systems. Also referred to as cogeneration. (BC Climate Action Toolkit)

Closed-loop – A self-sustaining system whereby wastes/outputs of one system element is used as a resource/input for another system element.

Cogeneration – See CHP.

Combustion – Burning.

Community-Supported Agriculture (CSA) – A farming and food distribution model that consists of community members supporting a farm operation so that growers and consumers provide mutual support and share the risks and benefits of local food production. It usually involves weekly to monthly delivery of vegetables and fruit, and sometimes dairy products and meat.

Compost tea – A liquid that is made by steeping compost in water, generally used as a fertilizer for plants.

Design development process – The steps taken to create a physical plan that focuses on the physical form through design and engineering work.

Digestate – A solid by-product of anaerobic digestion that can be used as fertilizer.

District energy system – A shared system whereby heat (and possibly cooling) is distributed from centralized plants by circulating water (or low-pressure steam) through underground piping to multiple buildings. (BC Climate Action Toolkit)

Ecogastronomy – A concept of the "slow food" philosophy, which recognizes the strong connections between food and the environment.

Farm unit – A given area of land that is operated as a farm. Farm units can be small (less than 0.4 hectares, one acre) or large (more than 80 hectares, 200 acres).

Figure-ground relationship – A way of perceiving shapes with a tendency to see parts of a visual field as solid, well-defined objects that stand out against a less distinct background.

Food desert – An urban area such as a neighbourhood that has no or grossly insufficient access to healthy, affordable, and culturally-appropriate foods for local residents.

Food miles – The distance an agricultural product is transported from point of production to point of consumption.

Food security – Access by all people at all times to enough food for an active, healthy life. Food security includes at a minimum the ready availability of nutritionally adequate and safe foods (approximately 2,000 kilocalorie /day/ capita; and an assured ability to acquire acceptable foods in socially acceptable ways (e.g., without resorting to emergency food supplies, scavenging, stealing, or other coping strategies.

Food sovereignty – An approach to food security that includes the philosophy around social justice and sustainability in the food system. The six pillars of food sovereignty are: 1) Focuses on food for people 2) values food providers 3) Localizes food systems 4)Puts Control Locally 5) Builds knowledge and skills 6) Works with nature. (Source: Food Secure Canada).

Foodprint – The amount of space required to produce the resources and assimilate the wastes associated with the food system.

Gasification – A method extracting energy from organic materials through converting carbon-based materials such as biomass, coal or petroleum into carbon monoxide and hydrogen to produce fuel.

Genetically modified organism – A plant, animal or micro-organism (bacteria, fungus, etc.) That has been produced through genetic engineering. In its regulatory instruments, Canada uses a broader definition, which is a GMO being, in particular, an organism that presents a new characteristic that has never been observed in that organism, regardless of the method used to obtain that new characteristic. (Parliament of Canada).

Geoexchange – The use of energy stored in the earth (and in some cases surface or ground water) to heat and cool individual homes, multi-unit residences, commercial spaces, or industrial facilities. (BC Climate Action Toolkit)

Gleaning – The practice of harvesting food that otherwise might go to waste and channelling it to humanitarian agencies.

Global hinterland – A theoretical concept to describe the modern development of large-scale, international trading systems for natural resources (i.e. petroleum, food, fibre, water, energy).

Greenhouse gas (GHG) emissions – Components of the atmosphere that contribute to the "greenhouse effect." Some greenhouse gases occur naturally, while others come from activities such as the burning of fossil fuel and coal. Greenhouse gases include water vapor, carbon dioxide, methane, nitrous oxide, and ozone. (BC Climate Action Toolkit)

Groundwater recharge – The natural process of infiltration and percolation of rainwater from land areas or streams through permeable soils into water-holding rocks that provide underground storage. (PD, California Planning Roundtable).

Human-scaled agricultural systems – Farming systems that are planned and designed to be operated through human labour and small machinery.

Hydroponics – The cultivation of plants in a nutrient solution rather than in soil.

Infiltration area – The area in which the downward movement or seepage of water from the surface to the subsoil and/or groundwater occurs. (Adapted from PD, Grand Traverse County, Michigan).

Large material flows – The concept of large volumes of resources such as power, water, waste being moved from resource areas to and from urban areas.

Local multiplier effect – The concept that the initial spending or investment in a product or service will lead to more consumption that generates more spending and often associated with the idea of spin-off industries.

Looped – See closed-loop.

Market transformation – Is a process where innovations are introduced into the marketplace and over time penetrate a large portion of the eligible market. The innovations that are introduced can drive greener economies and contribute to positive change towards sustainability.

Monocropped quarter section – Cultivation of a single plant species on a unit of farm land whose dimensions are ¼ mile by a ¼ mile.

New Urbanism – The process of reintegrating the components of modern life – housing, workplace, shopping, and recreation – into compact, pedestrian-friendly, mixed-use neighbourhoods linked by transit and set in a larger regional open space framework. Initially dubbed "neotraditional planning", the principles that define new urbanism can be applied successfully to infill and redevelopment sites within existing urbanized areas (PD – Congress for the New Urbanism).

NGO – A non-government organization.

Open loop – A system that relies on inputs and provides outputs to the external environment, and is therefore not self-correcting.

Organic agriculture – Type of agriculture based on strict respect for the natural relations and balances between soil, plants and animals (i.e. Animals nourish the soil, which nourishes plants), and a prohibition against the use of synthetic chemicals. The term "organic farming" is generally regulated and/or subject to standards defined by the industry (i.e. Producers, processors, etc.), governments, or both. (Adapted from the Parliament of Canada).

Peak oil – The point in time when global oil production is at its highest, after which production goes into irreversible decline. Many experts believe peak oil has already occurred or will soon occur within the next few years.

Pedestrian-shed – An area that is centered on a common destination. Pedestrian Sheds are applied to structure communities and are commonly separated into three types: Standard Pedestrian Shed, which is an average of about the distance of a five-minute walk at a leisurely pace; a Long Pedestrian Shed, which is an average of about a ten-minute walk at a leisurely pace, and is often used when a transit stop (bus or rail) is present or proposed as the common destination; and a Linear Pedestrian Shed, which is about half of a kilometre and elongated along an important mixed use corridor such as a main street. (Adapted from City of Hayward, CA)

Permaculture – A design approach that mimics patterns and relationships found in nature, while yielding an abundance of food, fibre, and energy for the provision of local needs. (Holmgren, 2002)

Photosynthesis – A process whereby plants, in the presence of light, manufacture their food and build stores of energy. (Natural Resources Canada).

Photovoltaics – Active solar panels that produce electricity. (BC Climate Action Toolkit).

Placemaking – A design strategy to create public spaces that are attractive, interesting, and vibrant. Architecture, landscape, and connectivity to surrounding areas play an important role in placemaking.

Policy development process – The steps taken to create policy that focuses on dealing with concepts and words.

Public realm - Publicly owned streets, sidewalks, rights-of-ways, parks and other publicly accessible open spaces, and public and civic buildings and facilities. (City of Burlington, ON).

Resilience – The ability of a system to undergo change in response to external forces while retaining its basic structure and function.

Slow food movement – A group of individuals, some of whom form part of an international member-supported organization called "Slow Food", working to defend biodiversity in the food supply, spread taste education and connect producers of foods with co-producers through events and initiatives.

SPIN farming – A vegetable farming system, usually in urban settings, that make it possible to earn significant income from land bases under an acre in size. It is considered non-technical, easy to learn, and inexpensive to implement (adapted from www.spinfarming.com).

Stormwater conveyance system – A system for treating and dispursing stormwater.

Thermal conversion – Processes where heat is the dominant mechanism to convert the biomass into another chemical form, such as biogas.

Thermal storage – A number of technologies used to store heat.

Transect – The range of land uses from the urban core out to the rural boundary. The transect is the core framework for New Urbanist town planning and brings a focus to the importance of context to planning and design.

Transitional spaces – Areas that are situated between two or more different land uses or programs.

Transnational agribusiness – The global market and resource scope of large-scale agricultural business operations.

Twin – The act of developing programs and partnerships that connect cities in North America to those in unindustrialized or newly industrializing countries.

Urban aquaculture – The hatching, raising, and breeding of fish or other aquatic plants or animals, in an urban setting, for sale or personal use. (Adapted from PD – Asheville, N.C.)

Vermicomposting – The use of worms to consume and convert organic waste into a nutrient-rich soil, often used as plant fertilizer.

Endnotes

[1] This is demonstrated by the increased programs for funding local governments to create the necessary tools in order to become more sustainable. In Canada the Federation of Canadian Municipalities has brought in the Green Municipal Fund that provides local governments with significant resources to undertake plans, studies, and projects that benefit the environment, local economies and quality of life. http://www.sustainablecommunities.fcm.ca/GMF. Further, in the US, the ICLEI Star Community Index program is establishing a voluntary rating system for local governments to assess their sustainability performance http://www.icleiusa.org/star

[2] George Orwell as quoted in: William Buford (2006) Heat: An Amateur's Adventures as Kitchen Slave, Line Cook, Pasta-Maker, and Apprentice to a Dante-Quoting Butcher in Tuscany. Random House: New York, Toronto.

[3] Steel, Carolyn (2009). Hungry City: How Food Shapes Our Lives. Vintage: London. Pp 7.

[4] Pawlick, Thomas F (2006). The End of Food: How the Food Industry is Destroying our Food Supply- And What You Can do About it. Greystone Books: Vancouver BC. Pp 15-34.

[5] About 70% of all antibiotics used in the United States are fed to healthy pigs, poultry, and beef cattle to promote growth and to compensate for the crowded, unsanitary conditions of intensive livestock operations. This contributes to the growth of antibiotic-resistant bacterial strains that cause serious illness in humans. Union of Concerned Scientists. Accessed Oct 11-09: http://www.ucsusa.org/assets/documents/catalyst/Catalyst-Spring02.pdf

[6] Statistics Canada(2004). Canadian Community Health Survey. Accessed November 3-09: http://www.statcan.ca/english/research/82-620-MIE/2005001/charts/child/chart2.htm

[7] Starky, Sheena (2005). The Obesity Epidemic in Canada. The Library of Parliament. Accessed March-08: http://www.parl.gc.ca/information/library/prbpubs/prb0511-e.htm#economictxt

[8] Other causes of the world food crisis include increased demand for food due to population growth and consumer demands as well as a decrease in supply due to land degradation and environmental conditions.

[9] As noted by Michael Pollan, major food corporations are researching new ways to combine corn-based food molecules in such a way that they are indigestible, therefore by-passing the fixed stomach problem, enabling people to buy more and more food, creating the ultimate industrial eater. Pollan, Michael (2006). Omnivores Dilemma: A Natural History of Four Meals. Penguin: New York, NY. Pp 94.

[10] "The global proportion of urban population increased from a mere 13 per cent in 1900 to 29 per cent in 1950 and, according to the 2005 Revision of World Urbanization Prospects, reached 49 per cent in 2005. Since the world is projected to continue to urbanize, 60 per cent of the global population is expected to live in cities by 2030." UN Department of Economic and Social Affairs: Population Division (2005). Accessed Nov 16-09: http://www.un.org/esa/population/publications/WUP2005/2005wup.htm

[11] Cruz, María Caridad, Roberto Sánchez Medina (2003). Agriculture in the City: A Key to Sustainability in Havana Cuba. Ian Randle & IDRC: Kingston, Jamaica.

[12] The Food and Agriculture Organization of the United Nations estimated in 2005 that global cereal production was about 2.2 billion tonnes, enough for over 2000 calories per day for everyone on the planet. (FAO as in Lang, Tim, Erik Millstone (2008). Atlas of Food: Who Eats What, Where, and Why. University of California Press: Berkeley.)

[13] Webber, Christopher, H. Scott Matthews (2008). Food-Miles and the Relative Climate Impacts of Food Choices in the United States. Environment, Science, and Technology. 42 (10), pp 3508–3513.

[14] Purvis in Pothukuchi, K. and Kaufman, J.L. (Spring 2000). The Food System: A Stranger to the Planning Field. American Planning Association. 66:2. Pp 113-124.

[15] Environment Canada (2008). Canada's Greenhouse Gas Emissions: Understanding the Trends, 1990-2006. Available on-line: http://www.ec.gc.ca/pdb/ghg/inventory_report/2008_trends/trends_eng.cfm#toc_1_2

[16] One hundred years ago the average person from a developed country ate significantly less meat than they do today with an average of 25 kg of meat per year compared to 80 kg today (FAO as in Steel 2009)

[17] Christian Peters, M.S. '02, Ph.D. '07 http://www.news.cornell.edu/stories/Oct07/diets.ag.footprint.sl.html

[18] Ipsos- Mori survey (1997). Kids Confused over Food Facts. Accessed Feb-08: http://www.ipsos-mori.com/researchpublications/researcharchive/poll.aspx?oItemId=2175

[19] Farmers' Markets Canada (2009). National Farmers' Market Impact Study. Available on-line: http://www.farmcentre.com/File.aspx?id=541aadd6-20ce-4324-8955-46a21ff0e95b

[20] The works of many authors have laid important ground work for understanding the modern context of food. In particular, the writing of authors such as Micheal Pollan, Vandanna Shiva, Thomas Pawlick, Wendell Berry, Frances Moore Lappe, Marion Nestle, and others have created a platform for change towards more sustainable food and agriculture systems.

[21] Ronald Wright in Homer-Dixon, T. (2009). Carbon Shift: How the Twin Crises of Oil Depletion and Climate Change Will Define the Future. Random House Canada.

[22] Purvis in Pothukuchi, K. and Kaufman, J.L. (Spring 2000). The Food System: A Stranger to the Planning Field. American Planning Association. 66:2. Pp 113-124.

[23] See the Economic Development Strategy for Comox BC that positions the agri-food industry as a key pillar of the strategy. Available on-line: http://www.investcomoxvalley.com/keySectors/agrifood.htm

[24] Sheena Starky (2005). The Obesity Epidemic in Canada. Library of Parliament. Available on-line http://www.parl.gc.ca/information/library/prbpubs/prb0511-e.htm

[25] Pothukuchi, K. and Kaufman, J.L. (Spring 2000). The Food System: A Stranger to the Planning Field. American Planning Association. 66:2. Pp 113-124.

[26] The Land Conservancy (2009). A Guide to Farmland Access Agreements. Available on-line: http://ffcf.bc.ca/programs/farm/Farmland Access Agreement Guide 2009 FINAL.pdf

[27] USDA (2009). Accessed October 15-09: http://www.ers.usda.gov/Briefing/farmstructure/Questions/aging.htm.

[28] CSR Wire (2009) Organic Valley Farmer-Owners Celebrate $528 Million in 2008 Sales While Keeping 58 Million Pounds of Synthetic Chemicals Off the Land. Accessed Sept-09: http://www.csrwire.com/press/press_release/20450-Organic-Valley-Farmer-Owners-Celebrate-528-Million-in-2008-Sales-While-Keeping-58-Million-Pounds-of-Synthetic-Chemicals-Off-the-Land

[29] Altieri, Miguel (1995). Agroecology: The Science of Sustainable Agriculture Second Edition. Westview Press, Boulder Colorado.

30 McDonough, William, Michael Braungart (2002). Cradle to Cradle: Remaking the Way We Make Things. North Point Press: New York. Pp 35.

31 For those not familiar with the scope of farming equipment that a typical farm may need, a quick peruse of something as simple as the Wikipedia list of farm equipment is an interesting start. http://en.wikipedia.org/wiki/List_of_farm_implements

32 Harris, Andrea, Murray Fulton (2000). Farm Machinery Co-operatives: An Idea Worth Sharing. Centre for the Study of Co-operatives University of Saskatchewan. Available on-line: http://www.usaskstudies.coop/pdf-files/Idea Worth Sharing.pdf

33 Mougeot, Luc (2006). Growing Better Cities: Urban Agriculture for Sustainable Development. IDRC: Ottawa. Pp xiv

34 Altieri, Miguel (1995). Agroecology: The Science of Sustainable Agriculture Second Edition. Westview Press, Boulder Colorado.

35 Mollison, Bill (1988). Permaculture, A Designers' Manual. Tagari, Tyalgum Australia.

36 Holmegren, David (2002). Permaculture: Principles and Pathways Beyond Sustainability. Holmgren Design Services: Victoria Australia.

37 Coleman, Elliot (1989). The Organic Grower: A Masters Manual of Tools and Techniques for the Home and Market Gardener. Chelsea Green Publishing Company: White River Junction, Vermont. Pp 21.

38 This number has been adjusted to reflect today's rates of exchange. Coleman, Elliot (1989). The Organic Grower: A Masters Manual of Tools and Techniques for the Home and Market Gardener. Chelsea Green Publishing Company: White River Junction, Vermont. Pp 22.

39 The Land Conservancy (2009). A Guide to Farmland Access Agreements. Available on-line: http://ffcf.bc.ca/programs/farm/Farmland Access Agreement Guide 2009 FINAL.pdf

40 Canada, the US, France and Spain, some of the most affluent countries, spend an average of $1,000 or more per person, per year on food and alcohol away from home. In the US, the average annual spent per person per year is $2500. Lang, Tim, Erik Millstone (2008). Atlas of Food: Who Eats What, Where, and Why. University of California Press: Berkeley. Pp 92.

41 EPA (2009). Organic Materials. Accessed March-09: http://www.epa.gov/organicmaterials

42 Source: Hartley Rosen, EYA Personal communication

43 Slow Food (2007). Food and Taste Education. Accessed Aug-09: http://www.slowfood.ca/about_education.php

44 One World. Accessed Oct-09: http://uk.oneworld.net

45 FAO. Accessed Nov-2: http://www.fao.org

46 One World. Accessed Oct-09: http://uk.oneworld.net

47 Amena Bakr (2009). Emirates Investment Group to buy Pakistan Farmland. Food Crisis and the Global Land Grab. Accessed Oct 9-09: http://farmlandgrab.org/2951

48 Food Sovereignty. Accessed October 9-09: http://www.foodsovereignty.org

49 Hunger in America. Accessed October 9-09: http://www.hungerinamerica.org

50 EPA. Accessed October 9-09: http://www.epa.gov/organicmaterials

51 Hunger in America. Accessed October 9-09: http://www.hungerinamerica.org

[52] Hunger in America. Accessed October 9-09: http://www.hungerinamerica.org

[53] Quest Outreach. Accessed October 9-09: http://www.questoutreach.org

[54] Green Daily. Accessed October 9-09: http://www.greendaily.com

[55] Consider that 25% of all US freshwater used each year goes towards making food that Americans waste (January 2010 Harper's Index, page 13)

[56] Fabos, J. G. (1995). Introduction and Overview: The Greenway Movement, Uses and Potentials of Greenways. Landscape and Urban Planning, 33, 1-13.

[57] This percentage range is somewhat arbitrary but is based on an approximation of what the maximum possible area for gardens could be in a high density context (i.e. four stories or more). Another way to quantify the garden space requirements for high density environments is to use the LEED ND 2009 rating system, which designates garden space per dwelling as proportionate to the density. For example, in a density of 4-7 units per acre, the garden space requirement is 200 square feet and in a 35 units per acre context, the requirement is for 60 square feet.

[58] Statistics Canada data as cited in Is Farming Sustainable by Wendy Holm. Accessed Nov 15-09: http://www.theholmteam.ca

[59] Canadian Wheat Board (June/July 2006). Grain Matters. Accessed Nov 15-09: http://www.cwb.ca

[60] George Penfold (2009), Thoughts on Regional Food Security and Self-Reliance. Accessed Sept 15-09: http://communitytransition.blogspot.com/2009/09/thoughts-on-regional-food-security-self.html

[61] EPA (2009). Bulletin How Does Your Garden Grow- Brownfield Development and Local Agriculture. Available on-line: http://www.epa.gov/brownfields/success/local_ag.pdf

[62] Urban Partners, Farming in Philadelphia: Feasibility Analysis and Next Steps (Institute for Innovations in Local Farming: December 2007),

[63] Annie Myers (2008). Vitalizing the Vacant– The Logistics and Benefits Of Middle- to Large-Scale Agricultural Production on Urban Land. CP252, Professor Fred Etzel University of California, Berkeley, Department of Urban and Regional Planning.

[64] United States Department of Agriculture. Adding Values to Our Food System: An Economic Analysis of Sustainable Community Food Systems, Sustainable Agriculture Research and Education Program, Utah State University, prepared by Integrity Systems Cooperative and Sustainability Ventures Group, Feb. 1997.

[65] Saanich Organics, A Model for Sustainable Agriculture Through Cooperation, by Robin Tunnicliffe, B.C. Institute for Cooperative Studies, 2008.

[66] Are the Farmers' Markets Really More Expensive? Neighborhood Farmers' Market Alliance, http://www.seattlefarmersmarkets.org/ripe-n-ready/are-the-farmers-markets-really-more-expensive

[67] USDA (1997). Adding Values to Our Food System: An Economic Analysis of Sustainable Community Food Systems. Department of Agriculture Sustainable Agriculture Research and Education Program, Utah State University, prepared by Integrity Systems Cooperative and Sustainability Ventures Group, Feb. 1997.

[68] Grow Biointensive. Accessed Sept-09: http://growbiointensive.org/about_history.html

[69] John Jeavons (2002). How to Grow More Vegetables Than You Ever Thought Possible on Less Land Than You Can Imagine. Berkeley: Ten Speed Press. Pp xii-xiii., quoted in Annie Myers (2008). Vitalizing the Vacant– The Logistics and Benefits Of Middle- to Large-Scale Agricultural Production on Urban Land. CP252, Professor Fred Etzel University of California, Berkeley, Department of Urban and Regional Planning.

[70] Michael Ableman (2005). Fields of Plenty: A Farmer's Journey in Search of Real Food and the People Who Grow It, Chronicle Books.

[71] Urban Partners (2007). Farming in Philadelphia: Feasibility Analysis and Next Steps. Prepared for: Institute for Innovations in Local Farming by Urban Partners, December. Available On-line: http://www. spinfarming.com/common/pdfs/STF_inst_ for_innovations_exec_summary_dec07.pdf

[72] New York Times Magazine, Sept. 2008

[73] Interview with the author

[74] Adding Values to Our Food System: An Economic Analysis of Sustainable Community Food Systems, United States Department of Agriculture Sustainable Agriculture Research and Education Program, Utah State University, prepared by Integrity Systems Cooperative and Sustainability Ventures Group, Feb. 1997.

[75] Rick Preutz (2003). Accessed Sept 3-09: http://www.beyondtakingsandgivings.com/ tdr.htm.

[76] Corporation de Gestion de Marches Publics. Accessed Sept 5-09: http://www. marchespublics-mtl.com

[77] Albright L (2004). CEA: Controlled Environment Agriculture. Accessed Sept 10-09: http://www.cornellcea.com/about_ CEA.htm

[78] New York Times Magazine, Sept. 2008

[79] Solviva (1998). How to Grow $500,000 on One Acre and Peace on Earth. 2nd Printing. Trailblazer Press, Martha's Vineyard, Massachusetts, http://www.solviva.com, solviva@vineyard.net

[80] Solviva, p. 156

[81] Solviva, p. 158

[82] Food, Nutrition, Science Lempert Report Newsletter, Oct. 26, 2009,

[83] Vertical Farms. Advantages of Vertical Farming . Accessed Sept 15-09: http:// verticalfarms.com

[84] Davis, D.R., M.D. Epps, and H.D. Riordan (2004). Changes in USDA Food Composition for 43 Garden Crops, 1950 to 1999. Journal of the American College of Nutrition. 23(4): 669–682.

[85] Rich, D. K.(2006). Organic Fruits and Vegetables Work Harder for their Nutrients. SFGate. Accessed Sept 20-09: http:// articles.sfgate.com/2006-03-25/home-and-garden/17286248_1_nutrients-fruits-and-vegetables-organic-center

[86] Heffernan, W. (2005) What is Happening in our Agri-Food System. In K. Mullinix (ed.). The Next Agricultural Revolution: Revitalizing Family Based Agriculture and Rural Communities. Proceedings of the Washington State Family Farm Summit. Yakima, WA: Good Fruit Grower.

[87] Goldschmidt, W. (1978) As You Sow: Three Studies in the Social Consequences of Agribusiness. Montclair, N.J.: Allanheld, Osmun & Co.

[88] The Hartman Group Inc. (2007) Consumer Understanding of Buying Local. Seattle WA. Accessed Nov 10-09 http://www.hartman-group.com

[89] The Hartman Group Inc. (2008) Thinking on Organic. Seattle WA. Accessed Nov 10-09 http://www.hartman-group.com

90 Mullinix, K. Ed. (2005). The Next
Agricultural Revolution: Revitalizing Family
Based Agriculture and Rural Communities
Proceedings of the Washington State Family
Farm Summit. Good Fruit Grower, Yakima,
WA.

91 Carlson, A. (2008) Agrariansim Reborn:
The Curious Return of the Small Family Farm.
The Intercollegiate Review. 43(1): 13-23.

92 Heinberg R. (2006). Fifty Million Farmers.
Twenty-Sixth Annual E. F. Schumacher
Lectures. E. F. Schumacher Society,
Stockbridge, Massachusetts.

93 Mullinix, K. Ed. (2005). The Next
Agricultural Revolution: Revitalizing Family
Based Agriculture and Rural Communities
Proceedings of the Washington State Family
Farm Summit. Good Fruit Grower, Yakima,
WA.

94 The Eight Pillars of a Sustainable
Community. Mark Holland. Accessed
Sept-23: http://www.hblanarc.ca/
attachments/8pillars_matrix_HBL.pdf

95 Davis, Kim (2002). Green Roof Inventory:
Preface Report for the Greater Vancouver
Regional District . Available On-Line:
http://www.gvrd.bc.ca/BuildSmart/pdfs/
gvrdgreenroofinventory.pdf. Pg 17.

96 Barrs, Robert (2002). Southeast False
Creek Urban Agriculture Strategy. Prepared
for the City of Vancouver. Prepared by
Holland-Barrs Planning Group in association
with Lees + Associates Sustainability
Ventures Group. Available on-line at
http://homepage.mac.com/cityfarmer/
SEFCUrbanAgStudyFINAL.pdf

97 Davis, Kim (2002). Green Roof Inventory:
Preface Report for the Greater Vancouver
Regional District. Available On-Line:
http://www.gvrd.bc.ca/BuildSmart/pdfs/
gvrdgreenroofinventory.pdf. Pg 17.